Learn to Speak Burmese Quickly!

EASY
Burmese

KENNETH WONG

Department of South and Southeast Asian Studies
University of California, Berkeley

T0151218

TUTTLE Publishing

Tokyo | Rutland, Vermont | Singapore

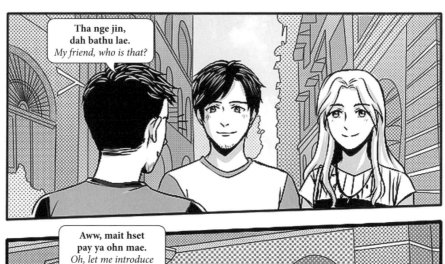

Contents

The Shwedagon Pagoda

Marionette puppets

A foodstall
in Yangon

Dah kyanawt amyo thamee Samantha bah.
This is my girlfriend Samantha

Dah kyama amyo thar Win Naing bah.
This is my boyfriend Win Naing

CHAPTER 1

A Basic Introduction

Colloquial Burmese—the spoken Burmese you can use to barter with local merchants, order tea in a teashop, or introduce yourself to someone—is not that difficult. You don't have to learn a whole lot of grammar; you can master a few basic patterns and you can recycle them to suit your needs.

The chapters in this book are designed to expose you to the most useful structures. The plot introduces you to Naing Oo, a Burmese-American returning to Yangon to start a travel business; Naing Oo's girlfriend Samantha, who wants to improve her Burmese; and Naing Oo's childhood friend Win San, who serves as their local contact. As you follow in their footsteps and eavesdrop on their conversations, you pick up useful expressions for self-introduction, going around town, shopping, talking about local culture, conducting business, and much more.

You might notice that the way Naing Oo addresses his childhood friend Win San, and the way Win San addresses Naing Oo's girlfriend Samantha are distinctly different. In his dialogues with Win San, Naing Oo tends to use the pronouns ငါ nga for *I*, မင်း min for *you*. On the other hand, Win San usually addresses Samantha by name, not with a pronoun. And when Samantha speaks to Win San, she uses the pronouns ကျွန်မ kyama for *I*, and Win San's own name as a substitute for *you*.

These differences highlight one of the most important aspects of spoken Burmese: You use a different set of pronouns based on your gender, how well you know the other person, how much older or younger you are, and how much respect you wish to convey.

Casual and Formal Styles

The casual and formal styles are defined primarily by the pronouns you use and how you end your sentences. These function as respect markers in your conversation. You may safely use the casual style if you meet *both* conditions below:

1. You have a close or intimate relationship with the other person;
2. You and the other person are of the same age group (i.e. the age difference between you is no more than five or six years).

If you know the other person well, but he or she is significantly older than you, the casual style is not recommended. By the same token, if you're speaking to a stranger or an acquaintance, even if you're both the same age, the casual style is not recommended. In those instances, the formal or polite speech is the safer bet.

Basically, in the casual style, you use ငါ **nga** for *I* and မင်း **min** for *you*, if you're male; and ငါ **nga** for *I* and နင် **nin** for *you*, if you're female.

In formal or polite style, you use ကျွန်တော် **kyanaw** for *I* and ခင်ဗျား **khamyar** for *you*, if you're male; ကျွန်မ **kyama** for *I* and ရှင် **shin** for *you*, if you're female. For extra politeness, you may also end your sentences with ခင်ဗျား **khamyar** if you're male, or ရှင် **shin** if you're female. **Note** that sometimes **khamyar** is pronounced **khamya** with a short final vowel for emphasis.

One curious feature of the formal or polite style is the speakers' tendency to minimize the use of the second-person pronoun *you*. Native speakers feel even the polite versions of *you*—ခင်ဗျား **khamyar** (used by men) and ရှင် **shin** (used by women)—sound extremely confrontational and accusatory. Therefore, whenever possible, they tend to use the name of the person as a substitute.

For example, when Samantha wants to ask Win San to give her Burmese lessons, she says:

ကိုဝင်းဆန်းကို အကူညီတောင်းချင်တယ်။ **Ko Win San go aku a nyi taung jin dae.**

It literally translates to, "I'd like to ask Mr. Win San a favor"—not "I'd like to ask *you* a favor." As you study the dialogues and listen to the audio clips, please take note of the correlation between the types of speech the speakers use and their social, personal, and professional relationships.

Statements, Requests, and Questions

The three types of sentences you'll likely encounter in your daily conversations are (1) statements, (2) requests or commands, and (3) questions. You can usually tell what type of sentence you're dealing with by looking at how it ends.

Statements about recent and past events

Statements about recent and past events usually end with တယ် **tae**, sometimes pronounced **dae**.
- စားတယ်။ **Sar dae.** (*I ate.*)
- သောက်တယ်။ **Thauk tae.** (*I drank.*)

For emphasis, statements about actions in the past may be marked with ခဲ့ **khaet**, also pronounced **gaet**, following the verb, but it's *not* mandatory.
- စားခဲ့တယ်။ **Sar gaet dae.** (*I ate*)
- သောက်ခဲ့တယ်။ **Thauk khaet dae.** (*I drank*)

Note: Just like in English, a simple present Burmese verb may also be used to describe habits and routine activities. So အမဲသားစားတယ်။ **Amae thar sar dae,** for example, may also mean, "I usually eat beef / I can eat beef."

Statements about future events

Statements about future events usually end with မယ် **mae.**

- စားမယ်။ **Sar mae.** *(I'll eat.)*
- သောက်မယ်။ **Thauk mae.** *(I'll drink.)*

Statements about actions in progress

Statements about actions in progress are marked with နေ **nay** following the verb.

- စားနေတယ်။ **Sar nay dae.** *(I'm eating.)*
- သောက်နေတယ်။ **Thauk nay dae.** *(I'm drinking.)*

Negative statements

Negative statements usually end with ဘူး **boo,** sometimes pronounced **phoo.**

- မစားဘူး။ **Ma sar boo.** *(I don't eat. / I didn't eat. / I won't eat.)*
- မသောက်ဘူး။ **Ma thauk phoo.**
  (I don't drink. / I didn't drink. / I won't drink.)

Requests and commands to do something

Requests and commands to do something usually end with ပါ **pah,** sometimes pronounced **bah.**

Requests and commands forbidding

Requests and commands for bidding you from doing something usually end with နဲ့ **naet.**

- စားပါ။ **Sar bah.** *(Please eat.)*
- သောက်ပါ။ **Thauk pah.** *(Please drink.)*
- မစားနဲ့။ **Ma sar naet.** *(Don't eat.)*
- မသောက်နဲ့။ **Ma thauk naet.** *(Don't drink.)*

Yes–no questions

Yes–no questions about past and present events usually end with လား **lar.** Yes–no questions about future events usually end with မလား **malar.**

- စားခဲ့လား။ **Sar gaet lar.** *(Did you eat?)*
- စားနေလား။ **Sar nay lar.** *(Are you eating?)*
- စားမလား။ **Sar ma lar.** *(Will you eat?)*

Who, what, where, when, why questions

Who, what, where, when, why questions about **past and present** events usually end with လဲ **lae.**

Who, what, where, when, why questions about **future** events usually end with မလဲ **malae.**

- ဘာစားခဲ့လဲ။ Bah sar gaet lae. *What did you eat?*
- ဘယ်မှာစားခဲ့လဲ။ Bae hmah sar gaet lae. *Where did you eat?*
- ဘာစားနေလဲ။ Bah sar nay lae. *What are you eating?*
- ဘာစားမလဲ၊ Bah sar malae. *What will you eat?*
- ဘယ်အချိန်စားမလဲ။ Bae a chain sar malae. *When will you eat?*

In English, there are the five Ws for formulating questions: Who, What, Where, When, Why. In Burmese, there are five **bas**—question words spelled with the letter သ **ba.** They are:

- ဘယ်သူလဲ။ Bae thu lae. *Who's that?*
- ဘာလဲ။ Bah lae. *What's that?*
- ဘယ်မှာလဲ။ Bae hmar lae. *Where is it?*
- ဘယ်တော့လဲ။ Bae dawt lae. *When is it?*
- ဘာလို့လဲ or ဘာဖြစ်လို့လဲ or ဘာကြောင့်လဲ။
  Bah lo lae or **Bah phit lo lae** or **Bah jaunt lae.** *Why is that?*

Time Markers

In English, you conjugate the verb to match the past, present, or future tense: the time of the action. In Burmese, the verb remains unchanged. The verb စား **sar** (to eat) or သောက် **thauk** (to drink) remains the same whether you're talking about eating something in the past, present, or future. But you use time markers to indicate when the action takes place. For example:

- မနေ့က ခေါက်ဆွဲ စားတယ်။ <u>Ma nayt ga</u> khauk swe sar dae.
  I ate noodles yesterday.
- မနက်က ခေါက်ဆွဲ စားတယ်။ <u>Ma net ka</u> khauk swe sar dae.
  I ate noodles this morning.
- မနက်ဖြန် ခေါက်ဆွဲ စားမယ်။ <u>Ma net phyan</u> khauk swe sar mae.
  I'll eat noodles tomorrow.

In the first example sentence, the time indicator **ma nayt ga** (yesterday) anchors the action in the past. In the second example sentence, the phrase **ma net ka** (morning) places in the action in the recent past. In the last example sentence, both **ma net phyan** (tomorrow) and the future sentence end particle **mae** put the action in the future. You'll find a list of commonly used time indicators in the Glossary.

Common Auxiliary Verbs

Auxiliary verbs are a handy way to clarify your mood, willingness, desire, or capacity. For example:

- Beer သောက်တယ်။ **Beer thauk tae.**
  I drink beer / I drank beer. (Without auxiliary verb)
- Beer သောက်ချင်တယ်။ **Beer thauk chin dae.**
  I'd like to drink beer. (With auxiliary verb)
- Mandalay သွားတယ်။ **Mandalay thwar dae.**
  I go to Mandalay / I went to Mandalay. (Without auxiliary verb)
- Mandalay သွားနိုင်တယ်။ **Mandalay thwar naing dae.**
  I can go to Mandalay / I'm able to go to Mandalay. (With auxiliary verb)

The auxiliary verb usually comes *after* the main verb (not before, as in English). Here are some basic auxiliary verbs:

ချင် *chin*, sometimes pronounced *jin*. "Want to, would like to"

- San Francisco သွားချင်တယ်။ **San Francisco thwar jin dae.**
  I want to go to San Francisco.
- Pizza စားချင်တယ်။ **Pizza sar jin dae.** *I'd like to eat pizza.*
- Soda သောက်ချင်တယ်။ **Soda thauk chin dae.** *I'd like to drink soda.*

နိုင် *naing*, "Can, able to"

- မနက်ဖြန် လာနိုင်တယ်။ **Ma net phyan lah naing dae.**
  I can come tomorrow.
- နေပြည်တော် သွားနိုင်တယ်။ **Naypyidaw thwar naing dae.**
  I can go to Naypyidaw.
- ကားမောင်းနိုင်တယ်။ **Kar maung naing dae.** *I can drive.*

ရ *ya*, "Must, have to, need to"

- Mandalay သွားရမယ်။ **Mandalay thwar ya mae.** *I must go to Mandalay.*
- ခေါက်ဆွဲ စားရမယ်။ **Khauk swe sar ya mae.** *I have to eat noodles.*
- ရေသောက်ရမယ်။ **Yay thauk ya mae.** *I need to drink some water.*

> **တတ်** *tut,* sometimes pronounced *dut,* "Have the know-how to, have the skill to"

- အင်္ဂလိပ်စကား ပြောတတ်တယ်။ Ingalaik zagar pyaw dut tae.
  I can speak English.
- Pasta ချက်တတ်တယ်။ Pasta chet tat tae. *I know how to make pasta.*

Note: that တတ် tat may also be used to indicate habits and tendencies, as in:

- သူ မနက်တိုင်း ကော်ဖီ သောက်တတ်တယ်။
  Thu ma net taing kaw phe thauk tat tae.
  He tends to drink coffee every morning.

Subject and Object Tags

In colloquial Burmese, you'll find that the subject is often omitted. Here's a typical exchange between two native speakers:

Speaker 1: နေကောင်းလား။
  Nay kaung lar.
  How are you? (Lit., Feeling well?)

Speaker 2: နေကောင်းပါတယ်။
  Nay kaung bah dae.
  I'm well. (Lit., Well.)

Speaker 1: ဘယ်သွားမလဲ။
  Bae thwar ma lae.
  Where're you going? (Lit., Where will go?)

Speaker 2: ဈေးသွားမယ်။
  Zay thwar mae.
  I'm going to the market. (Lit., Will go to market.)

Speaker 1 omits the subject *you* in "How are you?" because it's clear to whom he's directing the question. Speaker 2 omits the subject *I* in "I'm well" because it's abundantly clear he's talking about himself. In their subsequent exchange, they omit the *you* and *I* for the same reason. This manner of communication may be grammatically intolerable in English, but it's the norm in Burmese, where a lot of things are not explicitly stated but merely implied.

In cases where there could be confusion, Burmese speakers use subject and object tags to identify who's performing the action and who's receiving it. For example:

Kelly က Samantha ကို ဖုန်းဆက်တယ်။
Kelly ga Samantha go phone hset tae. *Kelly made a call to Samantha.*

In Burmese sentences, the verb usually comes at the end of the statement, not between the subject and the object (as verbs usually do in English). In the statement above, the subject tag က **ga** following Kelly identifies Kelly as the one who made the call; and the object tag ကို **go** following Samantha makes it clear Samantha is the one who received the call.

The use of subject and object tags allows the statement above to be recast as follows, without altering its meaning:

Samantha ကို Kelly က ဖုန်းဆက်တယ်။
Samantha go Kelly ga phone hset tae. *Kelly made a call to Samantha.*

Rearranging the order of the two nouns doesn't change the meaning of the statement at all, because the subject and object tags clarify who's made the call, and who received it.

You'll also find that people don't use subject and object tags in many cases. For example:

Kelly ရန်ကုန်သွားမယ်။ **Kelly Yangon thwar mae.** *Kelly will go to Yangon.*

Samantha ကော်ဖီသောက်ချင်တယ်။ **Samantha kaw phe thauk chin dae.** *Samantha wants to drink coffee.*

In these two sentences, no subject and object tags are needed, because common sense makes it clear only Kelly can travel to the city of Yangon; and only Samantha can desire a cup of coffee. No reasonable person would interpret that the city of Yangon will travel to Kelly, or that coffee desires to drink a cup of Samantha.

CHAPTER 2

A Guide to Burmese Pronunciation

Burmese is a tonal language. That means, a word can have different meanings depending on the *tone* or the amount of stress you put on the vowel. For example, if you pronounce **sa** with a short, abrupt stop, as if someone has interrupted you in the middle of your speech, it means "to begin" (verb). If you pronounce it with a long, lingering vowel, it means "letter or language" (noun). On the other hand, if you pronounce it with a raised tone, as if you're hollaring to get someone's attention, it means "to eat" (verb). In Burmese script, the difference is clear: စ (**sa**, to begin), စာ (**sah**, letter, language), စား (**sar**, to eat). But in Romanized Burmese, it's difficult (often impossible) to indicate such tonal differences.

Furthermore, there's no standard for Romanizing Burmese words. Therefore, to make the Romanized pronunciations intuitive, the author often chooses artificial ways to cut or raise the tones using English spelling conventions. For example, to indicate the short tone in မေ့ "to forget," it's Romanized as **mayt**; and to represent the high tone in the word စား "to eat," it's Romanized as **sar**.

Whereas many English words such as *cut, stop,* and *bone* have closing vowel sounds (closing in *t, p,* and *n,* respectively), Burmese words usually don't. But to Romanize Burmese words that must be pronounced with short, abrupt ends, English spellings with closing vowels prove to be the best equivalent. For instance, the word စာအုပ် "book" is best Romanized as **sah oak**. Keep in mind, however, that the ending **k** sound in **oak** should *not* be voiced. Similarly, the word ခေါက်ဆွဲ "noodles" is best Romanized as **khauk swe**. The closing **k** in **khauk** is there merely to signal to English readers of the short, abrupt end of ခေါက်; it should *not* be emphatically voiced, like you would with English words such as *smoke* or *fork.*

To further complicate matters, native Burmese speakers routinely pronounce many words and phrases differently from the way they're written. For example, the word ကစား "to play" (verb) is written **kasar**, but always pronounced **gazar**; similarly, the word ဘုရား "pagoda" is written **bu yar**, but always pronounced **phayar**.

Aiming for ease of use, the author employs a system driven by how the Burmese people themselves tend to Romanize their words; how native speakers usually pronounce certain words and expressions; and how English readers will mostly voice the Romanized sentences. *For best results, you should use the Romanized pronunciations provided as approximations and guidance, and look to the audio files as the vocal models to imitate.*

Consonant or Initial Sounds

a (အ) is like the *a* in "armor," e.g., အမိန့် **a-maint** (order, command)

b (ဗ or ဘ) is like the *b* in "band," e.g., ဗမာ **Bamah** (Burman, the ethnic majority of the country), ဘာသာ **bah thah** (faith, religion)

by (ျ or ဗ) is like the *b-y* sound in "beautiful" or "rebuke," e.g., ဗျည်း **byee** (consonant letter)

ch (ချ) is like the *ch* in "choose," e.g., ချစ် **chit** (to love)

d (ဒ and ဓ) is like the *d* in "do," e.g., ဒါ **dah** (this)

g (ဂ or ဃ) is like the *g* in "go," e.g., ဂီတ **gita** (music)

h (ဟ) is pronounced like the *h* in "he," e.g., ဟာသ **hah tha** (comedy)

j (ဂျ or ဂျ) is like the *j* in "jam," e.g., ဂြိုလ် **jo** (planet)

k (က) is like the unaspirated *k* in "skate," "skull," or "sky"; *not* like the aspirated *k* in "kill," "key," or "Kansas," e.g., ကု **ku** (to heal)

kh (ခ) is like the *k* in "kill," "key," or "Kansas," e.g., ခါး **khar** (bitter)

ky (ကျ) is similar to the *ch* in "chalk" or "chosen," but with less air escaping between the teeth, e.g., ကျောင်း **kyaung** (school)

l (လ) is like the *l* in "line," e.g., လ **la** (moon)

hl (လှ) is voiced with a breathy *h* preceding the *l* (make the exclamation *hmm*, but round it out with *l* instead), e.g., လှ **hla** (beautiful)

m (မ) is like the *m* in "moon," e.g., မိုး **moe** (rain)

hm (မှ) is voiced with a breathy *h* preceding the *m* (make the exclamation *hmm*, but round it out with *m* instead), e.g., မှား **hmar** (wrong)

my (မျ or မြ) is like the *my* in "music," e.g., မြင့် **myint** (high, tall)

n (န or ဏ) is like the *n* in "name," e.g., နေ **nay** (sun)

hn (နှ) is voiced with a breathy *h* preceding the *n* (make the exclamation *hmm*, but round it out with *n* instead), e.g., နှလုံး **hna-lone** (heart)

ng (င) is like the *ng* in "singer," e.g., ငါး **ngaa** (fish; five)

ny (ည) is like the Spanish *ñ* in *el niño*, which is pronounced *ny*, e.g., ည **nya** (night)

p (ပ) is like the unaspirated *p* from "spawn," "spool," or "Spain"; *not* like the aspirated *p* from "pawn," "pool," or "pain," e.g., ပန်း **pan** (flower)

ph (ဖ) is like the *p* from "pawn," "pool," or "pain," e.g., ဖား **phar** (frog)

py (ပျ or ပြ) is like the *py* sound in "spew," e.g., ပျား **phar** (bee)

phy (ဖျ or ဖြ) is like the *py* sound in "pew" or "pure," e.g., ဖျား **phyar** (to be ill)

r (ရ) is like the *r* in "run," e.g., အမရပူရ **A-ma-ra pu-ra** (Amarapura city)

s (စ) is like the *s* in "same," e.g., စား **sar** (to eat)

hs (ဆ) is like the *s* in "same" but with a sharper sibilant (emphasize the *sss*), e.g., ဆား **hsaa** (salt)

sh (ရှ) is like the *sh* in "she," e.g., ရှာ **shah** (to find)

t (တ) is like the unaspirated *t* in "stone," "stall," or "stable"; *not* like the aspirated *t* from "tone," "tall," or "table," e.g., တောင် **taung** (hill)

ht (ထ) is like the *t* in "tone," "tall," or "table," e.g., ထောင် **htaung** (prison)

tw (တွ) is similar to the *tw* sound in "twin," but the initial *t* should be like the *t* from stone, *not* like the *t* from tone, e.g., တွေး **tway** (to think)

htw (ထွ) is like the *tw* sound in "twin," e.g., ထွေး **htway** (to spit out)

th (သ) is like the *th* sound in "thought," e.g., သား **thar** (son)

thw (သွ) is like the *thw* sound in "thwart," e.g., သွား **thwaa** (to go)

w (ဝ) is like the *w* in "water," e.g., ဝါး **wah** (to chew)

y (ယ or ရ) is like the *y* in "yes," e.g., ရုံး **yone** (office)

z (ဇ or ဈ) is like the *z* in "zen," e.g., ဈေး **zay** (market)

Vowel Sounds

a is like the *a* in "spa," e.g., စ **sa** (to begin)

i, **e**, or **ee** is like the *e* in "me," e.g., သိ **thi** (to know)

u or **oo** is like the *u* in "blue," e.g., ကု **ku** (to heal)

ay is like the *ay* in "day," e.g., အမေ **a-may** (mother)

ae is like the *are* in "care," e.g., မယ် **mae** (future-tense indicator)

aw is like the *aw* in "flaw," e.g., ပေါ် **paw** (to appear)

o is like the *o* in "so," e.g., ပို **po** (extra)

in is like the *in* in "sin," e.g., ရင် **yin** (chest)

un or **an** is like the *un* in "fun," e.g., ပန် **pan** (to wear a flower)

on or **one** is like the *one* in "bone," e.g., ပုံ **pone** (image, picture)

aung is like the *oun* in "round," e.g., စောင် **saung** (blanket)

aing is like the *ine* in "dine," e.g., ပိုင် **paing** (to possess)

ain is like the *ain* in "stain," e.g., စိန် **sain** (diamond)

In Romanization, sometimes a **t** is added to the **ay, ae, aw, in, un, on, aung, aing,** or **ain** vowels to mark the short tone, pronounced with an abrupt end. Examples: မေ့ **mayt**, "to forget"; ပေါ့ **pawt**, "to be light in flavor"; ရင့် **yint**, "to be ripe, to be aging"; စောင့် **saungt**, "to wait."

In Romanization, sometimes an **h** is added to the **a** and **o** vowels to mark the long tone, pronounced with a lingering vowel. Examples: စာ **sah**, "letter, language"; ပို **poh**, "extra."

Sometimes an **r** is added to mark the high tone, pronounced with a raised voice. Example: စား **sar**, "to eat."

Sometimes an extra **e** is added to the **i, o,** and **ay** vowels to mark the high tone, pronounced with a raised voice. Examples: အသီး **a thee**, "fruit"; မိုး **moe**, "rain"; အေး **aye**, "cold."

The following vowels are *always* pronounced in the short tone with a hard stop:

> **ut** is like the *ut* in "hut," e.g., သတ် **thut** (to kill)
>
> **et** is like the *et* in "met," e.g., ခက် **khet** (difficult)
>
> **it** is like the *it* in "sit," e.g., ချစ် **chit** (to love)
>
> **oat** (or **ote**) is like the *oat* in "boat," e.g., ဟုတ် **hote** (true, yes)
>
> **aut** is like the *out* in "about," e.g., သောက် **thauk** (to drink)
>
> **ait** (or **aik**) is like the *ait* in "wait," e.g., စိတ် **sait** (mind)
>
> **ite** (or **ike**) is like the *ite* in "site," e.g., လိုက် **lite** (to follow)

A Note on Tone Shifting: Soft Consonants Sometimes Become Hard and Heavy

When voicing certain particles and auxiliary verbs, Burmese speakers frequently substitute the original **k, kh, s, hs, t, ht, p, and ph** consonants with harder, heavier counterparts—**g, z, d, b**. For example:

1A. သူရေသောက်တယ်။ **Thu yay thauk** tae. *He drank water.*

1B. သူခေါက်ဆွဲစားတယ်။ **Thu khauk swae sar** dae. *He ate noodles.*

2A. ကျွန်မ ရေသောက်ချင်တယ်။ **Kyama yay thauk** chin **dae.**
      I'd like to have some water.

2B. ကျွန်မ ခေါက်ဆွဲစားချင်တယ်။ **Kyama khauk swae sar** jin **dae.**
      I'd like to have some noodles.

In 1A, the affirmative sentence end particle တယ် is voiced **tae**. But in 1B, the same particle is voiced **dae**. In 2A, the auxiliary verb ချင် (want to) is voiced **chin**, but in 2B, it's voiced **jin**. This is what some call tone-shifting.

Tone shifting is not random. The specific instances in which it occurs can be identified and explained, but it won't make sense unless you know the written script and understand the spelling system. In this book, tone-shifted Romanized pronunciations are provided when appropriate, and the audio files also reflect the tone shifting. Therefore, if you follow the Romanized pronunciations and the audio files as your guide, you don't have to concern yourself with learning when to perform tone shifting.

CHAPTER 3

Greetings

Naing Oo grew up in Burma, but emigrated to the U.S. with his family in his teens. Today, he's back to visit his homeland with his girlfriend Samantha. The two are staying in downtown Yangon, in a guesthouse. Naing Oo's childhood friend Win San comes to meet them there.

DIALOGUE GREETINGS

Win San:	*Hey, Naing Oo, buddy!*
	Hey, Naing Oo, tha nge jin!
	ဟေ့ နိုင်ဦး သူငယ်ချင်း။
Naing Oo:	*Hey, Win San! How are you?*
	Hey, Win San! Nay kaung lar.
	ဟေ့ ဝင်းဆန်း၊ နေကောင်းလား။
Win San:	*Fine! And you?*
	Kaung dae. Min yaw.
	ကောင်းတယ်။ မင်းရော။
Naing Oo:	*Very good!*
	Kaung bah dae.
	ကောင်းပါတယ်။
Win San:	*It's been a while, hasn't it?*
	Kyah be naw.
	ကြာပြီနော်။
Naing Oo:	*Yes. It's been too long!*
	Hote tae. Kyah be.
	ဟုတ်တယ်။ ကြာပြီ။

VOCABULARY

tha nge jin	friend, buddy
kaung	great, good, well
nay kaung	to feel fine, to feel good
kyah be	it's been a while

Supplementary Vocabulary

kaung	good, well, fine
hote	true

pu	hot
aye	cold
chan	chilly
cho	sweet
khar	bitter

GRAMMAR NOTE Asking and responding to yes–no questions

Lar is the particle for posing yes–no questions. Let's look at this question from Win San:

နေကောင်းလား။ **Nay kaung lar.** *How are you?*

နေကောင်း	**nay kaung**	to feel fine
လား	**lar**	yes–no question particle

 PATTERN PRACTICE 1: YES–NO QUESTIONS

Practice saying these questions.

1. **Nay kaung lar.**   How are you / Are you feeling well?
2. **Kaung lar.**   Is it good?
3. **Hote lar.**   Is it true?
4. **Pu lar.**   Is it hot?
5. **Aye lar.**   Are you cold? / Is it cold here?
6. **Chan lar.**   Are you chilly?
7. **Cho lar.**   Is it sweet?
8. **Khar lar.**   Is it bitter?

When responding to yes–no questions in the **affirmative**, you end the statement with **tae** or **dae**:

နေကောင်းတယ်။ **Nay kaung dae.** *I'm doing fine.*

နေကောင်း	**nay kaung**	doing good, feeling well
တယ်	**dae**	affirmative sentence ending

PATTERN PRACTICE 2: AFFIRMATIVE REPLY

Practice saying these affirmative statements.

1. **Nay kaung dae.**   I'm doing fine.
2. **Kaung dae.**   I'm fine. / It's good.
3. **Hote tae.**   It's true.

4.	**Pu dae.**	It's hot.
5.	**Aye dae.**	It's cold.
6.	**Chan dae.**	It's chilly.
7.	**Cho dae.**	It's sweet.
8.	**Khar dae.**	It's bitter.

To respond to yes–no questions in the **negative**, you use the negative form of a verb or an adjective, followed by **boo** or **phoo**, the article to end negative statements. For example:

မဟုတ်ဖူး။ **Ma hote phoo.**   *It's not true.*

မဟုတ်	**ma hote**	not true
ဖူး	**phoo**	negative sentence end particle.

PATTERN PRACTICE 3: NEGATIVE REPLY

Practice saying these negative responses.

1.	**Nay ma kaung boo.**	I'm not feeling well.
2.	**Ma kaung boo.**	It's not good.
3.	**Ma hote phoo.**	It's not true.
4.	**Ma pu boo.**	It's not hot.
5.	**Ma aye boo.**	It's not cold.
6.	**Ma chan boo.**	It's not chilly.
7.	**Ma cho boo.**	It's not sweet.
8.	**Ma khar boo.**	It's not bitter.

GRAMMAR NOTE Asking tag questions

You can use **naw** to add a tag question for emphasis, or to seek agreement. This is what Win San did when he said

ကြာပြီနော်။ **Kyah be naw.**   *It's been a while, hasn't it?*

ကြာပြီ	**kyah be**	it's been a while
နော်	**naw**	hasn't it? (Tag question particle)

PATTERN PRACTICE 4: TAG QUESTIONS

Practice asking these tag questions.

1.	**Nay kaung dae naw.**	You're well, aren't you?
2.	**Kaung dae naw.**	It's good, isn't it?

3. **Hote tae naw.** It's true, isn't it?
4. **Pu dae naw.** It's hot, isn't it?
5. **Aye dae naw.** It's cold, isn't it?
6. **Chan dae naw.** It's chilly, isn't it?
7. **Cho dae naw.** It's sweet, isn't it?
8. **Khar dae naw.** It's bitter, isn't it?

EXERCISE 1: YES-NO QUESTIONS

Translate the following statements into Burmese:

1. It's true.
2. It's true, isn't it?
3. It's good.
4. It's good, isn't it?
5. I'm fine.
6. Is it hot?
7. Is it bitter?
8. It's not cold, is it?

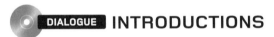

DIALOGUE INTRODUCTIONS

Win San notices Samantha, standing next to Naing Oo.

Win San: *My friend, who is that?*
Tha nge jin, dah bathu lae.
သူငယ်ချင်း၊ ဒါဘယ်သူလဲ။

Naing Oo: *Oh, let me introduce [you to her].*
Aww, mait hset pay ya ohn mae.
ဪ ... မိတ်ဆက်ပေးရဦးမယ်။
This is my girlfriend Samantha.
Dah nga amyo thamee Samantha bah.
ဒါ ငါ့အမျိုးသမီး Samantha ပါ။

Win San: [In English] *Hi Samantha! Nice to meet you!*

Samantha: *Nice to meet you!*
Twaet ya dah won thah bah dae.
တွေ့ရတာ ဝမ်းသာပါတယ်။

Win San: *Hey, you speak Burmese?*
Hah, Bamah zagar pyaw dut lah.
ဟာ ... ဗမာစကားပြောတတ်လား။

Samantha: *A little! Naing taught me.*
Nae Nae pyaw dut tae. Naing Oo thin pay lo.
နည်းနည်းပြောတတ်တယ်။ နိုင်ဦး သင်ပေးလို့။

Win San: *Ah, that's great!*
Aw, kaung dae.
ဪ ... ကောင်းတယ်။
Nice to meet you! I'm Win San.
Twaet ya dah won thah bah dae. Kyanaw Win San bah.
တွေ့ရတာ ဝမ်းသာပါတယ်။ ကျွန်တော် ဝင်းဆန်းပါ။

VOCABULARY

dah	that
bathu	who
mait hset	to introduce
amyo thamee	girlfriend, fiancée
twaet	to meet
won thah	happy, glad
Bamah zagar	Burmese language
pyaw	to speak
tut, dut	[auxiliary verb] have the skill to [do something]
pyaw dut	can speak
nae nae	a little bit, some
thin	to teach

Supplementary Vocabulary

ma pyaw dat	cannot speak
nar lae	understand
nar ma lae	don't understand
thaik	too much, very much, a lot
amyo thar	boyfriend, fiancé
aphae	father
amae	mother
ako	older brother
nyi	younger brother (if you're a man)
maung	younger brother (if you're a woman)
nyi ma	sister
a htet ayah shi	supervisor
loke phaw kaing bet	coworker
hsayah	teacher / mentor

kyaung nay bet tha nge jin	schoolmate / classmate
tha nge jin	friend

CULTURAL NOTE The familiar vs. the formal

There are several ways to say *you, I, me, my, he,* or *she* in Burmese, depending on the degree of formality required, how well you know the other person, and your gender, among other things. For the scenario in this lesson, let's concentrate on the *casual and formal* pronouns; and the *male and female* pronouns.

Old friends like Naing Oo and Win San will most likely use familiar, informal first-person and second-person pronouns with each other.

 ### Casual, familiar pronouns

ngah	I, me (used by both male and female speakers)
nga (short tone)	my (used by both male and female speakers)
min	you, your (used primarily by men)
nin	you (used primarily by female speakers)
nint	your (used primarily by female speakers)
thu	he/she, him/her (used by both male and female speakers)
thu (short tone)	him, his/her (used by both male and female speakers)

But these are not appropriate for strangers who have just met. That's why Samantha and Win San must use the formal, respectful pronouns.

Formal, respectful pronouns

kyanaw	I (used by male speakers)
kyanawt	me, my (used by male speakers)
kyama	I, me, my (used by female speakers)
khamyar	you (used by male speakers)
shin	you (used by female speakers)

PATTERN PRACTICE 1: INTRODUCING SOMEONE

When introducing his girlfriend Samantha to Win San, Naing Oo says:

ဒါင့်အမျိုးသမီး Samantha ပါ။   **Dah nga amyo thamee Samantha bah.**
This is my girlfriend Samantha.

ဒါ	**dah**	this
င့်အမျိုးသမီး	**nga amyo thamee**	my girlfriend (casual)

Samantha	Samantha	Samantha
ပါ။	bah	polite sentence end particle

When Naing Oo says **nga amyo thamee**, or *my girlfriend*, he's using the casual, familiar possessive **nga**. That's because he's known Win San for a long time. But if you're talking to a stranger or someone you've just met, you should use the formal equivalent **kyanawt** (if you're a man), or **kyama** (if you're a woman) for *my*. For example:

ဒါ ကျွန်တော့်အမျိုးသမီး Samantha ပါ။
Dah kyanawt amyo thamee Samantha bah. (Male speaker)
This is my girlfriend Samantha.

ဒါ	**dah**	this
ကျွန်တော့်	**kyanawt**	my (formal, male speaker)
အမျိုးသမီး	**amyo thamee**	girlfriend
Samantha	**Samantha**	Samantha
ပါ။	**bah**	polite sentence end particle

ဒါ ကျွန်မ အမျိုးသား ဝင်းနိုင် ပါ။
Dah kyama amyo thar Win Naing bah. (Female speaker)
This is my boyfriend Win Naing.

ဒါ	**dah**	this
ကျွန်မ	**kyama**	my (formal, female speaker)
အမျိုးသား	**amyo thar**	boyfriend (formal, female speaker)
ဝင်းနိုင်	**Win Naing**	Win Naing
ပါ။	**bah**	polite sentence end particle

Practice these phrases.
1. **Dah nga amyo thamee bah.**
    This is my girlfriend. (casual)
2. **Dah nga amyo thar bah.**
    This is my boyfriend. (casual)
3. **Dah kyanawt amyo thamee bah.**
    This is my girlfriend. (formal, male speaker)
4. **Dah kyama amyo thar bah.**
    This is my boyfriend. (formal, female speaker)
5. **Dah kyanawt tha nge jin bar.**
    This is my friend. (formal, male speaker)

6. **Dah kyama tha nge jin bar.**
   This is my friend. (formal, female speaker)
7. **Dah nga amyo thamee Jenny bah.**
   This is my my girlfriend Jenny. (casual)
8. **Dah nga amyo thar Jim bah.**
   This is my boyfriend Jim. (casual)
9. **Dah kyanawt amyo thamee Jenny bah.**
   This is my girlfriend Jenny. (formal, male speaker)
10. **Dah kyama amyo thar Jim bah.**
    This is my boyfriend Jim. (formal, female speaker)
11. **Dah kyanawt tha nge jin Jenny bah.**
    This is my friend Jenny. (formal, male speaker)
12. **Dah kyama tha nge jin Jim bah.**
    This is my friend Jim. (formal, female speaker)

PATTERN PRACTICE 2: SELF-INTRODUCTION

When introducing himself, Win San says:

ကျွန်တော် ဝင်းဆန်းပါ။ **Kyanaw Win San bah.** *I'm Win San.*

ကျွန်တော်	kyanaw	I (formal, male speaker)
ဝင်းဆန်း	**Win San**	Win San
ပါ။	**bah**	polite sentence end particle

Repeat the following:
1. **Kyanaw Jim bah.**   I'm Jim. (formal, male speaker)
2. **Kyama Samantha bah.**   I'm Samantha. (formal, female speaker)
3. **Kyanaw Henry bah.**   I'm Henry. (formal, male speaker)
4. **Kyama Jenny bah.**   I'm Jenny. (formal, female speaker)
5. **Kyanaw Jason bah.**   I'm Jason. (formal, male speaker)
6. **Kyama Jane bah.**   I'm Jane. (formal, female speaker)

PATTERN PRACTICE 3: "DO YOU SPEAK BURMESE?"

After hearing Samantha speaks Burmese, Win Naing asks:

ဗမာစကားပြောတတ်လား။ **Bamah zagar pyaw dut lar.**
Do you speak Burmese?

ဗမာစကား	**Bamah zagar**	Burmese language
ပြောတတ်	**pyaw dut**	can speak
လား	**lar**	yes–no question particle

Samantha replies:

နည်းနည်းပြောတတ်တယ်။   **Nae nae pyaw dut tae.**   *I can speak a little bit.*

နည်းနည်း	**nae nae**	a little bit
ပြောတတ်	**pyaw dut**	can speak
တယ်	**tae**	sentence end particle

Practice these exchanges with a partner:

a)   **Bamar zagar pyaw dut lar.**   Do you speak Burmese?
b)   **Nae nae pyaw dut tae.**   I can speak a little bit.

a)   **Ingalake zagar pyaw dut lar.**   Do you speak English?
b)   **Nae nae pyaw dut tae.**   I can speak a little bit.

a)   **Tayoke zagar pyaw dut lar.**   Do you speak Chinese?
b)   **Nae nae pyaw dut tae.**   I can speak a little bit.

a) **Japan zagar pyaw dut lar.**   Do you speak Japanese?
b) **Nae nae pyaw dut tae.**   I can speak a little bit.

a) **Jarmun zagar pyaw dut lar.**   Do you speak German?
b) **Nae nae pyaw dut tae.**   I can speak a little bit.

a) **Pyin thit zagar pyaw dut lar.**   Do you speak French?
b) **Nae nae pyaw dut tae.**   I can speak a little bit.

EXERCISE 2: INTRODUCING SOMEONE

1. You're meeting your childhood friend. Introduce *your girlfriend* to him. Remember to use the informal, familiar possessive **nga**. The word for *girlfriend* is **amyo thamee.**
2. You're meeting your supervisor. Introduce *your boyfriend* to her. Remember to use the formal respectful possessive **kyanawt** (if you're a man), or **kyama** (if you're a woman). The word for *boyfriend* is **amyo thar.**
3. Introduce *your classmate, James* to your supervisor. Remember to use the formal respectful possessive **kyanawt** (if you're a man), or **kyama** (if you're a woman). The word for *classmate* is **kyaung nay bet tha nge jin.**
4. Introduce *your childhood friend Kelly* to your sister. Remember to use the casual possessive **nga**. The word for *childhood friend* is **nge tha nge jin.**
5. Introduce *your coworker Ba Toe* to another stranger. Remember to use the formal respectful possessive **kyanawt** (if you're a man), or **kyama** (if you're a woman). The word for *coworker* is **loke phor kaing bet.**
6. Introduce *your teacher* to your brother. Remember to use the casual possessive **nga**. The word for *teacher* is **hsayah.**
7. Introduce *your supervisor* to your father. Remember to use the formal respectful possessive **kyanawt** (if you're a man), or **kyama** (if you're a woman). The word for supervisor is **a htet ayah shi.**
8. Introduce *your father* to your supervisor. Remember to use the formal respectful possessive **kyanawt** (if you're a man), or **kyama** (if you're a woman). The word for *father* is **aphae.**
9. Introduce *your mother* to your childhood friend. Remember to use the casual possessive **nga**. The word for *mother* is **amae.**
10. Introduce *your younger brother* to a stranger. Remember to use the formal respectful possessive **kyanawt** (if you're a man), or **kyama** (if you're a woman). The word for *younger brother* is **nyi** (if you're a man), or **maung** (if you're a woman).

Nyi lay, de hmah bah sar zayah shi lae.
What kind of food do you have here?

Pae byote naet naan byar shi dae; pout si shi dae; laphet thoke lae shi dae, ako.
We have boiled beans with naan bread, meat buns, also tealeaf salad.

Hsi htamin aw.
How about sticky rice?

Hsi htamin lae ya dae khamya.
We have sticky rice as well.

Dah so, pae byoke ne naan byah yu mae.
Then we'll take boiled beans with naan.

Si hta-min yu mae.
We'll take sticky rice.

CHAPTER 4

Visiting a Teashop

 **DIALOGUE** WHAT'S AVAILABLE AT THE
TEASHOP?

Naing Oo, Samantha, and Win San visit a teashop, where they are greeted by a
young waiter.

Waiter:	*Oh, come in, come in! Please sit over here.*
	Aww, lah bah, lah bah, di hmah htaing bah.
	ဪ ... လာပါ၊ လာပါ၊ ဒီမှာထိုင်ပါ။
Win San:	*What kind of food do you have here?*
	Nyi lay, de hmah bah sar zayah shi lae.
	ညီလေး ... ဒီမှာ ဘာစားစရာ ရှိလဲ။
Waiter:	*You can get boiled beans with* naan *bread, meat buns, cake, also tea leaf salad.*
	Pae byote naet naan byar shi dae; pout si shi dae; cake mote shi dae; laphet thoke lae shi dae, ako.
	ပဲပြုတ်နဲ့ နံပြားရှိတယ်။ ပေါက်စီရှိတယ်။ ကိတ်မုန့်ရှိတယ်။ လက်ဖက်သုပ်လည်းရှိတယ် အကို။
Naing Oo:	*Is* moke hingar *available as well?*
	Moke hingar aw ya lar.
	မုန့်ဟင်းခါးရောရလား။
Waiter:	*Moke hingar's not available.*
	Moke hingar dawt ma ya boo, ako.
	မုန့်ဟင်းခါးတော့ မရဘူးအကို။
Win San:	*How about sticky rice?*
	Hsi htamin aw.
	ဆီထမင်းရော။
Waiter:	*Sticky rice is available.*
	Hsi htamin dawt ya dae khamya.
	ဆီထမင်းတော့ရတယ် ခင်ဗျ။

Win San: *Then we'll take boiled beans with* naan.

Dah so, pae byoke ne naan byah yu mae.

ဒါဆို ပဲပြုတ်နဲ့နံပြားယူမယ်၊

We'll take sticky rice.

Si hta-min yu mae.

ဆီထမင်း ယူမယ်။

Also give us three cups of tea.

Naut, laphet yae thone gwet pah pay bah.

နောက် လက်ဖက်ရည် သုံးခွက်ပါ ပေးပါ။

VOCABULARY

de hmah	here
nyi lay	little brother
ako	big brother
sar zayah	food, eatables
lah	to come (verb)
ya	to be available (verb)
shi	to have (verb)
yu	to take (verb)
htaing	to sit (verb)
pae byote ne naan byah ya	boiled beans and *naan* bread
pout si	meat bun
cake mote	cake
laphet thoke	tea leaf salad (fermented tea leaves with nuts, dried shrimps, and condiments)
moke hingha	noodles with catfish chowder
hsi htamin	Burmese-style sticky rice
lephet yae	Burmese tea

Supplementary Vocabulary

ho hmah	there
nyi ma lay	little sister
ama	big sister
oo lay	uncle
aunty	aunt
sar	to eat (verb)
thauk	to drink (verb)
thwar	to go (verb)
thauk sayah	drinks

ohn no khaut swae	noodles with thick coconut soup
palata	paratha bread
paung mote htaw but thoke	buttered toast
kyet oo jaw	fried egg
kyet oo byote	boiled egg

CULTURAL NOTE **Using kinship terms to address strangers**

Speaking to the young waiter, Win San addresses him as **nyi lay** (little brother). In response, the waiter calls Win San, who is older than him, **ako** (big brother). This is fairly typical of how the Burmese teashop staff and their patrons interact. In fact, this is how Burmese people usually address strangers. Instead of the pronoun *you*, they address one another by kinship terms. The general sentiment is that, the formal pronoun **khamyar** (*you*, by male speakers) or **shin** (*you*, by female speakers) sounds too cold, even somewhat accusatory. Therefore, using a kinship term is a better approach.

ညီလေး ... ဒီမှာ ဘာစားစရာ ရှိလဲ။ Nyi lay, di hmah bah sar zayah ya lae.
Little brother, what kind of food do you have here?

ညီလေး	**nyi lay**	little brother
ဒီမှာ	**de hmah**	right here
ဘာစားစရာ	**bah sar zayah**	what food
ရှိ	**shi**	to have, to exist
လဲ။	**lae**	question particle

If the waiter were a young woman, Win San would say:

ညီမလေး ... ဒီမှာ ဘာစားစရာ ရှိလဲ။ Nyi ma lay, di hmah bah sar zayah ya lae.
Little sister, what kind of food do you have here?

On the other hand, if the waiter were older than him, Win San might say:

အကို ... ဒီမှာ ဘာစားစရာ ရှိလဲ။ Ako, de hmah bah sar zayah ya lae.
Big brother, what kind of food do you have here?

You do not usually address strangers as **aphae** (father) or **amae** (mother), even if they're about the same age as your own parents. Those terms are too intimate to be used for random strangers; therefore, it's better to use them only for one's own parents.

Waiters and waitresses may also address a male patron as **hsayah,** the word for *teacher*. But in that context, the term functions more like the word *boss* or *sir*.

 ## PATTERN PRACTICE 1: RELATIONSHIP TERMS

Practice these lines as if you're addressing a waiter / waitress.

1. **Nyi lay, de hmah bah sar zayah ya lae.** Little brother, what kind of food do you have here? (male speaker)
2. **Maung lay, de hmah bah sar zayah ya lae.** Little brother, what kind of food do you have here? (female speaker)
3. **Nyi ma lay, de hmah bah sar zayah ya lae.** Little sister, what kind of food do you have here?
4. **Ako, de hmah bah sar zayah ya lae.** Big brother, what kind of food do you have here?
5. **Ama, de hmah bah sar zayah ya lae.** Big sister, what kind of food do you have here?
6. **Oo lay, de hmah bah sar zayah ya lae.** Uncle, what kind of food do you have here?
7. **Aunty, de hmah bah sar zayah ya lae.** Aunty, what kind of food do you have here?

 Note: While men use **nyi lay** for *little brother*, women use **maung lay.**

GRAMMAR NOTE **Issuing requests or commands**

When Win San, Naing Oo, and Samantha entered, the young waiter said:

ေြသာ် ... လာပါ၊ လာပါ၊ ဒီမှာထိုင်ပါ။
Aww, lah bah, lah bah, de hmah htaing bah.
Oh, come, come, please sit here.

A verb followed by the particle **bah** or **pah** is a command or a request:

လာပါ၊ လာပါ။   **Lah bah, lah bah.**   *Come, come!*

လာ	**lah**	to come
ပါ။	**bah**	command / request particle

Strictly speaking, you can issue a command or a request simply by saying a verb, like **lah** (come) or **htaing** (sit). But that is considered to be extremely rude, because it gives the impression that you expect to be obeyed no matter what. Adding **bah** or **pah** makes the request more polite.

PATTERN PRACTICE 2: COMMANDS AND REQUESTS

Practice these commands and requests.

1. **Htaing bah.** Please sit!
2. **Lah bah.** Please come!
3. **Sar bah.** Please eat!
4. **Thauk pah.** Please drink!
5. **Thwar bah.** Please go!
6. **Yu bah.** Please take!

GRAMMAR NOTE "Here" and "there" — *de* vs. *ho*

To direct them to their seat, the waiter used **de hmah** (over here). If the seats were a bit farther away, the waiter would have used **ho hmah** (over there):

ဒီမှာထိုင်ပါ။   **Di hmah htaing bah.**   *Please sit over here.*

ဒီမှာ	de hmah	over here
ထိုင်	htaing	to sit
ပါ	bah	command / request particle

ဟိုမှာ ထိုင်ပါ။   **Ho hmah htaing bah.**   *Please sit over there.*

ဟိုမှာ	ho hmah	over there
ထိုင်	htaing	to sit
ပါ	bah	command / request particle

PATTERN PRACTICE 3: "HERE" AND "THERE"

Practice these commands and requests with place indicators.

1. **De hmah** htaing bah.   Please sit <u>over here</u>.
2. **Ho hmah** htaing bah.   Please sit <u>over there</u>.
3. **De hmah** sar bah.   Please eat <u>over here</u>.
4. **Ho hmah** sar bah.   Please eat <u>over there</u>.
5. **De hmah** thauk pah.   Please [have a] drink <u>over here</u>.
6. **Ho hmah** thauk pah.   Please [have a] drink <u>over there</u>.

GRAMMAR NOTE The Wh- question particle *lae*

You use the particle **lae** to pose *who, what, where, when, why* and *how* questions. When Win San wants to know what kind of food is available at the teashop, he asks the following question:

ဘာစားစရာ ရှိလဲ။ Bah sar zayah shi lae. *What kind of food do you have?*

ဘာ	bah	what
စားစရာ	sar zayah	food
ရှိ	shi	to have, to exist
လဲ။	lae	question particle

PATTERN PRACTICE 4: "WHAT DO YOU HAVE?"

Practice asking for these:

1. **De hmah** bah sar zayah shi lae.
   What kind of food do you have <u>here</u>?
2. **Ho hmah** bah sar zayah shi lae.
   What kind of food do you have <u>there</u>?
3. **De hmah** bah thauk sayah shi lae.
   What kind of drinks do you have <u>here</u>?
4. **Ho hmah** bah thauk sayah shi lae.
   What kind of drinks do you have <u>there</u>?
5. **De hsaing** hmah bah sar zayah shi lae.
   What kind of food is available at <u>this shop</u>?
6. **Ho hsaing** hmah bah sar zayah shi lae.
   What kind of food is available at <u>that shop</u>?
7. **De hsaing** hmah bah thauk sayah shi lae.
   What kinds of drinks are available at <u>this shop</u>?
8. **Ho hsaing** hmah bah thaunk sayah shi lae.
   What kinds of drinks are available at <u>that shop</u>?

GRAMMAR NOTE The verb *shi* (to have, to exist)

To tell Win San what was available to eat, the waiter said:

ပဲပြုတ်နဲ့ နံပြားရှိတယ်။ Pae byote naet naan byar shi dae.
There's boiled beans with naan *bread.*

ပဲပြုတ်	pae byote	boiled beans
နဲ့	naet	and

နံပြား	naan byar	*naan* bread
ရှိ	shi	to exist, to have
တယ်	dae	sentence-end particle

ကိတ်မုန့်ရှိတယ်။ Cake mont shi dae. *There's cake.*

ကိတ်မုန့်	cake mont	cake
ရှိ	shi	to exist, to have
တယ်	dae	sentence-end particle

လက်ဖက်သုပ်လည်းရှိတယ်။ Lephet thoke lae shi dae.
There's also tea leaf salad.

လက်ဖက်သုပ်	lephet thoke	tea leaf salad
လည်း	lae	also, as well, too
ရှိ	shi	to exist, to have
တယ်	dae	sentence-end particle

PATTERN PRACTICE 5: "THERE IS ..."

Practice saying these:
1. **Pout si shi dae.** There's meat buns.
2. **Moke hingar shi dae.** There's *moke hingar* (fish chowder and noodles).
3. **Ohn no khauk swae shi dae.** There's *ohn no khauk swe* (coconut noodles).
4. **Paung mote htaw bat thoke shi dae.** There's buttered bread.

PATTERN PRACTICE 6: "THERE'S ALSO ..."

Practice saying these with the particle **lae**:
1. **Pout si lae shi dae.** There's also meat buns.
2. **Palata lae ya dae.** There's also paratha.
3. **Kyet oo jaw lae ya dae.** There's also fried egg.
4. **Kyet oo byote lae ya dae.** There's also boiled egg.

GRAMMAR NOTE The verb *ya* (something to be available)

Naing Oo also uses the verb **ya** to ask if *moke hingar* is available:

မုန့်ဟင်းခါးရောရလား။ Moke hingar aw ya lar. *Is* moke hingar *also available?*

| မုန့်ဟင်းခါး | moke hingar | catfish chowder and noodles |
| ရော | yaw / aw | also, as well |

ရ	ya	available
လား	lar	question particle

Note: The particle **yaw** for *also* or *as well* may only be partially pronounced, as **aw**, in quick conversations.

PATTERN PRACTICE 7: "IS THIS ALSO AVAILABLE?"

Practice these questions:

1. **Moke hingar aw ya lar.**   Is *moke hingar* also available as well?
2. **Ohn no khauk swae aw ya lar.**   Is *ohn no khauk swe* available as well?
3. **Kyet oo jaw aw ya lar.**   Is fried egg available as well?
4. **Lepeht thoke ya lar.**   Is tea leaf salad available as well?

GRAMMAR NOTE "Give" and "take" (*pay* and *yu*)

Finally, to specify his order, Win San says:

ဆီထမင်း ယူမယ်။ **Hsi htamin yu mae.**   *I'll take* hsi htamin *(sticky rice).*

ဆီထမင်း	hsi htamin	sticky rice
ယူ	yu	to take
မယ်။	mae	future sentence end particle

Because Win San is stating what he wants to do, he ends the sentence with **mae**, the future sentence end particle. He doesn't use the sentence-end particle **tae**, which is for actions and events in the past or the present.

PATTERN PRACTICE 8: "I'LL TAKE THIS."

Practice these responses:

1. **Lephet thoke yu mae.**   I'll take tea leaf salad.
2. **Moke hingar yu mae.**   I'll take *moke hingar*.
3. **Kyet oo jaw yu mae.**   I'll take a fried egg.
4. **Pout si yu mae.**   I'll take a meat bun.

Win San rounds out his order with:

လက်ဖက်ရည် သုံးခွက် ပေးပါ။ **Laphet yay thone gwet pay bah.**
Please give us three cups of tea.

လက်ဖက်ရည်	laphet yay	tea

သုံးခွက်	thone gwet	three cups
ပေး	pay	to give
ပါ။	bah	request particle

PATTERN PRACTICE 9: "PLEASE GIVE ME THIS."

Practice these orders:

1. **Pout si pay bah.**   Please give me a meat bun.
2. **Pae byote naet naan byar pay bah.**
   Please give me boiled beans and naan bread.
3. **Kyet oo jaw pay bah.**   Please give me a fried egg.
4. **Moke hingar pay bah.**   Please give me *moke hingar*.

EXERCISE 1: STATING WHAT'S AVAILABLE

You're a waiter in a cafe. Tell the customer you have the following items. Remember to use the particle **lae** (also) for the last item.

1. Meat bun, *moke hingar* (catfish chowder and noodles), and a fried egg.
2. *Lephet thoke* (tea leaf salad), a meat bun, and *ohn no khauk swe* (coconut noodles).
3. *Hsi htamin* (sticky rice), tea leaf salad, and cake.

EXERCISE 2: "I'LL TAKE THIS AND THAT."

You're a customer in a teashop. Tell the waiter you'll take the following items. Remember to use the particle **lae** (also) for the last item.

1. Meat bun, *lephet thoke* (tea leaf salad), and *moke hingar* (catfish chowder and noodles).
2. *Hsi htamin* (sticky rice), a meat bun, and boiled beans and *naan* bread.
3. Tea, buttered toast, and cake.

CULTURAL NOTE The land of tea leaf salad and noodle stalls

Tea leaf salad or *lephet thoke*, is the quintessential Burmese snack. It comprises fermented tea leaves, fried scallions, chopped garlic, sesame seeds, peanuts, dried shrimps, and is flavored with lime juice, pungent fish sauce, and oil. The caffeine content makes it an ideal dish for students studying for exams. Other popular dishes include *moke hingar,* rice noodles served with catfish chowder; and *ohn no khauk swae,* egg noodles served in coconut-flavored soup with chicken. Local people tend to eat these dishes for breakfast or lunch at sidewalk noodle stalls. Vendors offer the option to add crumbled bean cakes and fritters to the broth for crunchiness. Customers sometimes ask the vendor to refill the bowl with extra broth to finish off the remaining noodles, and the vendor is usually happy to oblige.

Min agu bae hmah aloke loke lae.
Where are you working now?

Yangon ga in-teh-nay-shin-nae kyaung hmah Myanmar zah thin dae.
I teach Burmese at the International School in Yangon.

Hah, kaung dah pawt.
Oh, that's wonderful!

Min aw.
And you?

Nga ko baing loke ngan shi dae. Kha yee thwar loke ngan.
I've got my own business—a travel agency.

Tour kone pa-nee lar.
Is it a tour company?

Hote tae.
That's right.

CHAPTER 5

Small Talk

 **DIALOGUE** WHERE DO YOU WORK?

At the teashop, conversation turns to work and life. Win San reveals he's a Burmese
teacher for an international school in Yangon. Delighted, Samantha asks Win San
if she can get some Burmese lessons from him.

Naing Oo:	*Where are you working now?*
	Min agu bae hmah aloke loke lae.
	မင်း အခု ဘယ်မှာ အလုပ်လုပ်လဲ။
Win San:	*I teach Burmese at the International School in Yangon.*
	Yangon ga in-teh-nay-shin-nae kyaung hmah Myanmar zah thin dae.
	ရန်ကုန်က အင်တာနယ်ရှင်နယ်ကျောင်းမှာ မြန်မာစာသင်တယ်။
Naing Oo:	*Oh, that's wonderful!*
	Hah, kaung dah pawt.
	ဟာ ... ကောင်းတာပေါ့။
Win San:	*And you?*
	Min aw.
	မင်းရော။
Naing Oo:	*I've got my own business—a travel agency.*
	Nga ko baing loke ngan shi dae. Kha yee thwar loke ngan.
	ငါ့ကိုယ်ပိုင်လုပ်ငန်းရှိတယ်။ ခရီးသွားလုပ်ငန်း။
Win San:	*Is it a tour company?*
	Tour kone pa-nee lar.
	တိုးကုမ္ပဏီလား။
Naing Oo:	*That's right.*
	Hote tae.
	ဟုတ်တယ်။

VOCABULARY

agu	now
bah	what
aloke	job, work
kyaung	school

Myanmar zar	Burmese language
thin	to teach
loke ngan	business
ko baing	private, self-owned
kha yee thwar	traveling
sar thauk saing	restaurant
mun nay jah	manager
bae hmah le	where is it?
aku anyi	favor, help. assistance
taung	to ask for, request
pyaw	to speak
dagae	really, truly

Supplementary Vocabulary

ayin ga	before, previously
Ingalake sah	English language
Tayoke sah	Chinese language
Japan zah	Japanese language
Ko ree yan zah	Korean language
Pyinthit sah	French language
Jarmun zah	German language
set hmu loke ngan	manufacturing business
let hmu loke ngan	craft-making business, making homemade goods
anu pyin nyah loke ngan	art business
nee pyin nyah loke ngan	technology business
lephet yay zaing	teashop
korphee zaing	coffee shop
yadanah zaing	jewelry shop
ayoke saing	toy shop
awut saing	clothing shop
ain jee zaing	shirt shop
pasoe zaing	man's *sarong* shop
htamain zaing	woman's *sarong* shop
zabin hnyut saing	hairdresser
aat chote saing	tailoring shop
ayet saing	bar, place that serves alcohol
kon zone zaing	grocer, shop selling general goods

sah oak saing	bookshop
wun dan	staff, clerk
paing shin	owner

<hr>

CULTURAL NOTE **Prefixes and honorifics**

When addressing someone by his / her name in polite conversations, it's important to add the age-appropriate honorifics. This is why Samantha addresses **Win
San** as **Ko Win San**. If you're older than the other party, you could choose to omit
the honorifics, but if you're the younger one, it's good manner to use them. Here
are the honorifics:

Prefix	who is it for	example
Maung	for young boys, young men	Maung Win San
Ko	for adult males	Ko Win San
U (pronounced **Oo**)	for older gentlemen	U Win San
Ma	for young girls, young women	Ma Khin Lay
Daw	for older women	Daw Khin Lay

CULTURAL NOTE **Using someone's name as a pronoun**

When asking Naing Oo about his current job, Win San said:

မင်း အခု ဘယ်မှာ အလုပ်လုပ်လဲ။   Min agu bae hmah aloke loke lae.
Where do you work now?

မင်း	**min**	you (casual, familiar)
အခု	**agu**	right now
ဘယ်မှာ	**bae hmar**	where at
အလုပ်	**aloke**	job, work
လုပ်	**loke**	to do, work
လဲ။	**lae**	question particle

Win San used the informal, familiar pronoun **min** for *you* because he and Naing
Oo have known each other for a long time. To pose the same question to strangers
or people you have just met, you should use the polite pronoun **khamyar** (if you're
a male speaker) or **shin** (if you're a female speaker).

(Formal, male speaker) ခင်ဗျား အခု ဘယ်မှာ အလုပ်လုပ်လဲ။
Khamyar agu bae hmah aloke loke lae.   *Where do you work now?*

ခင်ဗျား	khamyar	you (formal, male speaker)
အခု	agu	right now
ဘယ်မှာ	bae hmah	where at
အလုပ်	aloke	job, work
လုပ်	loke	to do, work
လဲ။	lae	question particle

(Formal, female speaker) ရှင် အခု ဘယ်မှာ အလုပ်လုပ်လဲ။
Shin agu bae hmar aloke loke lae.   *Where do you work now?*

ရှင်	shin	you (formal, female speaker)
အခု	agu	right now
ဘယ်မှာ	bae hmah	where at
အလုပ်	aloke	job, work
လုပ်	loke	to do, work
လဲ။	lae	question particle

But there's another—arguably more polite—alternative. That is, to use the other person's name instead of the pronoun *you*. In polite, formal exchanges, native speakers tend to favor this option over the pronouns **khamyar** or **shin**. For example, if you're speaking to Win San, you may instead ask the same questions as:

ကိုဝင်းဆန်း အခု ဘယ်မှာ အလုပ်လုပ်လဲ။
Ko Win San agu bae hmah aloke loke lae.
Where does Ko Win San work now?

ကို	**Ko**	respectful prefix for adult male
ဝင်းဆန်း	**Win San**	Win San (person's name instead of the pronoun you)
အခု	**agu**	right now
ဘယ်မှာ	**bae hmah**	where at
အလုပ်	**aloke**	job, work
လုပ်	**loke**	to do, to work
လဲ။	**lae**	question particle

And if you're speaking to, say, a woman named Moe Moe, you can say:

မမိုးမိုး အခု ဘယ်မှာ အလုပ်လုပ်လဲ။
Ma Moe Moe agu bae hmah aloke loke lae.
Where does Ma Moe Moe work now?

မ	Ma	respectful prefix for adult female
မိုးမိုး	Moe Moe	(person's name instead of the pronoun you)
အခု	agu	right now
ဘယ်မှာ	bae hmah	where at
အလုပ်	aloke	job, work
လုပ်	loke	to do, to work
လဲ။		

GRAMMAR NOTE Talking about the present and the past

In Win San's question above, the phrase **agu** specifies the time: *now* or *currently*. In Burmese, you can use the same verb to talk about events in the past or the present. You do *not* need to transform the verb **loke** (to do) into a different form to talk about the past, the way you must in English. So you can use the same structure to pose a question about the past by simply replacing the word **agu** (now) with **ayin ga** (before, previously).

(Formal, male speaker, asking about someone's current job)
    ခင်ဗျား အခု ဘယ်မှာ အလုပ်လုပ်လဲ။   **Khamyar agu bae hmar aloke loke lae.**
    Where do you work now?

ခင်ဗျား	khamyar	you (formal, male speaker)
အခု	agu	right now
ဘယ်မှာ	bae hmah	where at
အလုပ်	aloke	job, work
လုပ်	loke	to do, to work
လဲ။	lae	question particle

(Formal, male speaker, asking about someone's previous job)
    ခင်ဗျား အရင်က ဘယ်မှာ အလုပ်လုပ်လဲ။
    Khamyar ayin ga bae hmar aloke loke lae.   *Where did you work before?*

ခင်ဗျား	khamyar	you (formal, male speaker)
အရင်က	ayin ga	previously, before
ဘယ်မှာ	bae hmah	where at
အလုပ်	aloke	job, work
လုပ်	loke	to do, to work
လဲ။	lae	question particle

PATTERN PRACTICE 1:
ASKING ABOUT SOMEONE'S WORK

Practice these questions:

1. <u>Khamyar</u> agu bae hmah aloke loke lae.
   Where do you work now? *Polite form, male speaker*
2. <u>Shin</u> agu bae hmah aloke loke lae.
   Where do you work now? *Polite form, female speaker*
3. <u>Khamyar</u> ayin ga bae hmah aloke loke lae.
   Where did you work before? *Polite form, male speaker*
4. <u>Shin</u> ayin ga bae hmah aloke loke lae.
   Where did you work before? *Polite form, female speaker*

PATTERN PRACTICE 2:
USING SOMEONE'S NAME INSTEAD OF "YOU"

Let's practice asking Min Lu, an adult man, and Moe Moe, an adult woman, about where they currently work now, and where they used to work. This time, we will use their names instead of the pronouns **khamyar** or **shin**.

Since Min Lu is an adult male, you should address him with the prefix **Ko** before his name in polite conversations. By the same token, you should address Moe Moe with the prefix **Ma** before her name.

1. <u>Ko</u> Min Lu agu bae hmah aloke loke lae.
   Where do you work now, Mr. Min Lu?
2. <u>Ma</u> Moe Moe agu bae hmah aloke loke lae.
   Where do you work now, Miss Moe Moe?
3. <u>Ko</u> Min Lu ayin ga bae hmah aloke loke lae.
   Where did you work before, Mr. Min Lu?
4. <u>Ma</u> Moe Moe ayin ga bae hmah aloke loke lae.
   Where did you work before, Miss Moe Moe?

Let's also practice asking Bo Bo, an older gentleman, and Thidar, an older lady, about where they currently work now, and where they used to work. Since Bo Bo is an older gentleman, you should address him with the prefix **U** (pronounced **oo**) before his name in polite conversations. By the same token, you should address the lady with the prefix **Daw** before her name.

1. <u>U</u> Bo Bo agu bae hmah aloke loke lae.
   Where do you work now, Mr. Bo Bo?
2. <u>Daw</u> Thidar agu bae hmah aloke loke lae.
   Where do you work now, Ms. Thidar?

3. <u>U</u> Bo Bo ayin ga bae hmah aloke loke lae.
    Where did you work before, Mr. Bo Bo?
4. <u>Daw</u> Thidar ayin ga bae hmah aloke loke lae.
    Where did you work before, Ms. Thidar?

PATTERN PRACTICE 3: USING KINSHIP TERMS TO ASK ABOUT SOMEONE'S WORK

Burmese people also tend to use kinship terms to address strangers. So let's practice asking the same questions above, using kinship terms.

1. <u>Ako</u> agu bae hmah aloke loke lae. <u>Big brother</u>, where do you work now?
2. <u>Ako</u> ayin ga bae hmah aloke loke lae. <u>Big brother</u>, where did you work before?
3. <u>Nyi lay</u> agu bae hmah aloke loke lae. <u>Little brother</u>, where do you work now? *Male speaker*
4. <u>Maung lay</u> agu bae hmah aloke loke lae. <u>Little brother</u>, where do you work now? *Female speaker*
5. <u>Nyi lay</u> ayin ga bae hmah aloke loke lae. <u>Little brother</u>, where did you work before? *Male speaker*
6. <u>Maung lay</u> ayin ga bae hmah aloke loke lae. <u>Little brother</u>, where did you work before? *Female speaker*
7. <u>Ama</u> agu bae hmah aloke loke lae. <u>Big sister</u>, where do you work now?
8. <u>Ama</u> ayin ga bae hmah aloke loke lae. <u>Big sister</u>, where did you work before?
9. <u>Nyi ma</u> agu bae hmah aloke loke lae. <u>Little sister</u>, where do you work now?
10. <u>Nyi ma</u> ayin ga bae hmah aloke loke lae. <u>Little sister</u>, where did you work before?
11. <u>Oo lay</u> agu bae hmah aloke loke lae. <u>Uncle</u>, where do you work now?
12. <u>Oo lay</u> ayin ga bae hmah aloke loke lae. <u>Uncle</u>, where did you work before?
13. <u>Aunty</u> agu bae hmah aloke loke lae. <u>Aunty</u>, where do you work now?
14. <u>Aunty</u> ayin ga bae hmah aloke loke lae. <u>Aunty</u>, where did you work before?

EXERCISE 1: CURRENT WORK, PREVIOUS WORK

How would you say the following in Burmese?

1. Little brother, where did you work before?
2. Big sister, where do you work now?
3. Little sister, where do you work now?
4. Little sister, where did you work before?
5. Mr. Chan Aye, where do you work now? (Mr. Chan Aye is an adult male.)
6. Miss Lwin Lwin, where did you work before? (Miss Lwin Lwin is an adult female.)

7. Mr. Kan Paw, where did you work before? (Mr. Kan Paw is an older man.)
8. Ms. Khin Oo, where do you work now? (Ms. Khin Oo is an older woman.)

GRAMMAR NOTE The particle *hmah* (in, at)

Describing his work, Win San says:

အင်တာနယ်ရှင်နယ်ကျောင်းမှာ မြန်မာစာသင်တယ်။
In-tah-nay-shin-nae kyaung hmah Myanmar zah thin dae.
I teach Burmese at the International School.

မှာ	hmah	at, in
အင်တာနယ်ရှင်နယ်ကျောင်း	In-tah-nay-shin-nae kyaung	International School
မြန်မာစာ	Myanmar zah	Burmese
သင်	thin	to teach
တယ်။	dae	sentence end particle

The particle **hmah** functions like *at* or *in* to indicate the place where Win San is teaching. It comes after the noun, the name of the place. For example:

ရန်ကုန်မှာ	Yangon hmah	in Yangon
မန္တလေးမှာ	Mandalay hmah	in Mandalay
မေမြို့မှာ	Maymyo hmah	in Maymyo
အမေရိကားမှာ	A may ri ka hmah	in America
ဂျပန်မှာ	Japan hmah	in Japan

 **PATTERN PRACTICE 4:
USING THE PLACE INDICATOR *HMAR***

Practice these sentences:
1. **Yangon hmah Myanmar zah thin dae.**   I teach Burmese in Yangon.
2. **Mandalay hmah Myanmar zah thin dae.**   I teach Burmese in Mandalay.
3. **Maymyo hmah Myanmar zah thin dae.**   I teach Burmese in Maymyo.
4. **Amay ri ka hmah Myanmar zah thin dae.**   I teach Burmese in America.
5. **Japan hmah Myanmar zah thin dae.**   I teach Burmese in Japan.

Also practice some variations of the type of language taught, using the list of languages in the supplementary vocabulary on page 46:
1. **Yangon hmah Ingalake sah thin dae.**   I teach English in Yangon.
2. **Yangon hmah Tayoke sah thin dae.**   I teach Chinese in Yangon.

Yangon hmah Myanmar zah thin lar.
Do you teach Burmese in Yangon?

3. **Yangon hmah Japan zah thin dae.**   I teach Japanese in Yangon.
4. **Yangon hmah Ko ree yan zah thin dae.**   I teach Korean in Yangon.
5. **Yangon hmah Jarmun zah thin dae.**   I teach German in Yangon.
6. **Yangon hmah Pyinthit sah thin dae.**   I teach French in Yangon.
7. **Yangon hmah Ko ree yan zah thin dae.**   I teach Korean in Yangon.

EXERCISE 2: "WHERE I TEACH A CERTAIN LANGUAGE"

Say the following in Burmese:
1. I teach Burmese in Mandalay.
2. I teach French in Maymyo.
3. I teach German in America.
4. I teach Japanese in Yangon.
5. I teach English in Mandalay.
6. I teach Burmese at the International School.
7. I teach Korean at the International School.

PATTERN PRACTICE 5: "DO YOU TEACH THIS?"

In Chapter 3: Greetings, you learnt a simple way to formulate yes–no questions with the particle **lar**:

နေကောင်းလား။   **Nay kaung lar.**   *How are you?*

| နေကောင်း | nay kaung | to feel fine |
| လား | lar | yes–no question particle |

You can use the same question-making particle **lar** to ask someone what language he/she teaches:

မြန်မာစာ သင်လား။   **Myanmar zar thin lar.**   *Do you teach Burmese?*

မြန်မာစာ	Myanmar zah	Burmese language
သင်	thin	to teach
လား	lar	yes–no question particle

Practice the following questions:
1. **Ingalake sah thin lar.** Do you teach English?
2. **Tayoke sah thin lar.** Do you teach Chinese?
3. **Japan zah thin lar.** Do you teach Japanese?
4. **Ko ree yan zah thin lar.** Do you teach Korean?
5. **Pyinthit sah thin lar.** Do you teach French?
6. **Jarmun zah thin lar.** Do you teach German?

GRAMMAR NOTE Converting statements into yes–no questions

Let's compare the affirmative statement "I teach Burmese" and the question "Do you teach Burmese?"

မြန်မာစာသင်တယ်။   **Myanmar zah thin dae.**
I teach Burmese. (affirmative statement)

မြန်မာစာ	Myanmar zah	Burmese language
သင်	thin	to teach
တယ်	dae	affirmative sentence end particle.

Note that the subject pronoun *I* is suppressed or implied. This is a perfectly acceptable omission: If you can safely assume people know what or who you're talking about, you don't have to state it explicitly.

မြန်မာစာသင်လား။   **Myanmar zah thin lar.**
Do you teach Burmese? (yes–no question)

မြန်မာစာ	**Myanmar zah**	Burmese language
သင်	**thin**	to teach
လား	**lar**	yes–no qestion particle.

Note that, here, the subject pronoun *you* is also suppressed or implied. With these types of sentences, the only difference between the affirmative statement and the yes–no question is the final particle—**tae** or **dae** for affirmative statements; **lar** for yes–no questions.

Knowing this secret allows you to turn many *affirmative statements* into *yes–no questions*. For example:

ရန်ကုန်မှာ မြန်မာစာသင်တယ်။   **Yangon hmah Myanmar zah thin dae.**
I teach Burmese in Yangon. (affirmative statement)

ရန်ကုန်မှာ မြန်မာစာသင်လား။   **Yangon hmah Myanmar zah thin lar.**
Do you teach Burmese in Yangon? (yes–no question)

EXERCISE 3: TURNING STATEMENTS INTO QUESTIONS
Convert the following statements into yes–no questions in Burmese:
1. **Tayoke sah thin dae.**   I teach Chinese.
2. **Ingalake sah thin dae.**   I teach English.
3. **Japan zah thin dae.**   I teach Japanese.
4. **Amay ri ka hmah Myanmar zah thin dae.**   I teach Burmese in America.
5. **Mandalay hmah Tayoke sah thin dae.**   I teach Chinese in Mandalay.
6. **Maymyo hmah Ingalake sah thin dae.**   I teach English in Maymyo.

Samantha ga aw.
How about you, Samantha?

Bah aloke loke lae.
What kind of work do you do?

Sar thauk hsaing man nay jah bah.
I'm a restaurant manager.

Aww, hsaing ga bae hmah lae.
Oh, where's the restaurant?

San Francisco hmah.
In San Francisco.

Ko Win San go aku anyi taung jin dae.
I'd like to ask you a favor, Win San.

Ya bah dae.
Of course.

Myanmar zah thin pay bah.
Teach me Burmese.

Hin, dagae lar.
Hmm, really?

Dagae bah shint.
Really.

🔘 DIALOGUE WHAT DO YOU DO?

The three friends continue their conversation about work. Now it's Win San's turn to find out what Samantha does for a living.

Win San:	*How about you, Samantha?*
	Samantha ga aw.
	Samantha ကရော
	What kind of work do you do?
	Bah aloke loke lae.
	ဘာအလုပ် လုပ်လဲ॥
Samantha:	*I'm a restaurant manager.*
	Sar thauk hsaing man nay jah bah.
	စားသောက်ဆိုင် မန်နေဂျာ ပါ॥
Win San:	*Oh, where's the restaurant?*
	Aww, hsaing ga bae hmah lae.
	ၾသော် ... ဆိုင်က ဘယ်မှာလဲ॥
Samantha:	*In San Francisco.*
	San Francisco hmah.
	San Francisco မှာ॥
Win San:	*Hah, great!*
	Hah, kaung dae.
	ဟာ ... ကောင်းတယ်॥
Samantha:	*I'd like to ask you a favor, Win San.*
	Ko Win San go aku anyi taung jin dae.
	ကိုဝင်းဆန်းကို အကူညီတောင်းချင်တယ်॥
Win San:	*Of course.*
	Ya bah dae.
	ရပါတယ်॥
Samantha:	*Teach me Burmese.*
	Myanmar zah thin pay bah.
	မြန်မာစာ သင်ပေးပါ॥
Win San:	*Hmm, really?*
	Hin, dagae lar.
	ဟင် ... တကယ်လား॥
Samantha:	*Really.*
	Dagae bah shint.
	တကယ်ပါ ရှင့်॥

GRAMMAR NOTE Asking "what" questions with *bah*

Turning to Samantha, Win San asks:

ဘာအလုပ် လုပ်လဲ။   **Bah aloke loke lae.**   *What kind of work do you do?*

ဘာ	bah	what
အလုပ်	aloke	job, work
လုပ်	loke	to do, to work
လဲ	lae	question particle

In reply, Samantha says:

စားသောက်ဆိုင် မန်နေဂျာ ပါ။   **Sar thauk hsaing man nay jah bah.**
I'm a restaurant manager.

စားသောက်ဆိုင်	sar thauk hsaing	restaurant
မန်နေဂျာ	man nay jar	manager
ပါ	bah	sentence-end particle

GRAMMAR NOTE

When to use *tae* (or *dae*); when to use *pah* (or *bah*)

The particles **tae** (or **dae**) and **pah** (or **bah**) usually appear at the end of affirmative sentences. The general rule is, **tae** (or **dae**) follows a *verb* or *adjective*; and **pah** (or **bah**) usually follows a *noun*. For example:

Myanmar zah thin dae. *I teach Burmese.* (**Thin**, *to teach*, is a verb, so the sentence ends in **dae**.)

Sar thauk hsaing man nay jah bah. *I'm a restaurant manager.* (**Man nay jar**, *manager*, is a noun, so the sentence ends in **bah**.)

PATTERN PRACTICE 6: "WHAT I DO FOR WORK."

Practice these variations:
1. **Sar thauk hsaing wun dan bah.**
   I'm a restaurant employee (waiter or waitress).
2. **Sar thauk hsaing paing shin bah.**   I'm a restaurant owner.
3. **Sar oak hsaing man nay jah bah.**   I'm a bookstore manager.
4. **Korphee zaing wun dan bah.**   I'm a cafe employee.
5. **Lephet yay zaing paing shin bah.**   I'm a teashop owner.

6. **Yadanah zaing man nay jah bah.**   I'm a jewelry shop owner.
7. **Awut hsaing paing shin bah.**   I'm a clothing shop owner.

Just like the affirmative sentences ending with **tae** or **dae**, you can also easily convert affirmative sentences ending with **pah** or **bah** into yes–no questions by changing the last particle. For example:

Sar thauk hsaing man nay jah bah.   *(I'm a) restaurant manager.*

Sar thauk hsaing man nay jah lar.   *(Are you) a restaurant manager?*

EXERCISE 4: "IS THIS YOUR JOB?"
Now convert these into yes–no questions:
1. **Korphee zaing wun dan bah.**   I'm a cafe employee.
2. **Yadanah zaing man nay jah bah.**   I'm a jewelry shop owner.
3. **Sar thauk hsaing wun dan bah.**   I'm a restaurant staffer (waiter or waitress)
4. **Sar thauk hsaing paing shin bah.**   I'm a restaurant owner.
5. **Lephet yay zaing paing shin bah.**   I'm a teashop owner.
6. **A-wut hsaing paing shin bah.**   I'm a clothing shop owner.
7. **Sar oak hsaing man nay jar bah.**   I'm a bookstore manager.

CHAPTER 6

Getting Around

 **DIALOGUE** GOING PLACES

As they are getting ready to leave the teashop, Samantha tells Naing Oo she wants to visit the famous Shwedagon Pagoda. Since Naing Oo isn't sure how to get there, he asks Win San for directions.

Naing Oo: *Say, Win San, Samantha wants to go to Shwedagon.*
Kae, Win San, Samantha Shwedagon thwar jin dae.
ကဲ ဝင်းဆန်း၊ Samantha ရွှေတိဂုံ သွားချင်တယ်။
How do we get there?
Bae lo thwar ya lae.
ဘယ်လိုသွားရလဲ။

Win San: *Hmm, don't you know how to get there?*
Hah, min ma thwar dut phoo lar.
ဟာ ... မင်း မသွားတတ်ဘူးလား။

Naing Oo: *I don't remember it [the way to get there].*
Nga ma hmut mi boo.
ငါ မမှတ်မိဘူး။

Win San: *Well, well, Mr. Traveler, I'll tell you.*
Kae, kae, khayee thae gyi.
ကဲ၊ ကဲ၊ ခရီးသည်ကြီး၊
Walk straight for about three blocks.
Shayt taet daet thone balauk shaut.
ရှေ့တည့်တည့် သုံးဘလောက် လျှောက်။

Naing Oo: *OK.*
Kaung bi.
ကောင်းပြီ။

Win San: *Then turn right at the traffic light.*
Naut, mee point hmah nyah choe.
နောက် မီးပွိုင့်မှာ ညာချိုး။

Naing Oo: *And then?*
Pee dawt.
ပြီးတော့ ...

Win San: *Next, take the number 43 bus from A-Mait Ain bookshop.*

Pee yin, Amayt Ain sah oak hsaing shaet hmah lay zae thone kar see thwar.

ပြီးရင် အမေ့အိမ် စာအုပ်ဆိုင်ရှေ့မှာ ၄၃ ကားစီး။

You'll get there after seven stops.

Khon-na hmut taing hso yaut pe.

၇ မှတ်တိုင်ဆို ရောက်ပြီ။

Naing Oo: *Thanks! Well, I'll be going now.*

Kyay zoo bae. Kae, thwar mae naw.

ကျေးဇူးပဲ၊ ကဲ သွားမယ်နော်။

Samantha: *Please excuse us.*

Khwint pyu bah ohn.

ခွင့်ပြုပါဦး။

Win San: *Of course, of course!*

Hote kaet, hote kaet.

ဟုတ်ကဲ့ ၊ ဟုတ်ကဲ့

VOCABULARY

thwar jin dae	want to go
bae lo	how
thwar dut dae	know how to go
ma thwar dut phoo	don't know how to go
hmut mi dae	remember
ma hmut mi boo	don't remember
khayee thae	traveler/tourist
shayt taet daet	straight ahead
balauk	block
shaut	walk
naut	next, then
mi point	traffic light
nyah choe	turn right
shaet hmah	in front of
sah oak hsaing	bookshop
lay zae thone kar	number 43 bus
hmut taing	bus stop
khon-na hmut taing	seven stops
yaut pe	will arrive, would have arrived, have arrived

Supplementary Vocabulary

sar jin dae	want to eat
thauk chin dae	want to drink
lah jin dae	want to come
ait chin dae	want to sleep
nar jin dae	want to rest
twayt jin dae	want to meet
htaing jin dae	want to sit
bae choe	turn left
naut hlaet	turn around, turn back
lephet yae zaing	teashop
mont zaing	snack shop
akyaw zaing	fritter shop

 **GRAMMAR NOTE** "Want to go somewhere"

When Naing Oo tells Win San that Samantha wants to go to Shwedagon, he says:

Samantha ရွှေတိဂုံ သွားချင်တယ်။ Samantha Shwedagon thwar jin dae.
Samantha wants to go to Shwedagon.

Samantha	**Samantha**	Samantha
ရွှေတိဂုံ	**Shwedagon**	Shwedagon (pagoda)
သွား	**thwar**	to go
ချင်	**jin**	want to (auxiliary verb)
တယ်	**dae**	sentence-end particle

 Notice how the desired destination, **Shwedagon**, appears before the phrase **thwar jin dae** (wants to go). Using this pattern, you can say:

- **Jonathan Mandalay thwar jin dae.** Jonathan wants to go to Mandalay.
- **Kelly Yangon thwar jin dae.** Kelly wants to go to Yangon.
- **Moe Moe Kan Daw Gyi thwar jin dae.** Moe Moe wants to go to Kan Daw Gyi.

PATTERN PRACTICE 1: I WANT TO GO TO ...

Practice saying these:
1. **John Mandalay thwar jin dae.** <u>John</u> wants to go to <u>Mandalay</u>.
2. **Min Min Yangon thwar jin dae.** <u>Min Min</u> wants to go to <u>Yangon</u>.

3. **Julie Singapore thwar jin dae.** Julie wants to go to Singapore.
4. **Naing Oo Shwedagon thwar jin dae.** Naing Oo wants to go to Shwedagon.
5. **Win San Taung Gyi thwar jin dae.** Win San wants to go to Taung Gyi.

GRAMMAR NOTE "Don't want to ..."

To convert the expression **thwar jin dae** (want to go) from affirmative to negative, add the negative-maker **ma** at the front, then end with **boo**, the particle for ending negative sentences.

Affirmative: **thwar jin dae** (want to go)

Negative: **ma thwar jin boo** (don't want to go)

With *some* verbs, the auxiliary verb is written and pronounced **chin**, not **jin:**.

Affirmative: **thauk chin dae** (want to drink)

Negative: **ma thauk chin boo** (don't want to drink)

EXERCISE 1: HOW TO SAY "DON'T WANT TO ..."

Change these verbs from the affirmative form to their negative form.

1. **sar jin dae**   want to eat
2. **thauk chin dae**   want to drink
3. **lah jin dae**   want to come
4. **ait chin dae**   want to sleep
5. **nar jin dae**   want to rest
6. **twaet jin dae**   want to meet
7. **htaing jin dae**   want to sit
8. **pyan jin dae**   want to go home, want to leave

PATTERN PRACTICE 2: COUNTING BLOCKS

When Win San gives direction to Naing Oo, he starts off with:

ရှေ့တည့်တည့်သုံးဘလောက် လျှောက်။ **Shayt taet daet thone ba-lauk shaut.**
Walk straight ahead for three blocks.

တည့်တည့်	shayt taet daet	straight ahead
သုံး	thone	three
ဘလောက်	balauk	block
လျှောက်	shaut	walk

First, let's practice saying one to ten blocks in order.

1. **da balauk** (one block)
2. **hna balauk** (two blocks)

3. **thone balauk** (three blocks)
4. **lay bakauk** (four blocks)
5. **ngar balauk** (five blocks)
6. **chauk balauk** (six blocks)
7. **khon-na balauk** (seven blocks)
8. **shiq balauk** (eight blocks)
9. **koe balauk** (nine blocks)
10. **hsae balauk** (ten blocks)

Now, try saying these in Burmese:
1. **Shayt taet daet da balauk shaut.** Walk straight ahead for **one block.**
2. **Shayt taet daet lay balauk shaut.** Walk straight ahead for **four blocks.**
3. **Shayt taet daet chauk balauk shaut.** Walk straight ahead for **six blocks.**
4. **Shayt taet daet koe balauk shaut.** Walk straight ahead for **nine blocks.**
5. **Shayt taet daet hsae balauk shaut.** Walk straight ahead for **ten blocks.**

GRAMMAR NOTE Turn left, turn right

Win San's instruction also included the following:

မီးပွိုင့်မှာ ညာချိုး Mee point hmah, nyah choe. *At the traffic light, turn right.*

မီးပွိုင့်	**mee point**	traffic light
မှာ	hmah	at
ညာ	nyah	right
ချိုး	choe	turn

The word for *left* is **bae**, so if you want someone to turn *left* instead, you'd say:

မီးပွိုင့်မှာ ဘယ်ချိုး။ Mee point hmah, bae choe. *At the traffic light, turn left.*

မီးပွိုင့်	**mee point**	traffic light
မှာ	hmah	at
ဘယ်	bae	left
ချိုး	choe	turn

EXERCISE 2: DIRECTIONS

Give these directions in Burmese. (The Burmese words you need for businesses and landmarks are provided.)

1. At the traffic light (**mee point**), turn left.
2. At the bus stop (**hmut taing**), turn right.
3. At the bus stop (**hmut taing**), turn left.
4. At the bookshop (**sah oak hsaing**), turn left.
5. At the teashop (**laphet yay zaing**), turn right.
6. At the fritter shop (**akyaw zaing**), turn left.
7. At the traffic light (**mee point**), turn right.

PATTERN PRACTICE 3: COUNTING BUS STOPS

Giving instructions for the bus ride, Win San tells Naing Oo:

ရ မှတ်တိုင်ဆို ရောက်ပြီ။ Khon-na hmut taing hso yaut pe.
After seven stops, you're there.

ရ	**khon-na**	seven
မှတ်တိုင်	**hmut taing**	bus stops
ဆို	**hso**	after
ရောက်ပြီ	**yaut pe**	have arrived

 Note: In the context of this sentence, the particle **hso** is best understood as *after*. But that's not quite accurate. **Hso** is a reference particle that sums up the noun **khon-na hmut taing** (seven stops). Literally, the Burmese sentence means, "If / when there are seven bus stops, you've arrived."

Practice the phrases below to count from one to ten bus stops:

*   **ta hmut taing** (one stop)
*   **hna hmut taing** (two stops)
*   **thone hmut taing** (three stops)
*   **lay hmut taing** (four stops)
*   **ngar hmut taing** (five stops)
*   **chauk hmut taing** (six stops)
*   **khon-na hmut taing** (seven stops)
*   **shiq hmut taing** (eight stops)
*   **koe hmut taing** (nine stops)
*   **hsae hmut taing** (ten stops)

EXERCISE 3: "AFTER EIGHT STOPS, YOU'RE THERE."
Try saying these in Burmese:
1. After **eight** stops, you're there.
2. After **two** stops, you're there.
3. After **six** stops, you're there.
4. After **three** stops, you're there.
5. After **nine** stops, you're there.

EXERCISE 4: "AFTER THREE BLOCKS, YOU'RE THERE."
Try saying these in Burmese:
1. After **three** blocks, you're there.
2. After **six** blocks, you're there.
3. After **four** blocks, you're there.
4. After **two** blocks, you're there.
5. After **nine** blocks, you're there.

CULTURAL NOTE Common Burmese landmarks

Pagodas, schools, monasteries, and teashops are the most common landmarks in urban and rural Burmese settings. Therefore, if you ask a hotel receptionist, a shopkeeper, or a bystander for walking directions to somewhere, you're bound to hear them mentioned. To help you recognize them, here they are:

ဘုရား	**phayar**	pagoda
ကျောင်း	**kyaung**	school
ဘုန်းကြီးကျောင်း	**phone gyi kyaung**	monastery
လက်ဖက်ရည်ဆိုင်	**lephet yay zaing**	teashop

The teashop waitstaff are particularly knowledgeable about their neighborhoods. Due to frequent contact with overseas travelers, many of them can speak at least some English. So if you ever get lost or need directions, you should try approaching them.

Sam. Dah Shwedagon Phayah.
Sam, this is Shwedagon Pagoda.

A kyi ji bae!
It's huge!

A myint ji bae!
It's so tall!

Hote tae.
Yes.

Inn.
Mm hm.

Thaik hla dae.
So beautiful!

Inn.
Mm hm.

CHAPTER 7

Sightseeing

DIALOGUE WHAT'S IT CALLED IN BURMESE?

Visiting the famous Shwedagon Pagoda for the first time, Samantha has some questions about the features of the stupa and the temple complex. The visit quickly turns into a vocabulary lesson.

Samantha: *Naing, what's a pagoda in Burmese?*
Naing, Pagoda go bamah lo bah khaw lae.
နိုင်၊ Pagoda ကို ဗမာလို ဘာခေါ်လဲ။

Naing Oo: *A pagoda is called* phayah. *It's also called* zedi.
Pagoda go phayar lo khaw dae. Zedi lo lae khaw dae.
Pagoda ကို ဘုရားလို့ခေါ်တယ်။ စေတီလို့လည်းခေါ်တယ်။

Samantha: *That's why it's called Shwedagon Phayar.*
Dah jaungt dah Shwedagon Phayar.
ကြောင့် ဒါ ရွှေတိဂုံဘုရား။

Naing Oo: *That's right. This is called Shwedagon Phayar.*
Hote tae, Sam. Dah Shwedagon Phayah khaw dae.
ဟုတ်တယ် Sam, ဒါ ရွှေတိဂုံဘုရား လို့ခေါ်တယ်။

Samantha: *It's huge!*
A kyi ji bae!
အကြီးကြီးပဲ။

Naing Oo: *Yes.*
Hote tae.
ဟုတ်တယ်။

Samantha: *It's so tall!*
A myint ji bae!
အမြင့်ကြီးပဲ။

Naing Oo: *Mm hm.*
Inn.
အင်း

Samantha: *So beautiful!*
Thaik hla dae.
သိပ်လှတယ်။

Naing Oo *Mm hm.*
Inn.
အင်း

Samantha: *What's a walkway called?*
Walkway go bah khaw lae.
Walkway ကို ဘာခေါ်လဲ။

Naing Oo: *It's called* zaung dan.
Zaung dan lo khaw dae.
စောင်းတန်း လို့ခေါ်တယ်။

Samantha: *What's this?*
Dah bah lae.
ဒါဘာလဲ။

Naing Oo: *That's the entrance.*
Dah win baut.
ဒါ ဝင်ပေါက်။
The front gate, of course.
A Shayt Gate pawt.
အရှေ့ Gate ပေါ့။
It's called A Shayt Moke.
A Shayt Moke lo khaw dae.
အရှေ့မုခ် လို့ခေါ်တယ်။

Samantha: *There're so many vendors in the walkway.*
Zaung dan hmah vendor dwae amyar ji naw.
စောင်းတန်းမှာ vendor တွေ အများကြီးနော်။

Naing Oo: *Vendors are called* zay thae.
Vendor go zay thae lo khaw dae.
Vendor ကို ဈေးသည်လို့ခေါ်တယ်။

Samantha: *There are so many vendors in the corridor.*
Zaung dan hmah zay thae dwae amyar ji.
စောင်းတန်းမှာ ဈေးသည်တွေ အများကြီး။

Naing Oo: *Definitely!*
A hote pae.
အဟုတ်ပဲ။

VOCABULARY

phayar	pagoda
zedi	shrine, pagoda
a kyi ji	really big!
a myint ji	really tall!

thaik hla dae	very beautiful.
zaung dan	walkway (in a religious site)
dah	this
win baut	entrance
a shayt	east, eastern
moke	gate (of a religious site)
zay thae	vendors, merchants

Supplementary Vocabulary

phone ji kyaung	monastery
thi la shin kyaung	nunnery
zay	market
saing	store, shop
kyaung	school
zin gyan	walkway (nonreligious)
a shay gi	really long
thae thae lay	really small
pu pu lay	really short (in height)
to to lay	really short (in length)
di har	this object
ho har	that object
anaut	west, western
taung bet	south, southern
myaut phet	north, northern
myit	river
da-dar	bridge
sar kyi daik	library

🔘 GRAMMAR NOTE The verb "to call" — *khaw*

Let's take a look at one of Samantha's *what* questions for Naing Oo, whom she affectionately calls Naing:

Pagoda ကို ဗမာလို ဘာခေါ်လဲ။ Pagoda go bamah lo bah khaw lae.
What's a pagoda in Burmese?

Pagoda	**pagoda**	pagoda
ကို	**go**	object tag
ဗမာလို	**Bamah lo**	in Burmese

ဘာ	**bah**	what
ခေါ်	**khaw**	called
လဲ	**lae**	question particle

The operative verb in her question is **khaw**, the verb *to call* or *to name.*

Here are other ways to use this verb:

ကျွန်တော့်ကို Ken လို့ခေါ်ပါ။ **Kyanawt go Ken lo khaw bah.**
Please call me Ken.

ကျွန်တော့်	**kyanawt**	me (male speaker, object case)
ကို	**go**	object marker
Ken လို့	**Ken lo**	as "Ken"
ခေါ်	**khaw**	to call, to name
ပါ	**bah**	polite request marker

ကျွန်မကို Sam လို့ ခေါ်ပါ။ **Kyama go Sam lo khaw bah.** *Please call me Sam.*

ကျွန်မ	**kyama**	me (female speaker, object case)
ကို	**go**	object marker
Sam လို့	**Sam lo**	as "Sam"
ခေါ်	**khaw**	to call, to name
ပါ	**bah**	polite request marker

PRONUNCIATION NOTE **Dropped tones in object case pronouns**
When used as objects, pronouns with long, lingering vowel tones like **kyanaw** (I, male speaker, formal) or **nin** (you, primarily female speaker, casual) are usually voiced with short, dropped tones. That's why **kyanaw** (I) becomes **kyanawt** (me) in the example "Please call me Ken." On the other hand, the pronoun **kyama** (I, female speaker, formal) is already in dropped tone. That's why there's no change when it's used as an object in the example "Please call me Sam."

PATTERN PRACTICE 1: "WHAT'S IT CALLED?"

To find out the Burmese word for pagoda, Samantha asks:

Pagoda ကို ဗမာလို ဘာခေါ်လဲ။ **Pagoda go bamah lo bah khaw lae.**
What's a pagoda in Burmese?

Pagoda	**pagoda**	pagoda
ကို	**go**	object tag
ဗမာလို	**Bamah lo**	in Burmese
ဘာ	**bah**	what
ခေါ်	**khaw**	called
လဲ	**lae**	question particle

If you want to know the Burmese words for *monastery, mango*, or *jasmine*, you can use the same pattern:

- ***Monastery* go Bamah lo bah khaw lae.** What do you call a monastery in Burmese?
- ***Mango* go Bamah lo bah khaw lae.** What do you call a mango in Burmese?
- ***Jasmine* go Bamah lo bah khaw lae.** What do you call jasmine in Burmese?

Now, try asking the Burmese words for these:

1. museum
2. nunnery
3. shop
4. market
5. school
6. river
7. bridge
8. library

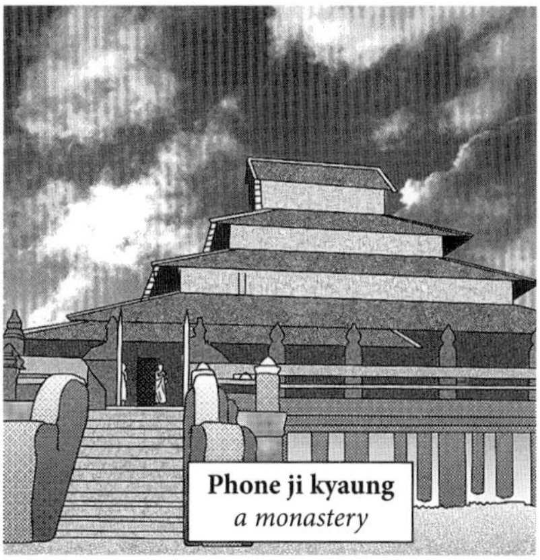

Phone ji kyaung
a monastery

PATTERN PRACTICE 2: "WHAT'S IT CALLED?" (Shorter Form)

After the first question, Samantha doesn't feel the need to repeat **Bamah lo** (in Burmese) in her next questions. When asking for the word for *corridor*, she says:

> Walkway ကို ဘာခေါ်လဲ။ **Walkway go bah khaw lae.**
> *What's a walkway called?*

Now, try asking how these items are called, using the shorter format:

1. shop
2. school
3. vendors
4. market
5. gate

PRONUNCIATION NOTE Tone shifting—*tae* or *dae, ko* or *go*?

Native Burmese speakers routinely pronounce many particles spelled with soft consonants (such as **ka, pa, ta,** and **sa**) with their heavier counterparts (such as **ga, ba, da,** and **za**). This is called *tone-shifting*. Tone shifting tends to occur in most cases, *except* when following words with glottal stops. A glottal stop is characterized by an abrupt stop in the vowel (like the way you'd pronounce *uh* in *uh-oh!*). When glottal stops occur, the particle that follows is voiced as written *without* tone shifting. That's why the sentence-end particles **tae** and **pah** are frequently pronounced **dae** and **bah**; and the object marker **ko** is frequently pronounced **go**.

GRAMMAR NOTE The reference particle *lo*

When Samantha's asks the Burmese word for *pagoda*, Naing Oo says:

Pagoda ကို ဘုရားလို့ခေါ်တယ်။
Pagoda go phayar lo khaw dae. Zedi lo lae khaw dae.
A pagoda is called phayah. *It's also called* zedi.

Pagoda	pagoda	pagoda
ကို	go	object marker
ဘုရား	phayar	pagoda
လို့	lo	reference particle
ခေါ်	khaw	called
တယ်။	dae	sentence-end particle

The particle **lo** is a reference particle. It usually follows a quote or a specific phrase that needs to be singled out or highlighted. In this case, the word **phayar** (the Burmese word for *pagoda*) needs to be treated as a separate word, or a quoted word. That's why it's set off with the particle **lo**.

PATTERN PRACTICE 3: "IT'S CALLED ..."

Based on the exchanges between Samantha and Naing Oo in this episode, you learn that:

- A *pagoda* is called **phayar**.
- A *walkway* is called **zaung dan**.
- *Vendors* are called **zay thae**.
- An *entrance* is called **win baut**.

The structure Naing Oo uses could be summed up as follows:

[English word] + **go** (the Burmese term for English word) **lo khaw dae**. For example:

- **(Walkway) go (zaung dan) lo khaw dae.** A *walkway* is called **zaung dan**.
- **(Vendors) go (zay thae) lo knor dae.** *Vendors* are called **zay thae**.
- **(Entrance) go (win baut) lo khaw dae.** An *entrance* is called **win baut**.

a walkway (religious site) with lots of vendors selling fruits, flowers, etc.

Now, use this "formula" to say the following in Burmese:

1. A monastery is called **phone ji kyaung.**
2. A nunnery is called **thi la shin kyaung.**
3. A market is called **zay.**
4. A school is called **kyaung.**
5. A shop is called **hsaing.**
6. A river is called **myit.**
7. A bridge is called **da-dar.**
8. A library is called **sar kyi daik.**

CULTURAL NOTE Terms for religious sites only

The word **zaung dan** is used almost exclusively for the walkways in religious sites. Therefore, a walkway connecting two office buildings, for example, would not be called **zaung dan**. It's called **zin gyan**.

Likewise, the word **moke**, as in the **A Shayt Moke of the Shwedagon** (Shwedagon's Eastern Gate), is strictly for the grand entrance of religious sites. You should not refer to the entrance of someone's house or even an office building as **moke**. The more appropriate word for the entrance to your home, a friend's home, or a non-religious place is **win baut**.

PATTERN PRACTICE 4: "THIS" AND "THAT"

Approaching the grand entrance of the Shwedagon, the following exchange takes place between Samantha and Naing Oo:

Samantha: **Dah** bah **lae.** *What's this?*
Naing Oo: **Dah win baut.** *This is the entrance.*

Dah is the generic word to refer to people and things within reach, someone or something you can point to. Remember the exchange from the first time Win San met Samantha?

Win San: **Dah ba thu lae.** *Who's this?*
Naing Oo: **Dah nga amyo thamee.** *This is my girlfriend.*

Dah's companion words are:
de hah (this item, this thing, this object, this person, ...)
ho hah (that item, that thing, that object, that person, ...)

Note: In normal speech and fast-paced conversations, people tend to pronounce **de hah** as **de-ah**, and **ho hah** as **ho-ah**.

Practice these exchanges with a partner.
a) **Dah bah lae.** What's this?
b) **Dah Shwedagon Phayar.** This is Shwedagon Pagoda.

a) **De hah bah lae.** What's this thing?
b) **De hah phone ji kyaung.** This is a monastery.

a) **Ho hah bah lae.** What's that thing?
b) **Ho hah zaung dan.** That's the corridor.

a) **De hah bah lae.** What's this thing?
b) **De hah thi la shin kyaung.** This thing is a nunnery.

a) **Dah bah lae.** What's this?
b) **Dah win baut.** This is the entrance.

a) **De hah bah lae.** What's this thing?
b) **De hah sah kyi daik.** This thing is a library.

a) **Ho hah bah lae.** What's that thing?
b) **Ho hah da-dar.** That thing is a bridge.

PATTERN PRACTICE 5: CARDINAL DIRECTIONS

When identifying the gate of Shwedagon where they're at, Naing Oo specifies:

အရှေ့မုခ်　**A Shayt Moke**　*the Eastern Gate*

| အရှေ့ | **a shayt** | the East |
| မုခ် | **moke** | gate, entrance (of a holy site) |

Practice the following:

1. **a nauk moke**　the west gate
   myauk phet moke　the north gate
   taung bet moke　the south gate

2. **a shayt win baut**　the east entrance
   a nauk win baut　the west entrance
   myauk phet win baut　the north entrance
   taung bet win baug　the south entrance

3. **a shayt da-dar**　the eastern bridge
   a nauk da-dar　the western bridge
   myauk phet da-dar　the northern bridge
   taung bet da-dar　the southern bridge

4. a shayt zaung dan   the eastern walkway
    a nauk zaung dan   the western walkway
    myauk phet zaung dan   the northern walkway
    taung bet zaung dan   the southern walkway

EXERCISE 1: CARDINAL DIRECTIONS

Select the correct translation of the following terms:

1. **a shayt moke**
    a) the eastern gate
    b) the western gate
    c) the north gate
    d) the south gate

2. **taung bet zaung dan**
    a) the eastern walkway
    b) the western walkway
    c) the northern walkway
    d) the southern walkway

3. **myauk phet da-dar**
    a) the eastern bridge
    b) the western bridge
    c) the northern bridge
    d) the southern bridge

4. **a nauk phet win baut**
    a) the east entrance
    b) the west entrance
    c) the north entrance
    d) the south entrance

GRAMMAR NOTE

Kyi and **thay**, suffixes for "greatness" and "smallness"

Confronted with the towering pagoda, Samantha exclaims:

အကြီးကြီး!   **a kyi ji**   *really big!*
အကြီး (a kyi, bigness) +   ကြီး (ji, suffix for *greatness*)

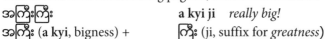

အမြင့်ကြီး   **a myint ji**   *really tall!*
အမြင့် (a myint, tallness) +   ကြီး (ji, suffix for *greatness*)

Noticing the corridor overflowing with shops and vendors, she exclaims:

အများကြီး   **a myar ji**   *so many!*

အများ (**amyar**, great quantity) + ကြီး (**ji**, suffix for *greatness*)

If Samantha were looking at a long line of pilgrims, she might have also said:

အရှည်ကြီး   **a shay ji**   *so long!*

အရှည် (**ashay**, length) +   ကြီး (**ji**, suffix for *greatness*)

The suffix **kyi**, often pronounced **ji**, marks something impressive in size or quality, such as *greatness, tallness, majesty,* etc. The opposite is the suffix **thay**, denoting *smallness, diminutiveness, cuteness, shortness,* and so on. For example:

သေးသေးလေး   **thay thay lay**   *so small!*

သေးသေး (**thay**, small) + လေး (**lay**, suffix for *smallness*)

တိုတိုလေး   **to do lay**   *so short! (length)*

တိုတို (**to**, short) +   လေး (**lay**, suffix for *smallness*)

ပုပုလေး   **pu bu lay**   *so short! (height)*

ပုပု (**pu**, short) +   လေး (**lay**, suffix for *smallness*)

It's a convention in exclamations to repeat or duplicate the adjective for emphasis. Thus **thay thay** (for *small*), **to do** (for *short length*), and **pu bu** (for *short height*).

PATTERN PRACTICE 6: BASIC EXCLAMATIONS
Practice the following:

- **De phone ji kyaung ga a kyi ji.** This monastery is so big!
- **De phayar ga amyint ji.** This pagoda is so tall!
- **De da-dar ga ashay ji.** This bridge is so long!
- **De sar kyi daik ka thay thay lay.** This library is so small!
- **De myit ka to do lay.** This river is so short!
- **De lu ga pu bu lay.** This person is so short!

EXERCISE 2: LEARNING TO EXCLAIM
What is the appropriate exclamation in Burmese for the following?

1. a tall building
2. a long bridge
3. a large mountain
4. a short teacher
5. a tiny cake
6. a short sarong

CHAPTER 8

Shopping and Bargaining
Part 1

DIALOGUE **HOW MUCH IS THAT?**

At Shwedagon, Naing Oo and Samantha decide to make some flower offerings. Entering a flower vendor's stall, Naing Oo begins negotiating the price.

Naing Oo: *How much for a bunch of eugenia?*
Aung thabyay da zee balauk lae.
အောင်သပြေ တစ်စည်း ဘယ်လောက်လဲ။

Vendor: *It's 500, big brother.*
Ngar yah bah ako.
၅၀၀ ပါအကို။

Naing Oo: *How much for a string of jasmine?*
Zabae da gone balauk lae.
စံပယ်ပန်း တစ်ကုံးဘယ်လောက်လဲ။

Vendor: *300.*
Thone yah bah.
၃၀၀ ပါ။

VOCABULARY

balauk / bae lauk	how much
aung thabay	eugenia (leaves used as sacred offering)
zabae	jasmine
ya ma lar	Can I get it? Is it doable?
kaung bi	All right, OK.
yu mae	I'll take it.

Supplementary Vocabulary

hnin ze	rose
kha yay	starflower
nay jah ban	sunflower
pan thee	apple
thayet thee	mango

phayae the	watermelon
ngapyaw thee	banana
khway	dog
lu	person

Numbers 1–10 (when used by themselves without classifiers)
1. ၁ **tit** (one)
2. ၂ **hnit** (two)
3. ၃ **thone** (three)
4. ၄ **lay** (four)
5. ၅ **ngar** (five)
6. ၆ **chauk** (six)
7. ၇ **khon** or **khonnit** (seven)
8. ၈ **shiq** (eight)
9. ၉ **koe** (nine)
10. ၁၀ **ta hsae** (ten)

Numbers 1–10 (when used with classifiers)
1. ၁ **ta** or **da** (one)
2. ၂ **hna** (two)
3. ၃ **thone** (three)
4. ၄ **lay** (four)
5. ၅ **ngar** (five)
6. ၆ **chauk** (six)
7. ၇ **khona** (seven)
8. ၈ **shiq** (eight)
9. ၉ **koe** (nine)
10. ၁၀ **hsae** (ten)

 GRAMMAR NOTE Classifiers for counting

When Naing Oo is asking for the price of a bunch of eugenia, he says **aung tha bay da zee**. When he is asking about a strand of jasmine, he says, **zabae da gone**.

Zee and **gone** are unit classifiers—words used for counting different types of objects. These are similar to words like *bunch* in *a bunch of bananas*, *cup* in *a cup of tea*, or *bouquet* in *a bouquet of roses*. The variety of classifiers in Burmese is quite extensive, and mastering the repertoire is a challenge even for native Burmese speakers. But you need them to refer to things or people in specific numbers.

For example:

yay ta khwet *(a cup of water)*, where **khwet** is the classifier for liquid measured in cups

khway da gaung *(a dog)*, where **gaung** is the classifier for animals

lu ta yaut *(a person)*, where **yaut** is the classifier for humans

Here are the most important classifiers for daily use:
- **khwet** or **gwet** for liquid measured in cups
- **palin** or **balin** for liquid measured in bottles
- **pwe** or **bwe** for food servings
- **khu** or **gu** for lifeless, inanimate objects in general
- **yauk** for people
- **kaung** or **gaung** for animals
- **lone** for round objects (like fruit and balloons; also used for some common furniture like beds, tables, chairs)
- **see** or **zee** for vegetables in tied-up bunches
- **kone** or **gone** for items in wreaths, strands, and strings
- **htae** or **dae** for clothings

A note on the pronunciation variants: The spelling variants account for the tone shifting mentioned in Chapter 7: Sightseeing (see pronunciation note on page 72). For example, for five strings of jasmine, native speakers say **zabae ngar gone**, instead of **zabae ngar kone**. For ten servings of rice, they'd say **htamin hse bwe**, instead of **htamin hsae pwe**. For one bottle of Coke, they'd say **Coke da balin**, instead of **Coke ta palin**.

If you're a beginner to Burmese, using the first pronunciation variant for all instances may be the most effective solution. You may sound slightly different from the native speakers, but you'll be understood. Over time, as you interact more with native speakers and hear how they speak, you can develop an instinct for tone shifting, even if you never learn to read or write.

To use the classifiers, you follow this "formula":

Noun + number + classifier
1. **yay** (water) **ta** (one) **khwet** (cup) = a cup of water
2. **Coke** (Coke) **hna** (two) **palin** (bottle) = two bottles of Coke
3. **htamin** (rice) **thone** (three) **bwe** (serving) = three servings of rice

4. **keyboard** (keyboard) **lay** (four) **gu** (classifier for things) = four computer keyboards
5. **lu** (person) **nga** (five) **yauk** (classifier for people) = five people
6. **khway** (dog) **chaut** (six) **kaung** (classifier for animal) = six dogs
7. **panthee** (apple) **khonna** (seven) **lone** (classifier for round objects) = seven apples
8. **aung thabyay** (eugenia) **shiq** (eight) **see** (bunch) = eight bunches of eugenia
9. **zabae** (jasmine) **koe** (nine) **gone** (strands) = nine strands of jasmine
10. **T-shirt** (T-shirt) **htae** (ten) **dae** (classifier for clothes) = ten T-shirts

PATTERN PRACTICE 1: NUMBERS AND CLASSIFIERS

Practice these phrases:

1. **lu ta yauk**	one person
2. **khway hna kaung**	two dogs
3. **Coke thone balin**	three bottles of Coke
4. **keyboard lay gu**	four keyboards
5. **T-shirt ngar dae**	five T-shirts
6. **panthee chauk lone**	six apples
7. **aung thabyay khonna see**	seven bunches of eugenia
8. **zabae shiq kone**	eight strands of jasmine
9. **yay koe gwet**	nine cups of water
10. **htamin hsae bwe**	ten servings of rice

EXERCISE 1: LEARNING TO COUNT

Say the following in Burmese. (For numbers and counters that have two spelling variants, just use the first.)

1. a cup of Coca Cola
2. two keyboards
3. three people
4. four apples
5. five strings of jasmine
6. six dogs
7. seven bunches of eugenia
8. eight T-shirts
9. nine bottles of water
10. ten servings of rice

GRAMMAR NOTE Asking "how much" with *balauk/bae lauk*

Let's take a closer look at Naing Oo's first question to the flower seller:

အောင်သပြေ တစ်စီး ဘယ်လောက်လဲ။   **Aung thabyay da zee balauk lae.**
How much is a bunch of eugenia?

အောင်သပြေ	aung thabyay	eugenia
တစ်	da	one
စည်း	zee	bunch (classifier)
ဘယ်လောက်	balauk	how much
လဲ	lae	question particle

The question word **balauk** is written **bae lauk**, but often pronounced **balauk**.

CULTURAL NOTE Offering flowers at a shrine

At pagodas and temples, Burmese pilgrims traditionally offer bunches of eugenia at the altars and shrines around the main stupa. The lush green leaves are usually sold in neatly tied bunches at the flower stalls along the steps and walkways leading to the pagoda entrance.

PATTERN PRACTICE 2: "HOW MUCH IS ...?" (PRICE/COST)

Practice these questions:

1. **Coke da balin balauk lae.**   How much is a bottle of Coke?
2. **T-shirt hna htae balauk lae.**   How much is two T-shirts?
3. **Zabae thone gone balauk lae.**   How much is three strands of jasmine?
4. **Htamin lay bwe balauk lae.**   How much is four servings of rice?
5. **Aung thabyay hgar zee balauk lae.**   How much is five bunches of eugenia?
6. **Kor phee chauk khwet balauk lae.**   How much is six cups of coffee?
7. **Panthee khonna lone balauk lae.**   How much is seven apples?
8. **Keyboard shiq khu balauk lae.**   How much is eight keyboards?
9. **Thayet thee koe lone balauk lae.**   How much is nine mangoes?
10. **Khayay hsae gone balauk lae.**   How much is ten strands of star flowers?

 **DIALOGUE BARGAINING**

Naing Oo: *Can I get six bunches of eugenia for 2,500?*
             Aung thabyay chauk hsee hna htaungt ngar yah naet ya ma lar.
             အောင်သပြေ ခြောက်စည်း ၂၅၀၀ နဲ့ ရမလား။
Vendor: *Can't do it, big brother.*
             Ma ya boo ako.
             မရဘူးအကို။
             I'll give [it to you] for 2,800.
             Hna htaungt shiq yah naet pay mae.
             ၂၈၀၀ နဲ့ ပေးမယ်။
Naing Oo: *All right!*
             Kaung bi.
             ကောင်းပြီ။
             Then I'll take [them].
             Dah so yu mae.
             ဒါဆို ယူမယ်။

A note on counting money in larger numbers: Notice how Naing Oo omits the money counter **kyat** (the basic unit for Burmese currency) in his negotiations with the flower seller. When dealing in hundreds, thousands, or higher volumes in currency, native speakers tend to drop the classifier word **kyat**.

VOCABULARY

hsae or **zae**	ten (counting unit)
yah	hundred (counting unit)

htaung or **daung**   thousand (counting unit)

thaung   ten thousand (counting unit)

Counting in tens

၁၀	ta-hsae	10
၂၀	hna hsae	20
၃၀	thone zae	30
၄၀	lay zae	40
၅၀	ngar zae	50
၆၀	chauk hsae	60
၇၀	khona hsae	70
၈၀	shiq hsae	80
၉၀	koe zae	90

Counting in hundreds

၁၀၀	ta yah	100
၂၀၀	hna yah	200
၃၀၀	thone yah	300
၄၀၀	lay yah	400
၅၀၀	ngar yah	500
၆၀၀	chauk yah	600
၇၀၀	khona yah	700
၈၀၀	shiq yah	800
၉၀၀	koe yah	900

Counting in thousands

၁၀၀၀	ta htaung	1,000
၂၀၀၀	hna htaung	2,000
၃၀၀၀	thone daung	3,000
၄၀၀၀	lay daung	4,000
၅၀၀၀	hgar daung	5,000
၆၀၀၀	chauk htaung	6,000
၇၀၀၀	khona htaung	7,000
၈၀၀၀	shiq htaung	8,000
၉၀၀၀	koe daung	9,000
၁၀၀၀၀	ta thaung	10,000

PRONUNCIATION NOTE Dropped tones in mixed–unit numbers

In numbers that mix numerical units such as thousands, hundreds, and tens, the vowel sound for the unit words (**htaung** for thousands, **yah** for hundreds, and **hsae** for tens) are lowered, or dropped, with the exception of the final number. For example:

- ၂၃၀၀ or 2,300 is <u>not</u> **hna htaung thone yah** but **hna htaungt thone yah**
- ၁၅၀၀ or 1,500 is <u>not</u> **ta htaung ngar yah** but **ta htaungt ngar yah**
- ၆၅၀ or 650 is <u>not</u> **chauk yah ngar zae** but **chauyk ya** (short tone) **ngar zae**
- ၃၅ or 35 is <u>not</u> **thone zae ngar** but **thone zaet ngar**

GRAMMAR NOTE Transactions with the particle *naet*

The flower seller's price for a bunch of eugenia is 500 kyats. At this rate, the total for six bunches comes to 3,000. Naing Oo wonders if he might get a discount for buying six bunches. So his counter-offer is:

အောင်သပြေ ခြောက်စည်း ၂၅၀၀ နဲ့ ရမလား။

Aung thabyay chauk hsee hna htaungt ngar yah naet ya ma lar.

Can I get six bunches of eugenia for 2,500?

အောင်သပြေ	aung thabyay	eugenia
ခြောက်	chauk	six
စည်း	see	bunch (classifier)
၂၅၀၀	hna htaungt ngar yah	2,500
နဲ့	naet	with
ရမလား	ya malar	can I get?

Pay attention to the use of the particle **naet**, or *with*. Whereas in English, such an offer would involve the particle **for** (Can I get it **for** 2,800?), in Burmese, the appropriate particle is **naet**.

PATTERN PRACTICE 3: MAKING COUNTER–OFFERS

Practice the following:

1. **Ta thaung naet ya malar.**   Can I get it for 10,000?
2. **Koe daung naet ya malar.**   Can I get it for 9,000?
3. **Shiq htaung naet ya malar.**   Can I get it for 8,000?
4. **Khona htaung naet ya malar.**   Can I get it for 7,000?
5. **Chauk htaung naet ya malar.**   Can I get it for 6,000?
6. **Ngar daung naet ya malar.**   Can I get it for 5,000?

7. **Lay daung naet ya malar.**   Can I get it for 4,000?
8. **Thone daung naet ya malar.**   Can I get it for 3,000?
9. **Hna htaung naet ya malar.**   Can I get it for 2,000?
10. **Ta htaung naet ya malar.**   Can I get it for 1,000?

PATTERN PRACTICE 4: MIXED–UNIT COUNTER–OFFERS
Practice the following:
1. **Ta htaungt hna yah naet ya malar.**   Can I get it for 1,200?
2. **Hna thaung thone daung naet ya malar.**   Can I get it for 23,000?
3. **Thone thaung lay daung naet ya malar.**   Can I get it for 34,000?
4. **Ngar daungt chauk yah naet ya malar.**   Can I get it for 5,600?
5. **Chauk ya khona hsae naet ya malar.**   Can I get it for 670?
6. **Khona ya shiq hsae naet ya malar.**   Can I get it for 780?
7. **Shiq htaungt koe yah naet ya malar.**   Can I get it for 890?
8. **Koe ya ta hsae naet ya malar.**   Can I get it for 910?

EXERCISE 2: COUNTING LARGE NUMBERS
Say these numbers in Burmese:
1. 2,900
2. 3,800
3. 470
4. 360
5. 26,000
6. 37,000
7. 4,200
8. 5,100

EXERCISE 3: COUNTERS AND COUNTER–OFFERS
Say the following in Burmese:
1. six bottles of Coke
2. seven cups of water
3. three T-shirts
4. two apples
5. 3,500
6. 920
7. 51,000
8. Can I get six strands of jasmine for 4,000?
9. Can I get two servings of rice for 2,500?
10. Can I get ten bunches of eugenia for 8,500?

CHAPTER 9
Getting a Cab

 **DIALOGUE** WHERE TO?

As they leave Shwedagon, Naing Oo and Samantha decide to go shopping in Bogyoke Market downtown. At the taxi stand, Naing Oo and the driver negotiate the fare.

Cab driver: *Where do you want to go, boss?*
Bae thwar jin lae, hsayah.
ဘယ်သွားချင်လဲ ဆရာ။

Naing Oo: *I'd like to go to Bogyoke Market.*
Bogyoke Zay thwar jin dae.
ဗိုလ်ချုပ်ဈေး သွားချင်တယ်။
How much?
Balauk lae.
ဘယ်လောက်လဲ။

Cab driver: *Hmm, 5,000 [kyat].*
Inn, ngar htaung.
အင်း ... ၅၀၀၀။

Naing Oo: *Isn't it a bit much? Please make it 3,000.*
Ma myar boo lar. Thone daung htar like pah.
မများဘူးလား။ ၃၀၀၀ ထားလိုက်ပါ။

Cab driver: *Ha, I can't do it. But I can for 4,000.*
Hah, ma kait phoo bya. Lay daung daut ya dae.
ဟာ ... မကိုက်ဘူးဗျ။ ၄၀၀၀ တော့ ရတယ်။

Naing Oo: *All right. We'll go if it's 4,000.*
Kaung bi. Lay daung so thwar mae.
ကောင်းပြီ။ ၄၀၀၀ ဆို သွားမယ်။

Cab driver: *Please get in.*
Tet pah khamyar.
တက်ပါ ခင်ဗျား။

Naing Oo: *Sam, come, let's go.*
Sam, lah, thwar zo.
Sam ... လာ၊ သွားစို့။

VOCABULARY

bae	where
hsayah	boss, teacher, master
thwar jin	want to go
myar	many, much, a lot
... htar lite par	(slang) please make it ....
htaung or daung	(counting word) thousand
ma kait phoo	(slang) It's not doable. (Literally, it doesn't add up.)
thwar zo	let's go
tet pah	please climb up / come aboard

Supplementary Vocabulary

zay	market
yone	office
a loke	work, job
kyaung	school
pahsoe	man's *sarong*
htamain	woman's *sarong*

CULTURAL NOTE **The customer is the boss**

When the cab driver meets Naing Oo, he addresses him as **hsayah**. The word **hsayah** means *teacher* or *master*, but many service workers such as cab drivers, restaurant waitstaff, and hotel clerks also use it to address male patrons as a sign of respect—roughly the equivalent of calling a customer *boss* in English. By contrast, the term **hsayah ma**, for *female teacher*, is *not* used in the same way to address female patrons.

GRAMMAR NOTE **The auxiliary verb "want to"—*jin***

To indicate where he wants to go, Naing Oo says:

ဗိုလ်ချုပ်ဈေး သွားချင်တယ်။   **Bogyoke Zay thwar jin dae.**
I'd like to go to Bogyoke Market.

ဗိုလ်ချုပ်ဈေး	**Bogyoke Zay**	Bogyoke Market
သွား	**thwar**	to go
ချင်	**jin**	want to (auxiliary verb)
တယ်	**dae**	sentence-end particle

Adding the auxiliary verb **chin** or **jin** after the main verb lets you express the desire to perform the action in the main verb. Study the chart below: *Note: the affirmative sentences should end with* **tae** *or* **dae**; *the negative sentences should end with* **phoo** *or* **boo**.

Bogyoke Market

Main verb	Auxiliary verb	Meaning of the phrase
သွား (thwar, to go)	+ ချင် (jin, want to)	= သွားချင် (thwar jin, want to go)
စား (sar, to eat)	+ ချင် (jin, want to)	= စားချင် (sar jin, want to eat)
သောက် (thauk, to drink)	+ ချင် (chin, want to)	= သောက်ချင် (thauk chin, want to drink)
ထိုင် (htaing, to sit)	+ ချင် (jin, want to)	= ထိုင်ချင် (htaing jin, want to sit)

The negative forms of these are:

မသွား (ma thwar, not go)	+ ချင် (jin, want to)	= မသွားချင် (ma thwar jin, don't want to go)
မစား (ma sar, not eat)	+ ချင် (jin, want to)	= မစားချင် (ma sar jin, don't want to eat)

မသောက် (ma thauk, + ချင် (chin, want to) = မသောက်ချင် (ma thauk chin, don't want to drink)

မထိုင် (ma htaing, not sit) + ချင် (jin, want to) = မထိုင်ချင် (ma htaing jin, don't want to sit)

PATTERN PRACTICE 1: "I WANT TO, I DON'T WANT TO"

Practice the following exchanges:

a) **Yangon thwar jin lar.**   Do you want to go to Yangon?
b) **Thwar jin dae.**   I want to go.

a) **Mandalay thwar jin lar.**   Do you want to go to Mandalay?
b) **Ma thwar jin boo.**   I don't want to go.

a) **Moke hingar sar jin lar.**   Do you want to eat *moke hingar*?
b) **Sar jin dae.**   I want to eat (it).

a) **Ice cream sar jin lar.**   Do you want to eat ice cream?
b) **Ma sar jin boo.**   I don't want to eat (it).

a) **Beer thauk chin lar.**   Do you want to drink beer?
b) **Thauk chin dae.**   I want to drink (beer).

a) **Coca Cola thauk chin lar.**   Do you want to drink Coca Cola?
b) **Ma thauk chin boo.**   I don't want to drink (Coca Cola).

EXERCISE 1: "I WANT TO GO THERE."

Let's take another look at what Naing Oo says to the cab driver:

Bogyoke Zay thwar jin dae.   *I'd like to go to Bogyoke Market.*

Bogyoke Zay, or Bogyoke Market, is the name of the desired destination. The second part, **thwar jin dae**, is *want to go*. In this scenario, the fact that Naing Oo is the one who wants to go to Bogyoke Market is obvious, so the word for *I*, **kyanaw**, is not explicitly stated.

So if you'd like to go to **Botataung Phayar** (Botataung Pagoda), you can say:

Botataung Phayar thwar jin dae.   *I'd like to go to Botataung Pagoda.*

And if you'd like to go to **Shwedagon Phayar** (Shwedagon Pagoda), you can say:

Shwedagon Phayar thwar jin dae. *I'd like to go to Shwedagon Pagoda.*

Now, use this format to say the following in Burmese:
1. I'd like to go to Bogyoke *Panjan*. (Bogyoke Park, short for Bogyoke Aung San Park)
2. I'd like to go to Bandoola Panjan. (Bandoola Park)
3. I'd like to go to Mingalah Zay. (Mingalar Market)
4. I'd like to go to Inya Kan. (Inya Lake)
5. I'd like to go to Kandaw Ji. (Kandaw Gyi Lake)

GRAMMAR NOTE How much?—*balauk*

To ask how much his trip would cost, Naing Oo says:

ဘယ်လောက်လဲ။ **Balauk lae.** *How much is it?*

ဘယ်လောက် (**balauk**, about how much) + လဲ (**lae**, question particle)

When speaking to cab drivers, to get the estimated fare to go somewhere, you can also use this phrase in conjunction with the name of the place you want to go. For example:

ဗိုလ်ချုပ်ဈေး ဘယ်လောက်လဲ။ **Bogyoke Zay balauk lae.**
How much for Bogyoke Market?

ဗိုလ်ချုပ်ဈေး	**Bogyoke Zay**	Bogyoke Market
ဘယ်လောက်	balauk	about how much
လဲ	lae	question particle

ရွှေတိဂုံ ဘယ်လောက်လဲ။ **Shwedagon balauk lae.** *How much for Shwedagon?*

ရွှေတိဂုံ	**Shwedagon**	Shwedagon Pagoda
ဘယ်လောက်	balauk	about how much
လဲ	lae	question particle

EXERCISE 2: "HOW MUCH TO GO TO ...?"

Use the format to ask the estimated cab fare in Burmese for these destinations:
1. Botataung Pagoda
2. Bandoola Park
3. Kandaw Gyi Lake
4. Inya Lake
5. Bogyoke Park

PATTERN PRACTICE 2: PROPOSING A CAB FARE

When making his counter-offer to negotiate with the cab driver, Naing Oo says:

၃၀၀၀ ထားလိုက်ပါ။ **Thone daung htar like pah.** *Please make it 3,000.*

၃၀၀၀	**Thone daung**	3,000
ထားလိုက်	**htar like**	keep it at, settle for
ပါ	**pah**	command / request particle

Practice the following:
1. **Ta yah htar like pah.** Please make it 100.
2. **Hna yah htar like pah.** Please make it 200.
3. **Thone yah htar like pah.** Please make it 300.
4. **Lay yah htar like pah.** Please make it 400.
5. **Ngar yah htar like pah.** Please make it 500.
6. **Chauk htaung htar like pah.** Please make it 6,000.
7. **Khona htaung htar like pah.** Please make it 7,000.
8. **Shiq htaung htar like pah.** Please make it 8,000.
9. **Koe htaung htar like pah.** Please make it 9,000.
10. **Ta thaung htar like pah.** Please make it 10,000.
11. **Koe htaungt ta yah htar like pah.** Please make it 9,100.
12. **Shiq htaungt hna yah htar like pah.** Please make it 8,200.
13. **Khona htaungt thone yah htar like pah.** Please make it 7,300.
14. **Chauk htaungt lay yah htar like pah.** Please make it 6,400.
15. **Ngar daungt ngar yah htar like pah.** Please make it 5,500.

EXERCISE 3: NEGOTIATING A CAB FARE

Say these sentences in Burmese. (If necessary, please refer to the vocabulary section in Chapter 8: Shopping and Bargaining to review the numbers.)
1. Please make it 2,000.
2. Please make it 4,200.

3. Please make it 6,400.
4. Please make it 7,100.
5. Please make it 8,000.

GRAMMAR NOTE Issuing requests and commands

As seen in the pattern on the previous page, the particle **pah** (or **bah**) is the particle for issuing commands and requests.

ထားလိုက် ... **htar like** (keep it, make it, settle it for) + ပါ **pah** (command particle) = ထားလိုက်ပါ။ **htar like pah**. *Please make the fare [this amount].*

The same particle also appears in the cab driver's words:
တက် **Tet pah**. *Please get in.*

တက် **Tet** (to come up) + ပါ **pah** (command particle) = တက်ပါ။ **Tet pah**. *Please come up / get in.*

Here are some requests and commands constructed with this particle:
1. **Sar bah.** Please eat.
2. **Thwar bah.** Please go.
3. **Thauk pah.** Please drink.
4. **Lah bah.** Please come.
5. **Wae bah.** Please buy.
6. **Pay bah.** Please give [something] to me.

PATTERN PRACTICE 3: "PLEASE DO THIS."
Practice these commands and requests.
1. **Zay thwar bah.** Please go to the market.
2. **Yone thwar bah.** Please go to the office.
3. **Aloke thwar bah.** Please go to work.
4. **Kyaung thwar bah.** Please go to school.
5. **T-shirt wae bah.** Please buy the T-shirt.
6. **Pa hsoe pay bah.** Please give me a man's *sarong*.
7. **Htamain pay bah.** Please give me a woman's *sarong*.
8. **Moke hingar sar bah.** Please eat *moke hingar*.
9. **Htamin sar bah.** Please have this meal / eat the rice.
10. **Beer thauk pah.** Please drink the beer.
11. **Kor phee thauk pah.** Please drink the coffee.
12. **Taung Gyi thwar bah.** Please go to [the city of] Taung Gyi.
13. **Lephet yay pay bah.** Please give me tea.
14. **A loke lah bah.** Please come to work.

CULTURAL NOTE Sentence-end politeness markers

When the cab driver tells Naing Oo and Samantha to get into the cab, he finishes off his sentence with **khamyar**, the polite sentence-end particle for male speakers.

တက်ပါ ခင်ဗျား။   **Tet pah khamyar.**   *Please get in.*

တက်ပါ (**tet pah**, get in) + ခင်ဗျား (**khamyar**, politeness marker, male)

Note that sometimes **khamyar** is pronounced **khamya** with a short vowel for emphasis.

The polite sentence-end particle for female speakers is **shin**. If the cab driver were a woman, she would have said:

တက်ပါ ရှင်။ **Tet pah shin.** *Please get in.*

တက်ပါ (**tet pah**, get in) + ရှင် (**shin**, politeness marker, female)

Note that sometimes **shin** is pronounced **shint** with a short vowel for emphasis.

In this scenario, the politeness marker is especially important. Since Naing Oo and Samantha are customers, the cab driver should show them respect. Issuing commands or requests without politeness markers is acceptable in casual conversations, among friends and social peers, but they're recommended when speaking to older folks, people of higher authority, or in formal conversations.

Politeness markers **khamyar** (for male speakers) and **shin** (for female speakers) usually come at the end of the sentences. Don't confuse them with the male and female speakers' way to say *you*. (Check out the *Cultural Note: The familiar vs. the formal* in Chapter 3: Greetings.) Even though the spellings and pronunciations are identical, politeness markers have a different function than the pronouns **khamyar** (how a male speaker says *you*) and **shin** (how a female speaker says *you*) in their purpose and function.

PATTERN PRACTICE 4: POLITE REQUESTS

Practice the same commands above, but this time with the appropriate politeness markers.

1. **Zay thwar bah khamyar.** Please go to the market. (male speaker)
2. **Yone thwar bah shin.** Please go to the office. (female speaker)
3. **Aloke thwar bah khamyar.** Please go to work. (male speaker)
4. **Kyaung thwar bah shin.** Please go to school. (female speaker)
5. **T-shirt wae bah khamyar.** Please buy the T-shirt. (male speaker)
6. **T-shirt wae bah shin.** Please buy the T-shirt. (female speaker)
7. **Pa hsoe pay bah khamyar.** Please give me a man's *sarong*. (male speaker)
8. **Htamain pay bah shin.** Please give me a woman's *sarong*. (female speaker)
9. **Moke hingar sar bah khamyar.** Please eat *moke hingar*. (male speaker)
10. **Htamin sarh bah shin.** Please have this meal / please eat the rice. (female speaker)
11. **Beer thauk pah khamyar.** Please drink the beer. (male speaker)
12. **Kor phee thauk pah shin.** Please drink the coffee. (female speaker)
13. **Taung Gyi thwar bah khamyar.** Please go to [the city of] Taung Gyi. (male speaker)
14. **Lephet yay pay bah shin.** Please give me tea. (female speaker)
15. **Aloke lah bah khamyar.** Please come to work. (male speaker)
16. **Aloke lah bah shin.** Please come to work. (female speaker)

Bah shah nay dah lae.
What're you looking for?

Minthamee yoke thay yoke lo jin dae.
I'd like a Minthamee marionette.

Shi lar.
Do you have one?

Shi bah dae shint.
We have one.

De hmah. Kyi bah.
Over here, look.

Hla dae. Dah kyait tae.
Lovely! I like this.

Nae nae thay dah shi lar.
Do you have something a bit smaller?

Shi bah dae.
We have it.

De hmah.
Here it is.

Thaik thay thwar bi.
That's too small.

Nae nae kyi dah aw.
How about something a bit bigger?

Dah so ataw bae.
This is perfect.

Balauk lae khamyar.
How much?

Thoung hna-htaung bah.
12,000.

Ta thaung naet ya ma lar.
Can I get it for 10,000?

Inn, zay oo baut mo lo pay like mae.
Hmm, well, I'll give it to you, since it's my first sale.

CHAPTER 10

Shopping and Bargaining
Part 2

 **DIALOGUE** WHAT ARE YOU LOOKING FOR?

At Bogyoke Market, Naing Oo and Samantha go into a souvenir shop. Naing Oo
wants to buy Samantha a traditional *minthamee* (princess) marionette.

Shopkeeper (female): *Come, big brother, come!*
Lah bah, ako ji, lah bah.
လာပါ၊အကိုကြီး၊ လာပါ။
What're you looking for?
Bah shah nay dah lae.
ဘာရှာနေတာလဲ။

Naing Oo: *I'd like a princess marionette. Do you have one?*
Minthamee yoke thay yoke lo jin dae. Shi lar.
မင်းသမီး ရုပ်သေးရုပ် လိုချင်တယ်။ ရှိလား။

Shopkeeper: *We have one. Over here, look.*
Shi bah dae shint. De hmah. Kyi bah.
ရှိပါတယ်ရှင့်။ ဒီမှာ ကြည့်.ပါ။

Naing Oo: *Lovely! I like this.*
Hla dae. Dah kyait tae.
လှတယ်။ ဒါကြိုက်တယ်။
Do you have something a bit smaller?
Nae nae thay dah shi lar.
နည်းနည်းသေးတာရှိလား။

Shopkeeper: *We have it. Here it is.*
Shi bah dae. De hmah.
ရှိပါတယ်။ ဒီမှာ။

Naing Oo: *That's too small.*
Thaik thay thwar bi.
သိပ်သေးသွားပြီ။
How about something a bit bigger?
Nae nae kyi dah aw.
နည်းနည်းကြီးတာရော။

Shopkeeper: *How about this one?*
Dah so yin aw.
ဒါဆိုရင်ရော။

Naing Oo: *This is perfect. How much?*
Dah so ataw bae. Balauk lae khamyar.
ဒါဆိုအတော်ပဲ။ ဘယ်လောက်လဲ ခင်ဗျား။

Shopkeeper: *12,000.*
Thoung hna-htaung bah.
၁၂၀၀၀ ပါ။

Naing Oo: *Can I get it for 10,000?*
Ta thaung naet ya ma lar.
၁၀၀၀၀ နဲ့ရမလား။

Shopkeeper: *Hmm, well, I'll give it to you, since it's my first sale.*
Inn, zay oo baut mo lo pay like mae.
အင်း ... ဈေးဦးပေါက်မို့လို့ ပေးလိုက်မယ်။

Naing Oo: *Wow, thanks a lot!*
Hah, kyay zu bae byah.
ဟာ ... ကျေးဇူးပဲဗျာ။

VOCABULARY

bah	what
shah	to find, to look for
minthamee	princess
yoke thay	marionette, puppet
lo jin dae	I'd like, I want
shi	to have, to exist
kyi	to look at
di hmah	right here
nae nae thay dah	something a bit smaller
nae nae kyi dah	something a bit bigger
zay oo bauk	first sale for the day

Supplementary Vocabulary

nah yi	watch
sah oak	book
minthar	prince
balu	demon
zawgyi	wizard
myin	horse

baji kar	painting
babu yoke	sculpture, carved figurines
let saung pyitsee	gift items
nae nae to dah	something a bit shorter
nae nae shay dah	something a bit longer
nae nae lay dah	something a bit heavier
nae nae pawt dah	something a bit lighter
a ni yaung	red, in red
a pyah yaung	blue, in blue
a sein yaung	green, in green
a wah yaung	yellow, in yellow
a net yaung	black, in black
a phyu yaung	white, in white

 **CULTURAL NOTE**

Shopkeepers may call you "big brother" or "big sister."

In the previous dialogue, you heard the cab driver addresses his customer Naing
Oo as **hsayah** (boss). In this dialogue, the shopkeeper addresses Naing Oo as **ako ji**
(big brother). Vendors, shopkeepers, teashop employees, and restaurant employees
often use relationship terms to address their customers as a sign of respect.

GRAMMAR NOTE *"Want" — lo jin*

To indicate what he is looking for, Naing Oo tells the shopkeeper:

မင်းသမီး ရုပ်သေးရုပ် လိုချင်တယ်။   Minthamee yoke thay yoke lo jin dae.
I'd like a princess marionette.

yoke thay
a marionette

မင်းသမီး	minthamee	princess
ရုပ်သေးရုပ်	yoke thay yoke	marionette / figurine
လိုချင်	lo jin	to want / to desire
တယ်	dae	sentence ending

The key word is the verb **lo jin dae**, which means, *I want [something]*. For example:

- **Fountain pen lo jin dae.**   *I want a fountain pen.*
- **Nah yi lo jin dae.**   *I want a watch.*
- **Sah oak lo jin dae.**   *I want a book.*
- **iPhone lo jin dae.**   *I want an iPhone.*

PATTERN PRACTICE 1: "I WANT THIS OBJECT."

Burmese marionettes represent iconic figures from folktales and Buddhist parables. The best-known are:

- **minthamee yoke thay yoke**   princess marionette
- **minthar yoke thay yoke**   prince marionette
- **balu yoke thay yoke**   demon marionette
- **zawji yoke thay yoke**   wizard marionette
- **myin yoke thay yoke**   horse marionette

Practice these requests:

1. **Minthar yoke thay yoke lo hin dae.** I'd like a prince marionette.
2. **Balu yoke thay yoke lo jin dae.** I'd like a demon marionette.
3. **Zawji yoke thay yoke lo jin dae.** I'd like a wizard marionette.
4. **Myin yoke thay yoke lo jin dae.** I'd like a horse marionette.
5. **Lephet yay lo jin dae.** I'd like some tea.
6. **Kor phee lo jin dae.** I'd like some coffee.
7. **Yay lo jin dae.** I'd like some water.
8. **Phone lo jin dae.** I'd like a phone.

CULTURAL NOTE **Something from Myanmar for your friends**

Because of their cultural significance and craftsmanship, Burmese marionettes dressed in elaborate outfits make great souvenirs for travelers. They're usually sold in major shopping areas, such as Yangon's Bogyoke Market or Mandalay's Zay Cho Market. In Bagan, the temple-dotted ancient capital in the middle of Myanmar, some souvenir vendors also make extra money by charging patrons a small fee for taking selfies with their meticulously arranged marionettes as backdrops.

With their elaborate designs and woven patterns, a Burmese sarong—a tubular cloth to wrap around one's waist and legs—also makes an impressive gift. Men's sarongs are called **pa hsoe** and women's are called **htamein**. Men's **pa hsoe** tend to be in darker, muted colors with checks and lines. By contrast, women's **htamein** tend to be in brighter, bolder colors, decorated with floral motifs.

Other popular gift items include:

မောင်း	maung	brass gong
ရင်ဖုံးအင်္ကျီ	yin bone ain ji	classic double-breasted shirt (for females)
ပင်နီတိုက်ပုံ	pin ni tike pone	classic red-cotton jacket (for males)
ချိပ်ထဘီ	chait htamain	decorative woven *sarong* (for females)
ကချင်လွယ်အိတ်	ka-chin lwae ait	*Kachin* satchel (with ethnic designs from the Kachin region)
ယွန်းထည်	yune dae	lacquer ware.
ရခိုင်ပုဆိုး	yakhaing pa hsoe	Rakhine *sarong* (decorative male *sarong*):
သနပ်ခါး	tha na khar	*thanakha* (aromatic woodbark paste, worn as a facial cosmetic)
စောင်းကောက်	saungg gaut	traditional Burmese harp
ဆွမ်းအုပ်	swun oat	traditional meal-carrying vessel
ယောထဘီ	yaw htamain	yaw *sarong*

EXERCISE 1: "I WANT THIS OBJECT."

Ask for these items in Burmese:
1. I'd like a prince marionette.
2. I'd like a demon marionette.
3. I'd like a horse marionette.
4. I'd like a wizard marionette.
5. I want coffee.
6. I'd like a watch.
7. I want tea.
8. I'd like a book.
9. I'd like a phone.
10. I want beer.

PATTERN PRACTICE 2:
"I WANT THIS IN THAT QUANTITY."

In Chapter 8: Shopping and Bargaining, Part I, you learnt some common classifiers for counting. So let's incorporate them here.

1. **Kor phee ta khwet lo jin dae.** I'd like one cup of coffee.
2. **Beer hna palin lo jin dae.** I'd like two bottles of beer.
3. **Nah yi thone lone lo jin dae.** I'd like three watches.
4. **Htamin lay bwe lo jin dae.** I'd like four servings of rice.
5. **iPhone ngar lone lo jin dae.** I'd like five iPhones.
6. **Khway chauk kaung lo jin dae.** I'd like six dogs.
7. **SIM kard khona khu lo jin dae.** I'd like seven SIM cards.

GRAMMAR NOTE Asking if something's there with *shi*

When Naing Oo wants to know if the shopkeeper has a particular marionette, he asks:

ရှိလား။   **Shi lar.**   *Do you have it?*

ရှိ (**shi**, to have, to exist) + လား (**lar**, yes–no question particle)

And the shopkeeper responds:

ရှိပါတယ်ရှင့်။   **Shi bah dae shint.**   *I have it.*

ရှိ (**shi**, to have, to exist) + ပါတယ်ရှင့် (**bah dae shint**, affirmative sentence ending, female speaker's politeness marker)

Depending on the context, the verb **shi** can mean *to have*, or *to exist*. In this case, both meanings are applicable: The shopkeeper has the figurine Naing Oo wants; it exists on the shop's premise.

Here are some variations in which the verb can be used:

- **Naing Oo de hmah shi dae.** *Naing Oo is here. (Literally: He exists here.)*
- **Samantha de hmah shi lar.** *Is Samantha here? (Literally: Does Samantha exist here?)*
- **De hsaing hmah pout si ma shi boo.** *This shop doesn't have meat buns.*
- **Nyi ma ta yauk shi dae.** *[I] have a sister.*
- **Tha nge jin ma shin boo.** *[I] don't have friends.*

PATTERN PRACTICE 3: SPECIFYING SIZE

To get a princess marionette in the right size, Naing Oo first said this:

နည်းနည်းသေးတာရှိလား။ **Nae nae thay dah shi lar.**
Do you have something a bit smaller?

နည်းနည်း	nae nae	a bit, a little
သေးတာ	thay dah	something small
ရှိ	shi	to have, to exist
လား	lar	question particle

Later, he also said:

နည်းနည်းကြီးတာရော။ **Nae nae kyi dah aw.**
How about something a bit bigger?

နည်းနည်း	nae nae	a bit, a little
ကြီးတာ	kyi dah	something big
ရော	syaw / aw	also, as well

The last part of his question, **shi lar** *(Do you have? Does it exist?)*, is not repeated but implied.

Practice the following:
1. **Nae nae to dah shi lar.** Do you have something a bit shorter (lengthwise)?
2. **Nae nae shay dah shi lar.** Do you have something a bit longer?
3. **Nae nae myint dah shi lar.** Do you have something a bit taller?
4. **Nae nae pu dah shi lar.** Do you have something a bit shorter (in height)?
5. **Nae nae lay dah shi lar.** Do you have something a bit heavier?
6. **Nae nae pawt dah shi lar.** Do you have something a bit lighter?

EXERCISE 2: TALKING ABOUT SIZE

Ask these questions in Burmese:
1. Do you have something a bit shorter (in length)?
2. Do you have something a bit longer?
3. Do you have something a bit taller?
4. Do you have something a bit shorter (in height)?
5. Do you have something a bit heavier?
6. Do you have something a bit lighter?

PATTERN PRACTICE 4: SPECIFYING COLOR

Also practice these questions with colors:

1. **A ni yaung shi lar.** Do you have it in red?
2. **A pyar yaung shi lar.** Do you have it in blue?
3. **A sein yaung shi lar.** Do you have it in green?
4. **A wah yaung shi lar.** Do you have it in yellow?
5. **A net yaung shi lar.** Do you have it in black?
6. **A phyu yaung shi lar.** Do you have it in white?
7. **Khayan yaung shi lar.** Do you have it in purple?
8. **Pan yaung shi lar.** Do you have it in pink?
9. **Mee go yaung shi lar.** Do you have it in gray?
10. **Lain maw yaung shi lar.** Do you have it in orange?

EXERCISE 3: TAKING ABOUT ATTRIBUTES

Ask these questions in Burmese:

1. Do you have it in yellow?
2. Do you have it in black?
3. Do you have it in green?
4. Do you have something a bit bigger?
5. Do you have something a little taller?
6. Do you have something a bit shorter (in length)?
7. Do you have something a bit lighter?

EXERCISE 4: MORE COLORS

What are these colors in English?

1. **a pyah yaung**
2. **a ni yaung**
3. **a wah yaung**
4. **a net yaung**
5. **a phyu yaung**
6. **a sein yaung**
7. **lainmaw yaung**
8. **khayan yaung**
9. **pan yaung**

CULTURAL NOTE Be sensitive to first sales

At the end of her negotiation, the shopkeeper says **zay oo baut mo lo** ("because it's the first sale"). Many Burmese shopkeepers believe that if their first sale of the day doesn't work out, business for the rest of the day could be ruined. It's a common superstition. Therefore, in their price negotiation during a first-sale transaction, they're usually much more willing to let you have the merchandise for a lower-than-usual price. If you're a customer who finds yourself with a shopkeeper trying to make his or her first sale of the day, it's good to show consideration for the shopkeeper's vulnerable position by not bargaining too aggressively. This is how many Burmese buyers and sellers show mutual respect for each other in **zay oo baut** or *first-sale* negotiations.

This is delicious.

Is that the first time you've tried Shan Kaukswe?

Yeah, I think so.

Ako, Ama, khauk swae bae lo nay lae.
Brother, sister, how is the noodle?

A hsin pyay lar.
OK?

Hah, hote lah.
Oh, really?

Pyin pay ya ma lah?
Shall I fix it for you?

Kyanawt a twet tawt ataw bae.
For me, it's just right.

Dah bae maet kyama a twet tawt nae nae sut tae.
But for me, it's a bit spicy.

Ma lo boo.
No need.

Sar naing dae.
I can eat it.

Nyi lay, di hmah wet thar pah lar.
Little Brother, is there pork in it?

Ma pah boo khamya.
No.

Kyet thar bae par dae.
Just chicken in it.

CHAPTER 11

Dining Out

DIALOGUE FLAVORS

After shopping, it's dinner time, so Naing Oo and Samantha go to a *Shan kaukswe* (Shan noodle) *shop.*

Samantha: *[in English] This is delicious.*

Naing Oo: *[in English] Is that the first time you've tried* Shan kaukswe*?*

Samantha: *[in English] Yeah, I think so.*

Waiter: *Brother, sister, how are the noodles?*
Ako, ama, khauk swae bae lo nay lae.
အကို၊ အမ ခေါက်ဆွဲ ဘယ်လိုနေလဲ။
OK?
A hsin pyay lar.
အဆင်ပြေလား။

Naing Oo: *For me, it's just right.*
Kyanawt a twet tawt ataw bae.
ကျွန်တော့် အတွက်တော့ အတော်ပဲ။

Samantha *But for me, it's a bit spicy.*
Dah bae maet kyama a twet tawt nae nae sut tae.
ဒါပေမယ့် ကျွန်မအတွက်တော့ နည်းနည်းစပ်တယ်။

Waiter: *Oh, really? Shall I fix it for you?*
Hah, hote lah. Pyin pay ya ma lah.
ဟာ ဟုတ်လား။ ပြင်ပေးရမလား။

Samantha: *It's OK. No need. I can eat it.*
Ya bah dae. Ma lo boo. Sar naing dae.
ရပါတယ်။ မလိုဘူး။ စားနိုင်တယ်။

Naing Oo: *Little brother, is there pork in it?*
Nyi lay, di hmah wet thar pah lar.
ညီလေး၊ ဒီမှာ ဝက်သားပါလား။

Waiter: *No. Just chicken in it.*
Ma pah boo khamya. Kyet thar bae par dae.
မပါဘူးခင်ဗျ။ ကြက်သားပဲ ပါတယ်။

VOCABULARY

bae lo nay lae	how is it?
a hsin pyay	going well, doing well, fine
kyanawt a twet	for me (male speaker)
kyama a twet	for me (female speaker)
ataw bae	just right
nae nae sut tae	a little bit spicy
pyin pay ya ma lar	shall I fix it for you?
ma lo boo	not necessary
sar naing dae	I can eat it.
wet thar	pork
kyet thar	poultry, chicken meat
pah dae	it's included; it's in there.

Supplementary Vocabulary

amae thar	beef
sait thar	goat meat
thoe thar	lamb
ngar	fish
bazun	shrimp
nga yoke thee	chili
thajar	sugar
acho hmont	artificial flavoring
thaghar a tu	artificial sweetener
thaik sut tae	very spicy
sut lun dae	too spicy
nae nae cho dae	a little bit sweet
thaik cho dae	very sweet
cho lun dae	too sweet
nae Nae chin dae	a little bit sour
thaik chin dae	very sour
chin lun dae	too sour
nae nae khar dae	a little bitter
thaik khar dae	very bitter
khar lun dae	too bitter
nae nae pyit tae	a little bit thick (as in liquid)
thaik pyit tae	very thick
pyit lun dae	too thick
nae nae kyae dae	a little bit thin (as in liquid)

thaik kyae dae	very thin
kyae lun dae	too thin
nae nae mar dae	a little bit hard
thaik mar dae	very hard
mar lun dae	too hard
nae nae pyawt dae	a little bit soft
thaik pyawt dae	very soft
pyawt lun dae	too soft

 **GRAMMAR NOTE** "As for me ..."

When the waiter worries that the dish might be too spicy, Naing Oo says:

ကျွန်တော့် အတွက်တော့ အတော်ပဲ။   **Kyanawt a twet tawt ataw bae.**
For me, it's just right.

ကျွန်တော့်	**kyanawt**	me (male speaker's *I* in object case)
အတွက်တော့	**a twet tawt**	as for
အတော်ပဲ	**a taw bae**	just right

Contrast with Samantha's answer:

ကျွန်မအတွက်တော့ နည်းနည်းစပ်တယ်။   **Kyamna a twet tawt nae nae sut tae.**
For me, it's a bit spicy.

ကျွန်မ	**kyama**	me (female speaker's *I* in object case)
အတွက်တော့	**a twet tawt**	as for
နည်းနည်း	**nae nae**	a little, a bit
စပ်တယ်	**sut tae**	spicy

In these instances, the phrases **kyanawt a twet tawt** and **kyama a twet tawt** correspond to "for me" or "as far as I'm concerned" (male and female speakers' versions). The particle **tawt** is roughly the equivalent of "though"—as in, "for me, though ..."

ကျွန်မအတွက်တော့ နည်းနည်းစပ်တယ်   **Kyama a twet tawt nae nae sut tae.**
For me though, it's a bit spicy.

For the statements above, the word **tawt** is not essential and can be omitted without affecting the meaning.

GRAMMAR NOTE "Very much, too much"

If the dish were very spicy or too spicy, Samantha may say:

သိပ်စပ်တယ် **Thaik sut tae.** *Very spicy.*

သိပ် (**thaik**, very) + စပ်တယ် (sut tae, spicy)

စပ်လွန်းတယ် **Sut lun dae.** *Too spicy.*

စပ် (**sut**, spicy) + လွန်း (**lun**, too, extremely) + တယ် (**dae**, affirmative sentence ending)

PATTERN PRACTICE 1: "AS FOR ME ..."

Practice these (with the gender-appropriate pronouns based on who you are). For simplicity, the particle **tawt** may be omitted.

1. Kyanawt/kyama a twet tawt <u>a hsin pyay dae</u>.   For me, it's <u>fine</u>.
2. Kyanawt/kyama a twet tawt <u>a hsin ma pyay boo</u>.   For me, it's <u>not fine</u>.
3. Kyawt/kyama a twet tawt <u>nae nae cho dae</u>.   For me, it's a <u>bit sweet</u>.
4. Kyanawt/kyama a twet tawt <u>thaik cho dae</u>.   For me, it's <u>very sweet</u>.
5. Kyanawt/kyama a twet tawt <u>cho lun dae</u>.   For me, it's <u>too sweet</u>.
6. Kyanawt/kyama a twet tawt <u>ma cho boo</u>.   For me, it's <u>not sweet</u>.
7. Kyawt/kyama a twet tawt <u>nae nae khar dae</u>.   For me, it's a <u>bit bitter</u>.
8. Kyanawt/kyama a twet tawt <u>thaik khar dae</u>.   For me, it's <u>very bitter</u>.
9. Kyanawt/kyama a twet tawt <u>khar lun dae</u>.   For me, it's <u>too bitter</u>.
10. Kyanawt/kyama a twet tawt <u>ma khar boo</u>.   For me, it's <u>not bitter</u>.
11. Kyawt/kyama a twet tawt <u>nae nae chin dae</u>.   For me, it's <u>a bit sour</u>.
12. Kyanawt/kyama a twet tawt <u>thaik chin dae</u>.   For me, it's <u>very sour</u>.
13. Kyanawt/kyama a twet tawt <u>chin lun dae</u>.   For me, it's <u>too sour</u>.
14. Kyanawt/kyama a twet tawt <u>ma chin boo</u>.   For me, it's <u>not sour</u>.

GRAMMAR NOTE "But"—*da bae maet*

Samantha begins her answer with the conjunction *but*—**dah bae maet:**

ဒါပေမယ့် ကျွန်မအတွက်တော့ နည်းနည်းစပ်တယ်။
Dah bae maet kyama a twet tawt nae nae sut tae. *But for me, it's a bit spicy.*

You can use the same conjunction to connect contrasting ideas and statements. For example:

ဒီကော်ဖီ ချိုတယ်။ ဒါပေတော့ ဟိုကော်ဖီ ခါးတယ်။

De kor phee cho dae. Dah bae maet ho kor phee khar dae.

This coffee is sweet, but that coffee is bitter.

ဒီကော်ဖီ	**de kor phee**	this coffee
ချိုတယ်။	**cho dae**	sweet
ဒါပေမယ့်	**dar bae maet**	but
ဟိုကော်ဖီ	**ho kor phee**	that coffee
ခါးတယ်။	**khar dae**	bitter

ကျွန်တော့်အတွက်တော့ အတော်ပဲ။ ဒါပေမယ့် သူ့အတွက် နည်းနည်းစပ်တယ်။

Kyanawt a twet tawt ataw bae. Dar bae maet thu a twet tawt nae nae sut tae.

For me, it's just right. But for him/her, it's a bit spicy.

ကျွန်တော့် အတွက်တော့	**kyanawt a twet tawt**	for me (male speaker)
အတော်ပဲ။	**a taw bae**	**just right**
ဒါပေမယ့်	**dah bae maet**	**but**
သူ့အတွက်	**thu a twet tawt**	**for him / her**
နည်းနည်းစပ်တယ်။	**nae nae sut tae**	a bit spicy

PATTERN PRACTICE 2: "BUT FOR HIM/HER ..."

Practice these. For simplicity, the particle **tawt** may be omitted.

1. **Dah bae maet thu a twet tawt ma khar boo.** But for him / her, it's not bitter.
2. **Dah bae maet thu a twet tawt nae nae sut tae.** But for him / her, it's a bit spicy.
3. **Dah bae maet thu a twet tawt cho lun dae.** But for him / her, it's too sweet.
4. **Dah bae maet kyanawt/kyama a twet tawt ma pyawt boo.** But for me, it's not soft.
5. **Dah bae maet kyanawt/kyama a twet tawt mar lun dae.** But for me, it's too hard.
6. **Dah bae maet kyanawt/kyama a twet tawt thaik pyit tae.** But for me, it's too thick.

EXERCISE 1: "FOR ME IT'S ..."

Say the following in Burmese. You may need to consult the supplementary vocabulary list for some of the flavors and texture-related words. Make sure to use the correct pronoun **kyanawt or kyama,** based on your gender.

1. For me, it's too spicy.
2. For me, it's a bit sweet.
3. For me, it's not sweet.
4. For me, it's a bit sour.
5. For me, it's very sour.
6. For me, it's not bitter.
7. For me, it's too bitter.
8. For me, it's a bit hard.
9. For me, it's very soft.
10. For me, it's too thick.

EXERCISE 2:
USING "BUT" TO SHOW CONTRASTING IDEAS

Say these sentences in Burmese:

1. It's fine for me, but for him/her, it's too bitter.
2. It's fine for me, but for him/her, it's very sweet.
3. It's fine for me, but for him/her, it's too sour.
4. It's soft for me, but for him/her, it's hard.
5. It's sweet for me, but for him/her, it's bitter.
6. It's bitter for me, but for him/her, it's not bitter.
7. It's not spicy for me, but for him/for her, it's a bit spicy.
8. It's not hard for me, but for him/her, it's a bit hard.
9. It's fine for him/her, but for me, it's very sour.
10. It's fine for him/her, but for me, it's a bit spicy.

GRAMMAR NOTE Is something/someone included?

When Naing oo wants to know if there's any pork in his dish, he asked:

ဒီမှာ ဝက်သားပါလား။ **De hmah wet thar pah lar.** *Is there pork in it?*

ဒီမှာ	de hmah	right here, in here
ဝက်သား	wet thar	pork
ပါ	pah	to include
လား	lar	yes–no question particle

Here are some other ways to use the verb **pah**:

ဒီရုပ်ရှင်မှာ Drew Barrymore ပါလား။
De yoke shin hmah, Drew Barrymore pah lar.
Is Drew Barrymore in this movie?

ဒီရုပ်ရှင်	di yoke shin	this movie
မှာ	hmah	in, at
ပါ	pah	to include, to be part of
လား	lar	yes–no question particle

ဒီသီချင်းပွဲမှာ ဖြူဖြူကျော်သိန်း ပါလား။
De thachin bwae hmah, Phyu Phyu Kyaw Thein pah lar.
Is [pop singer] Phyu Phyu Kyaw Thein [performing] in this concert?

ဒီသီချင်းပွဲ	de thachin bwae	this concert
မှာ	hmah	in, at
ဖြူဖြူကျော်သိန်း	Phyu Phyu Kyaw Thein	[name of pop singer] Phyu Phyu Kyaw Thein
ပါ	pah	to include, to be part of
လား	lar	yes–no question particle

EXERCISE 3: "IS THERE [SOMETHING] IN THIS DISH?"

Ask these questions in Burmese:

1. Is there goat meat (**sait thar**) in it?
2. Is there chicken (**kyet thar**) in it?
3. Is there beef (**amae thar**) in it?
4. Is there lamb (**thoe thar**) in it?

5. Is there chili (**nga yoke thee**) in it?
6. Is there sugar (**thajar**) in it?
7. Is there artificial sweetener (**thajar atu**) in it?
8. Is there artifical flavoring (**acho hmont**) in it?
9. Is there shrimp (**bazun**) in it?
10. Is there fish (**ngar**) **in it?**

GRAMMAR NOTE "Only this"—*pae/bae*

Responding to Naing Oo's question about pork being in the noodle dish, the waiter says:

ကြက်သားပဲပါတယ်။   **Kyet thar bae pah dae.**
Only chicken is included. / There's just chicken in it.

ကြက်သား	kyet thar	poultry, chicken meat
ပဲ	bae	only
ပါ	pah	included
တယ်	dae	affirmative sentence ending

Here are other ways to use the particle **pae/bae**:

ရေပဲသောက်မယ်။   **Yay bae thauk mae.**   *I'll drink only water.*

ရေ	yay	water
ပဲ	bae	only
သောက်	thauk	drink
မယ်	mae	future sentence end particle

ခေါက်ဆွဲပဲစားမယ်။   **Khauk swae bae sar mae.**   *I'll eat only noodles.*

ခေါက်ဆွဲ	khauk swae	noodles
ပဲ	bae	only
စား	sar	to eat
မယ်	mae	future sentence end particle

နည်းနည်းပဲယူမယ်။ Nae nae bae yu mae. *I'll take only a little.*

နည်းနည်း	nae nae	a little bit
ပဲ	bae	only
ယူ	yu	to take
မယ်	mae	future sentence end particle

EXERCISE 4: "ONLY THIS"

Say these phrases in Burmese:
1. Just fish (**ngar**) in it.
2. Just lamb (**thoe thar**) in it.
3. Just pork (**wet thar**) in it.
4. Just shrimp (**bazun**) in it.
5. Just beef (**amae thar**) in it.
6. Just goat meat (**sait thar**) in it.

CHAPTER 12

Taking a Burmese Class

 **DIALOGUE** TALKING TO THE TEACHER

Today, Samantha goes to Win San's Burmese class to get some lessons.

Win San:	*Greetings, Samantha!*
	Mingala bah, Samantha!
	မင်္ဂလာပါ Samantha.
Samantha:	*Greetings, Ko Win San.*
	Mingala bah, Ko Win San.
	မင်္ဂလာပါ ကိုဝင်းဆန်း။
Win San:	*In Burmese, the teacher is called* hsayah.
	Bamah lo *teacher* **go hsayah lo khaw dae.**
	ဗမာလို teacher ကို ဆရာလို့ခေါ်တယ်။
Samantha:	*Then, I shall call you* hsayah?
	Dah so, Ko Win San go hsayah lo khaw mae.
	ဒါဆို ကိုဝင်းဆန်းကိုဆရာလို့ခေါ်မယ်။
Win San:	*Yes.*
	Hote kaet.
	ဟုတ်ကဲ့။
Samantha:	*What's today's lesson about, teacher?*
	De nayt lesson ga bah a kyaung lae, hsayah.
	ဒီနေ့ Lesson က ဘာအကြောင်းလဲ ဆရာ။
Winsan:	*Today's lesson is on school-related vocabulary.*
	De nayt lesson ga kyaung thone waw hah ra.
	ဒီနေ့ Lesson က ကျောင်းသုံး ဝေါဟာရ။
Samantha:	*How about tomorrow's lesson?*
	Ma net phyan lesson ga yaw.
	မနက်ဖြန် Lesson ကရော။
Win San:	*Office-related vocabulary.*
	Yone thone waw hah ra.
	ရုံးသုံး ဝေါဟာရ။
Samantha:	*What is* waw hah ra?
	Waw hah ra **hso dah bah lae.**
	ဝေါဟာရ ဆိုတာ ဘာလဲ။

Win San: Waw hah ra *is vocabulary.*
               Waw hah ra hso dah *vocabulary* bah.
               ဝေါဟာရ ဆိုတာ vocabulary ပါ။
Samantha: *What's lesson* called?
               Lesson go bah khaw lae shint.
               Lesson ကို ဘာခေါ်လဲ ရှင့်။
Win San: *It's called* thin gan zar.
               Thin gan zar lo khaw bah dae.
               သင်ခန်းစာလို့ ခေါ်ပါတယ်။
Samantha: *How do you say* student *in Burmese,* Hsayah?
               Student go bah khaw lae, Hsayah.
               Student ကို ဘာခေါ်လဲ ဆရာ။
Win San: *You say* kyaung thar.
               Kyaung thar lo khaw dae.
               ကျောင်းသားလို့ခေါ်တယ်။
Samantha: *Then, I'm your* kyaung thar. *Correct?*
               Dah so, kyama ga hsaya yet kyaung thar. Hman lar.
               ဒါဆို ကျွန်မက ဆရာ့ရဲ့ကျောင်းသား။ မှန်လား။
Win San: *That's right.*
               Hman bah dae.
               မှန်ပါတယ်။
Samantha: *You are my* hsayah.
               Ko Win San ga kyama yet hsayah.
               ကိုဝင်းဆန်းက ကျွန်မရဲ့ ဆရာ။
Win San: *That's correct as well.*
               Dah lae hman dae.
               ဒါလည်းမှန်တယ်။
Samantha: *Thanks,* Hsayah!
               Kyay zu bah Hsayah.
               ကျေးဇူးပါ ဆရာ။

VOCABULARY

hsayah	teacher
kyaung	school (also monastery)
kyaung thone	school-related, used in school
yone	office, work
yone thone	office-related, used in the office
a kyaung	about
thone	to use

waw hah ra	vocabulary
di nayt	today
ma nayt ga	yesterday
ma net phyan	tomorrow
kyaung thar	student (can be male or female)
Myanmar zah	Burmese language
thin gan zah	lesson
taw dae	smart, clever, intelligent

Supplementary Vocabulary

hsayah ma	female teacher
kyaung thu	female student
sah oak	book
khae dan	pencil
baw pen	ballpoint pen
khone	desk
kala-htaing	chair
badin bauk	window
dagar	door
sah thin gan	classroom
phat sah oak	textbook
kyaung wut sone	school uniform
kyauk thin bone/kyauk thin mone	blackboard

CULTURAL NOTE Students, teachers, and gender politics

The word **kyaung thar** is a compound word formed with the word **kyaung** (school) and **thar** (son); therefore, it means *male student* by default. However, speaking of students generally, **kyaung thar** can be an all-inclusive word to refer to both male and female students. (A teacher might, for example, refer to a classroom full of male and female students as, "*These are my* **kyaung thar**.") But if you need to emphasize the female gender of a particular student, you may use **kyaung thu**, the word that specifically refers to *female students*.

Hsayah may be used for both male and female teachers, but by default it refers to male teachers. So if you need to emphasize the fact that a particular teacher is female, or if you're addressing a female teacher, you should use **hsayah ma**, the word for a *female teacher*.

In Burmese classrooms, the etiquette is to address the teacher as **hsayah** or **hsayah ma**. In fact, Burmese students continue to refer to their former teachers as **hsayah** or **hsayah ma** when they encounter them outside or when they meet them again, long after graduation.

GRAMMAR NOTE "About"—*a kyaung*

When Samantha asks Win Naing what she will be learning today, she says:

> ဒီနေ့ lesson က ဘာအကြောင်းလဲ။ **De nayt lesson ga bah a kyaung lae.**
> *What's today's lesson about?*

ဒီနေ့	**de nayt**	today
က	**ga**	subject marker
ဘာ	**bah**	what
အကြောင်း	**a kyaung**	about
လဲ	**lae**	question making particle

Here are some other ways the **a kyaung** particle can be used:

> ကျွန်တော်/ကျွန်မ ဒီအကြောင်း မသိဘူး။
> **Kyanaw / kyama de a kyaung ma-thi boo.** *I didn't know about this.*

ကျွန်တော်/ကျွန်မ	**kyanaw / kyama**	(male / female speaker)
ဒီအကြောင်း	**de a kyaung**	about this
မသိ	**ma thi**	don't know
ဘူး	**boo**	negative sentence ending

> San Francisco အကြောင်း ပြောပြပါ။ **San Francisco a kyaung pyaw pya bah.**
> *Tell me about San Francisco.*

San Francisco အကြောင်း	**San Francisco a kyaung**	about San Francisco
ပြောပြ	**pyaw pya**	tell / explain
ပါ	**bah**	polite command / request particle

> သူ့အကြောင်း မပြောချင်ဘူး။ **Thu a kyaung ma-pyaw jin boo.**
> *I don't want to talk about him.*

သူ့အကြောင်း	**thu a kyaung**	about him / her
မပြော	**ma pyaw**	not talk
ချင်	**jin**	want to (auxiliary verb)
ဘူး	**boo**	negative sentence ending

GRAMMAR NOTE Yesterday, today, tomorrow

When Samantha uses the following phrases about today and tomorrow's lessons:

| ဒီနေ့ lesson | de nayt lesson | today's lesson |
| မနက်ဖြန် lesson | manet phyan lesson | tomorrow's lesson |

If she wanted to know what was taught yesterday, she could have said:

| မနေ့က lesson | ma nayt ga lesson | yesterday's lesson |

Subsequently, Samantha learns that *lesson* is **thin gan zah** in Burmese. So from now on, she can start saying:

မနေ့က သင်ခန်းစာ	ma nayt ga thin gan zah	yesterday's lesson
ဒီနေ့ သင်ခန်းစာ	de nayt thin gan zar	today's lesson
မနက်ဖြန် သင်ခန်းစာ	manet phyan thin gan zah	tomorrow's lesson

GRAMMAR NOTE The reference particle *hso dah*

When Samantha doesn't understand a word in Win San's speech, she asks:

ဝေါဟာရ ဆိုတာ ဘာလဲ။   *Waw hah ra hso dah bah lae.*   *What's waw hah ra?*

ဝေါဟာရ	waw hah ra	vocabulary
ဆိုတာ	hso dah	so-called
ဘာ	bah	what
လဲ	lae	question particle

Hsayah!

The particle **hso dah** refers to the phrase **waw hah ra** as an unknown item that warrants clarification. Taken together, **waw hah ra hso dah** may be translated as "This so-called **waw hah ra** ..."

Here are other examples of its use:

Samantha ဆိုတာ ဘယ်သူလဲ။   Samantha hso dah ba thu lae.
Who is this Samantha? [Lit., Who is this so-called Samantha?]

Samantha ဆိုတာ ကျွန်တော့ အမျိုးသမီးပါ။
Samantha hso dah kyanawt amyo thamee bah.
Samantha is my girlfriend. [Lit., This so-called Samantha is my girlfriend.]

PATTERN PRACTICE 1:
LEARNING SCHOOL–RELATED WORDS

To teach the Burmese word for *teacher* to Samantha, Win San says:

Teacher ကို ဆရာလို့ခေါ်တယ်။   *Teacher* go hsayah lo khaw dae.
*A teacher is called **hsayah**.*

ကို	go	subject marker
ဆရာလို့	hsayah lo	as *hsayah*
ခေါ်	khaw	is called
တယ်	dae	sentence-end particle

Repeat the following to learn some classroom-related terms:
1. *Desk go khone* lo khaw dae.   A *desk* is called **khone**.
2. *School go kyaung* lo khaw dae.   A *school* is called **kyaung**.
3. *Teacher go hsayah* lo khaw dae.   A *teacher* is called **hsayah**.
4. *Textbook go phat sah oak* lo khaw dae.   A *textbook* is called **phat sah oak**.
5. *Window go badin bauk* lo khaw dae.   A *window* is called **badin bauk**.
6. *Door go dagar* lo khaw dae.   A *door* is called **dagar**.
7. *School uniform* go kyaung wut sone lo khaw dae.
   A *school uniform* is called **kyaung wut sone**.
8. *Classroom go sah thin gan* lo khaw dae.   A *classroom* is called **sah thin gan**.
9. *Homework ko ain zah* lo khaw dae.   *Homework* is called **ain zar**.
10. *Blackboard ko kyauk thin bone* lo khaw dae.
    A *blackboard* is called **kyauk thin bone** / **kyauk thin mone**.

PATTERN PRACTICE 2:
"WHAT'S IT CALLED? IT'S CALLED ..."
Practice these exchanges with a partner:
a) Desk **ko bah khaw lae.**   What is a *desk* called?
b) Desk **ko khone lo khaw dae.**   A *desk* is called **khone.**

a) School **go bah khaw lae.**   What is a *school* called?
b) Schook **go kyaung lo khaw dae.**   A *school* is called **kyaung.**

a) Teacher **go bah khaw lae.**   What is a *teacher* called?
b) Teacher **go Hsayah lo khaw dae.**   A *teacher* is called **hsayah.**

a) Student **go bah khaw lae.**   What is a *student* called?
b) Student **go kyaung thar lo khaw dae.**   A *student* is called **kyaung thar.**

a) Textbook **ko bah khaw lae.**   What is a *textbook* called?
b) Textbook **ko phat sah oak lo khaw dae.**   A *textbook* is called **phat sah oak.**

a) Homework **ko bah khaw lae.**   What is *homework* called?
b) Homework **ko ain zah lo khaw dae.**   *Homework* is called **ain zah.**

a) Lesson **go bah khaw lae.**   What is a *lesson* called?
b) Lesson **go thin gan zah lo khaw dae.**   A *lesson* is called **thin gan zah.**

a) Vocabulary **go bah khaw lae.**   What is *vocabulary* called?
b) Vocabulary **go waw hah ra lo khaw dae.**   *Vocabulary* is called **waw hah ra.**

EXERCISE 1: CLASSROOM VOCABULARY CHECK
Respond to these questions about school-related words in Burmese:
1. *Vocabulary* **go bah khaw lae.**   What is *vocabulary* called?
2. *Window* **go bah khaw lae.**   What is a *window* called?
3. *Lesson* **go bah khaw lae.**   What is a *lesson* called?
4. *Student* **go bah khaw lae.**   What is a *student* called?
5. *Homework* **ko bah khaw lae.**   What is *homework* called?
6. *Teacher* **go bah khaw lae.**   What is a *teacher* called?

GRAMMAR NOTE The possessive particle *yaet*

Trying out the new terms she has learned, Samantha says:

ကျွန်မက ဆရာ့.ရဲ့.ကျောင်းသား။ Kyama ga hsaya yaet kyaung thar.
I'm your student. [Lit., I'm teacher's student.]

ကျွန်မ	kyama	I (female speaker, polite)
က	ga	subject tag
ဆရာ	hsaya	teacher (substitute for *you*)
ရဲ့.	yaet	possessive particle
ကျောင်းသား	kyaung thar	student

ကိုဝင်းဆန်းက ကျွန်မရဲ့. ဆရာ။ Ko Win San ga kyama yaet hsayah.
You're my teacher. [Lit., Ko Win San is my teacher.]

ကိုဝင်းဆန်း	Ko Win San	Ko Win San (substitute for *you*)
က	ga	subject tag
ကျွန်မ	kyama	I (female speaker, polite)
ရဲ့.	yaet	possessive particle
ဆရာ	hsayah	teacher

Note that Samantha, who has picked up Burmese speaking habits from Naing Oo, uses both the word **hsayah** (teacher) and the name **Ko Win San** as substitutes for the pronoun **shin** (the female speaker's polite *you*).

PRONUNCIATION NOTE Dropped tones with possessive nouns

Nouns and pronouns with long, lingering vowel tones tend to morph into short, dropped tones when followed by the possessive particle **yaet**. That's why the word **hsayah** (teacher, long tone) becomes **hsaya** in **hsaya yaet** (teacher's, short tone).

(For a similar effect in object pronouns, refer to the Pronunciation Note on page 72)

PATTERN PRACTICE 3: HOW TO SAY "MY ..."
Practice these possessive phrases:
1. **kyanawt/kyama yaet khone**   my desk
2. **kyanawt/kyama yaet khaung**   my school
3. **kyanawt/kyama yaet hsayah**   my teacher

4. **kyanawt/kyama yaet tha nge jin**   my friend
5. **kyanawt/kyama yaet kor phee**   my coffee.
6. **kyanawt/kyama yaet phat sar oak**   my textbook
7. **kyanawt/kyama yaet ain zah**   my homework

PATTERN PRACTICE 4: HOW TO SAY "HIS/HER ..."
Practice the following phrases:
1. **thu yaet khone**   his / her desk
2. **thu yaet kyaung**   his / her school
3. **thu yaet hsayah**   his / her teacher
4. **thu yaet tha nge jin**   his / her friend
5. **thu yaet kor phee**   his / her coffee
6. **thu yaet phat sar oak**   his / her textbook
7. **thu yaet ain zah**   his / her homework
8. **thu yaet amyo thar**   his / her boyfriend
9. **thu yaet amyo thamee**   his / her girlfriend

PATTERN PRACTICE 5: THESE BELONG TO THEM
Practice the following phrases:
1. **hsaya yaet khone**   the teacher's desk
2. **hsaya yaet tha nge jin**   the teacher's friend
3. **tha nge jin yaet kor phee**   a friend's coffee
4. **tha nge jin yaet hsayah**   a friend's teacher
5. **kyaung thar yaet phat sar oak**   a student's textbook
6. **kyaung thar yaet kala htaing**   a student's chair
7. **kyaung thar yaet ain zah**   a student's homework

EXERCISE 2: SORTING OUT THE POSSESSIVES
Say the following in Burmese:
1. my student
2. his / her school
3. a friend's textbook
4. a friend's classroom
5. my lesson
6. a student's chair
7. the teacher's textbook
8. the teacher's homework

CHAPTER 13

Conducting Business

WHAT'S INCLUDED IN THE TOUR PACKAGE?

Today, Naing Oo meets a businessman named U Zaw Myint, who wants to buy a tour package from Naing Oo's travel agency.

Zaw Myint: *Are you Ko Naing Oo?*
             Ko Naing Oo lar.
             ကိုနိုင်ဦးလား။

Naing Oo: *Yes. Are you U Zaw Myint?*
             Hote par dae. U Zaw Myint lar.
             ဟုတ်ပါတယ်။ ဦးဇော်မြင့်လား။

Zaw Mying: *Yes, I called yesterday.*
             Hote pah dae. Ma nayt ga phone khaw dae.
             ဟုတ်ပါတယ်။ မနေ့က ဖုန်းခေါ်တယ်။

Naing Oo: *I remember.*
             Hmat mi bah dae.
             မှတ်မိပါတယ်။
             A pleasure to meet you.
             Twaet ya dah wun thah bah dae.
             တွေ့ရတာဝမ်းသာပါတယ်။
             Come, enter, please.
             Lah bah, win bah.
             လာပါ။ ဝင်ပါ။

Zaw Myint: *Our family wants to go to Bagan.*
             Kyanaw do mitharzu Bagan thwar jin dae.
             ကျွန်တော်တို့ မိသားစု ပုဂံသွားချင်တယ်။

Naing Oo: *Altogether how many people?*
             Arh lone bana yauk lae.
             အားလုံး ဘယ်နှစ်ယောက်လဲ။

Zaw Myint: *Four people.*
             Lay yauk pah.
             ၄ ယောက်ပါ။

Naing Oo:	*You want to visit the pagodas, I guess.*
	Phayar boo thwar mae htin dae.
	ဘုရားဖူးသွားမယ် ထင်တယ်။
Zaw Myint:	*That's right.*
	Hote pah dae.
	ဟုတ်ပါတယ်။
Naing Oo:	*In that case, 80,000 each.*
	Dah so tayauk ko shiq thaung bah.
	ဒါဆို တစ်ယောက်ကို ၈၀၀၀၀ ပါ။
Zaw Myint:	*Is it 320,000 for everything?*
	Arh lone thone thain hna thaung lar.
	အားလုံး ၃၂၀,၀၀၀ လား။
Naing Oo:	*That's correct.*
	Hote pah dae.
	ဟုတ်ပါတယ်။
Zaw Myint:	*How many days is the trip?*
	Kha yee ga bana yet lae.
	ခရီးက ဘယ်နှစ်ရက်လဲ။
Naing Oo:	*Eight days.*
	Shiq yet pah.
	၈ ရက်ပါ။
Zaw Myint:	*Is it by plane?*
	Lay yin naet lar.
	လေယာဉ်နဲ့လား။
Naing Oo:	*By car.*
	Kar naet bah khamya.
	ကားနဲ့ ပါ ခင်ျျ။
Zaw Myint:	*Does the car have air conditioning?*
	Kar ga air kon pah lar.
	ကားက အဲယားကွန်း ပါလား။
Naing Oo:	*It does.*
	Pah bah dae.
	ပါပါတယ်။
Zaw Myint:	*How about lodging?*
	Tae dah aw.
	တည်းတာရော။
Naing Oo:	*Included.*
	Pah bah dae.
	ပါပါတယ်။

Zaw Myint: *Are meals included?*
             Asar a thuak pah lar.
             အစားအသောက်ပါလား။
Naing Oo: *Breakfasts and lunches are included.*
             Manet sah naet nayt lae zah pah dae.
             မနက်စာနဲ့ နေ့လည်စာပါတယ်။
             But dinner is not.
             Dah bay maet nya nay zah ma pah boo.
             ဒါပေမယ့် ညစာမပါဘူး။

VOCABULARY

phone khaw	make a phone call
hmat mi	remember
mitharzu	family
arh lone	altogether, all, everything
bana (bae hna)	how many (persons/people)
phayar boo	pilgrimage, visiting shrines and temples
kha yee	trip, journey
lay yin	plane
ta yauk ko	for each person, per person
air kon	air conditioning / air conditioner
tae	to stay, to lodge somewhere
tae dah	lodging
pah	include
asar a thauk	food, meals, eating
manet sah	breakfast
nayt lae zah	lunch
nya nay zah/nya zah	dinner

Supplementary Vocabulary

ta khwet	each cup, per cup
ta htae	each item of clothing
da bwe	each serving
ta yet	each day
ta nya	each night
ta khu	each item (for inanimate objects like sculpture and toys)
ya htar	train
thin baw/thin maw	boat, ship

a hngar kar	taxi, cab
ko baing kar	private car
bus sakar	bus
kar hsayah	driver
win jay	entrance fee (collected at some prominent temples and popular tourist sites)
akyo apo	pickup and drop-off, transportation
lan bya	travel guide, tour guide
zagabyan	translator
thant shin yay	cleaning, cleanup

GRAMMAR NOTE All inclusive—*arh lone*

Before quoting the price of the tour package, Naing Oo asks the customer:

အားလုံး ဘယ်နှစ်ယောက်လဲ။   **Arh lone bana yauk lae.**
Altogether how many people?

အားလုံး	**arh lone**	altogether
ဘယ်နှစ်ယောက်	**bana yauk**	how many
လဲ	**lae**	question particle

Note: that the question word *how many*—**bana**—is actually written **bae hna** but often pronounced **bana** in conversation.

The word **arh lone** indicates an all-inclusive summary. Other examples using this word are:

အားလုံး နေကောင်းကြလား။   **Arh lone nay kaung ja lar.**
Is everybody well? / How's everyone?

အားလုံး	**arh lone**	everyone
နေကောင်း	**nay kaung**	feeling well
ကြ	**ja**	emphasizes plural action
လား	**lar**	question particle

အားလုံး ဝယ်ချင်တယ်။   **Arh lone wae jin dae.**
I'd like to buy everything/all.

အားလုံး	**arh lone**	everything

ဝယ်	wae	to buy
ချင်	jin	want to (auxiliary verb)
တယ်	dae	affirmative sentence ending

ကျွန်တော်တို့ အားလုံး လာမယ်။ Kyanaw do arh lone lah mae.
All of us will come.

ကျွန်တော်တို့	kyanaw do	we (plural, male speaker)
အားလုံး	arh lone	all, everyone
လာ	lah	to come
မယ်	mae	future sentence ending

GRAMMAR NOTE Pick a classifier to ask "How many?"

Because he wants to know the total number of passengers, Naing Oo asks his question with the classifier **yauk** (for people):

* ဘယ်နှစ်ယောက်လဲ။ **Bana yauk lae.** *How many people?*

   ဘယ်နှစ် (**bana**, how many) + ယောက် (**yauk**, classifier for humans) + လဲ (**lae**, question particle)

The counter to be used depends on the type of noun. For example:

* ဘယ်နှစ်ကောင်လဲ။ **Bana kaung lae** *How many creatures / animals?*

   ဘယ်နှစ် (**bana**, how many) + ကောင် (**kaung**, classifier for animals) + လဲ (**lae**, question particle)

* ဘယ်နှစ်ခုလဲ။ **Bana khu lae.** *How many items / objects?*

   ဘယ်နှစ် (**bana**, how many) + ခု (**khu**, classifier for objects) + လဲ (**lae**, question particle)

* ဘယ်နှစ်ခွက်လဲ။ **Bana khwet lae.** *How many cups?*

   ဘယ်နှစ် (**bana**, how many) + ခွက် (**khwet**, classifier for liquids, in cups) + လဲ (**lae**, question particle)

For more on classifiers, refer to page 83.

PATTERN PRACTICE 1: PRICE PER PERSON

When quoting the price for each traveler, Naing Oo says:

တစ်ယောက်ကို ၈၀၀၀၀ ပါ။   Ta yauk ko shiq thaung bah.
80,000 for each. (The currency unit **kyat** is implied, not stated.)

တစ်	ta	one
ယောက်	yauk	counting word for humans
ကို	ko	for
၈၀၀၀၀	shiq thaung	80,000 (kyat)
ပါ	bah	polite sentence ending

Because he was talking about people, Naing Oo used the counting word **yauk** in **ta yauk**, which literally means, *each person* or *per person*.

By the same token, if a teashop waiter is telling you the price of a cup of tea, he'll use the counting word **khwet** for liquid measured in cups: **Ta khwet ko chauk yah bah** (600 [kyat] for a cup).

And if a restaurant waitress is telling you the price for a meal, she'll use the counting word **pwe** or **bwe** for food servings: **Da bwe go koe yah bah** (900 [kyat] for a serving/plate/dish).

Practice these price quotes.

1. **Ta khwet ko balauk lae.**   How much for a cup (of the drink)?
2. **Ta htae go balauk lae.**   How much for a piece (of clothing)?
3. **Da bwe go balauk lae.**   How much for each serving (of food)?
4. **Ta yet ko balauk lae.**   How much for a day (of service or labor)?
5. **Ta nya go balauk lae.**   How much for a night?
6. **Ta khu go balauk lae.**   How much [is the price] for one item?
7. **Da gaung go balauk lae.**   How much [is the price] for one creature / animal? (This question can also be used for transactions involving fresh meat available in whole form, such as fish, crab, or chicken.)

EXERCISE 1: PRICE EACH

Based on the counting word in the Burmese sentence below, pick the correct translation of the sentence. (You can consult the classifiers in the supplementary vocabulary on page 133.)

1. **Ta yauk ko koe yah bah.**
   a. 900 per cup of tea.
   b. 900 per guest.
   c. 900 per meal.

2. **Ta khwet ko shiq yah bah.**
   a. 800 per cup of coffee.
   b. 800 per T-shirt.
   c 800 per toy.

3. **Ta khu go thone thaung bah.**
   a. 30,000 per sculpture.
   b. 30,000 for each traveler.
   c. 30,000 for a plate of caviar.

4. **Ta yet ko lay daung bah.**
   a. 4,000 for each *sarong*.
   b. 4,000 for each traveler.
   c. 4,000 for each day.

EXERCISE 2: A CLASSIFIER FOR EVERY OCCASION

Choose the correct Burmese tranlsation for each English phrase.

1. 600 for a cup of tea.
   a. Ta **htae go** chauk yah.
   b. Ta **yauk ko** chauk yah.
   c. Ta **khwet ko** chauk yah.

2. 90,000 per guest.
   a. Ta **yauk ko** koe thaung.
   b. Ta **htae go** koe thaung.
   c. Ta **yet ko** koe thaung.

3. 60,000 per night
   a. Ta **yauk ko** chauk thaung
   a. Da **bwe go** chauk thaung
   c. Ta **nya go** chauk thaung

4.   900 for a plate of *moke hingar*
  a.   Da **bwe go** koe yah
  b.   Ta **nya go** koe yah
  c.   Ta **yauk ko** koe yah

Ta khwet ko chauk yah bah.
600 (kyat) for a cup

Da bwe go koe yah bah
900 (kyat) for a serving/plate/dish

GRAMMAR NOTE The particle *naet* —"by means of"

Zaw Myint: လေယာဉ်နဲ့လား။ **Lay yin naet lar.** *By plane?*

လေယာဉ် (**lay yin**, plane) + နဲ့ (**naet**, with, by way of) + လား (**lar**, question particle)

Naing Oo: ကားနဲ့ ပါ ခင်ဗျ။ **Kar naet bah kha mya.** *By car.*

ကား (**kar**, car) + နဲ့ (**naet**, with, by way of) + ပါ ခင်ဗျ (**bah khamya**, polite sentence ending, male speaker)

In the exchange above, Zaw Myint and Naing Oo use the particle **naet** (with, and, by) to describe the manner in which something is done (in this case, the travel). Naing Oo uses the politeness marker **kyamya** because he is conducting business with a client. For a woman, the polite sentence-ending would be **shint**. In casual conversations, this could be omitted.

PATTERN PRACTICE 2: THE WAY TO GET THERE

Practice these exchanges with a partner.
a.   **Kar naet lar.**   By car?
b.   **Ya htar naet bah khamya/shint.**   By train.

a. **Lay yin naet lar.**   By plane?
b. **Kar naet bah khamya/shint.**   By car.

a. **A hngar kar naet lar.**   By rental car/taxi?
b. **Ko baing kar naet bah khamya/shint.**   By private car.

a. **Bus sakar naet lar.**   By bus?
b. **Thin baw naet bah kyamya/shint.**   By ship.

CULTURAL NOTE | **Taxi vs. private car**

The cabs or taxis you can flag down on the street for short rides are called **a hngar kar** (literally, rented car). But for longer journeys and overnight trips, tour companies usually arrange for you to travel in **ko baing kar** (literally, "private car"), meaning a car or van made available for your exclusive use for the duration of the trip. The price quoted for the so-called **ko baing kar** usually includes the service of a designated driver.

PATTERN PRACTICE 3: "WHAT'S INCLUDED IN THE TOUR PACKAGE?"

To clarify what's included and what's not in the package, Naing Oo tells the customer:

မနက်စာနဲ့ နေ့လည်စာပါတယ်။ ဒါပေမယ့် ညစာမပါဘူး။
Manet sah naet nayt lae zah pah dae. Dah bay maet nya zah ma pah boo.
Breakfasts and lunches are included. Dinner is not.

မနက်စာနဲ့ နေ့လည်စာ	manet sah naet nayt lae zah	breakfast and lunch
ပါတယ်	pah dae	is included
ဒါပေမယ့်	dah bae maet	but
ညစာ	nya zah	dinner
မပါဘူး	ma pah boo	is not included

Practice these exchanges with a partner.
a. **Manet sah pah lar.**   Is breakfast included?
b. **Ma pah boo. Dah bae maet nya zah pah dae.**   No, but dinner is included.

a. **Nayt lae zah pah lar.**   Is lunch included?
b. **Ma pah boo. Dah bae maet nya zah pah dae.**   No, but dinner is included.

a. **Zagabyan pah lar.**   Is a translator included?

b. **Ma pah boo. Dah bae maet lan bya pah dae.**
No, but a tour guide is included.

a. **Thant shin yay pah lar.**
Is cleaning included (in the price for an event-space rental)?

b. **Ma pah boo. Dah bae maet kar hsayah pah dae.**
No, but a driver is included (for transporting the guests).

a. **Akyo apo pah lar.**   Is pickup and drop-off [of passengers] included?

b. **Ma pah boo. Dah bae maet tae dah pah dae.**   No, but lodging is included.

EXERCISE 3: "HOW DO WE GET THERE?"

Try asking about these traveling options in Burmese:
1. Is it by bus (**bus sakar**)?
2. Is it by train (**ya htar**)?
3. Is it by ship (**thim maw**)?
4. Is it by taxi (**a hngar kar**)?
5. Is it by private car (**ko baing kar**)?

EXERCISE 4: "THIS IS HOW WE'LL GO."

Try saying the following:
1. It's by plane (**lay yin**).
2. It's by train (**ya htar**).
3. It's by private car (**ko baing kar**).
4. It's by taxi (**a hngar kar**).
5. It's by boat (**thimmaw**).

GRAMMAR NOTE Joining nouns with *naet*

To state that breakfasts and lunches are included in the package, Naing Oo says:

မနက်စာနဲ့ နေ့လည်စာပါတယ်။   Manet sah *naet* nay lae zah pah dae.
Breakfasts and lunches are included.

မနက်စာ	manet sah	breakfast
နဲ့	naet	and
နေ့လည်စာ	nayt lae zah	lunch
ပါတယ်	pah dae	is included

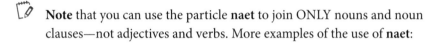 **Note** that you can use the particle **naet** to join ONLY nouns and noun clauses—not adjectives and verbs. More examples of the use of **naet**:

1. ကားနဲ့ ရထား   kar naet ya htar   car and train
2. လေယဉ်နဲ့ ရထား   lay yin naet ya htar   plane and train
3. ဘတ်စကားနဲ့ အငှားကား   bus sakar naet a hngar kar   bus and rental car
4. ကိုယ်ပိုင်ကားနဲ့ အငှားကား   ko baing kar naet a hngar kar
   private car and rental car
5. ရထားနဲ့ သင်္ဘော   ya htar naet thinmaw   train and ship

EXERCISE 5: JOIN THESE NOUNS, USING *NAET*.

Say these pairs in Burmese. Remember that you can join the items using **naet**. The phrase "is / are included" is **pah dae**.

1. Lunches (**nay lae zar**) and dinners (**nya nay zar**) are included.
2. A guide (**lan bya**) and a translator (**zagabyan**) are included.
3. A driver (**kar hsayah**) and a translator (**zagabyan**) are included.
4. Transportation (**akyo apo**) and cleanup (**thant shin yay**) are included.
5. Entrance fees (**win jay**) and meals (**asar athauk**) are included.

EXERCISE 6: "THIS AND THIS, BUT NOT THAT."

Practice saying these combinations in Burmese:

1. Lunches (**nay lae zah**) and dinners (**nya zah**) are included. But a driver (**kar hsayah**) is not.
2. A tour guide (**lan bya**) is included. But a translator (**zagabyan**) is not.
3. Transportation (**akyo apo**) is included. But cleanup (**thant shin yay**) is not.
4. Meals (**asar athauk**) are included. But pickup and drop-off (**akyo apo**) are not.
5. Lodging (**tae dah**) is included. But meals (**asar athauk**) are not.
6. Breakfasts (**manet sah**) and dinners (**nya zah**) are included. But lodging (**tae dah**) is not.

CHAPTER 14

Enjoying a Family Meal

 **DIALOGUE** CAN YOU HANDLE SPICY FOOD?

Win San invites Naing Oo and Samantha to his home for dinner.

Win San:	*Eat, OK? Eat.*
	Sar naw, sar.
	စားနော်၊ စား။
	No need to hold back.
	Arh ma-nah naet.
	အားမနာနဲ့။
Samantha:	*Yes!*
	Hote kaet bah shint.
	ဟုတ်ကဲ့ပါရှင့်။
Naing Oo:	*[in English] Oh, Sam, we've only been here for a month, but you're beginning to sound a lot more Burmese.*
Win San:	*Samantha, do you eat pork?*
	Samantha, wet thar sar lar.
	Samantha, ဝက်သားစားလား။
Samantha:	*I do.*
	Sar bah dae.
	စားပါတယ်။
Win San:	*This is fish curry.*
	Dah ngar hsee byan.
	ဒါက ငါးဆီပြန်။
	Do you like fish curry?
	Ngar hsee byan kyait lar.
	ငါးဆီပြန်ကြိုက်လား။
Samantha:	*Yes, I do.*
	Hote, kyait par dae.
	ဟုတ်။ ကြိုက်ပါတယ်။
Win San:	*Can you eat spicy food?*
	Asut sar naing lar.
	အစပ်စားနိုင်လား။

Samantha: *Yes, I can.*

                 Hote kaet, sar naing bah dae.

                 ဟုတ်ကဲ့၊ စားနိုင်ပါတယ်॥

Win San: *Is the saltiness OK?*

                 A ngan a taw bae lar.

                 အငံ အတော်ပဲလား॥

Samantha: *It's OK.*

                 A taw bah bae.

                 အတော်ပါပဲ॥

Win San: *This is fried beef.*

                 Dah amae thar jaw.

                 ဒါအမဲသားကြော်॥

                 Do you eat beef?

                 Amae thar sar lar.

                 အမဲသားစားလား॥

Samantha: *Hmm, I don't really eat beef, though.*

                 Aww, amae thar dawt ma sar boo shint.

                 အော်သြ ... အမဲသားတော့ မစားဘူးရှင့်॥

                 Sorry!

                 Sorry naw.

                 Sorry နော်॥

Win San: *How come?*

                 Bah phyit lo lae.

                 ဘာဖြစ်လို့လဲ॥

Samantha: *It's not that agreeable to me.*

                 Kyama naet ma taet lo bah.

                 ကျွန်မနဲ့ မတည့်လို့ပါ॥

VOCABULARY

arh nah dae*	sorry, forgive me.
arh ma nah naet	don't be sorry, don't hold back, don't hesitate
wet thar	pork
ngar hsee byan	fish curry
a sut	spicy food, spiciness
a ngan	saltiness
amae thar jaw	fried beef
ma taet boo	doesn't get along, is not agreeable

* See Cultural Note on next page.

Supplementary Vocabulary

acho	sweetness, sweet items
achin	sourness, sour items
a khar	bitterness, bitter items
thet thut lut	vegetarian food
kyet thar	poultry
kyet thar jaw	fried chicken
ngar	fish
ngar jaw/nga jaw	fried fish
bazun	shrimp, prawn
bazun jaw	fried shrimp, fried prawns
athee aywet	fruit and vegetables

 **CULTURAL NOTE**

Arh nah dae, the quintessential Burmese apology

Arh nah dae is an elusive Burmese phrase that doesn't have a direct English equivalent. Sometimes, it's used as an apology. For example, someone who needs to borrow money from you might say, "**Arh nah dae**, but can you lend me 10,000 kyat?" Sometimes, it's used as a way to apologetically refuse something. For example, if a stranger offers to buy you a lavish meal, you might say, "**Arh nah dae**, but I can't really let you do that."

In the dialogue in this chapter, Win San uses it to mean, "Don't feel that you're imposing." Therefore, he used it in the negative form, **arh ma nah naet** (Don't be **arh nah**). Burmese hosts usually use this expression to encourage their guests to take full advanage of the hospitality without holding back.

GRAMMAR NOTE Using *naet* to say "Don't ..."

When Win San wants to encourage Samantha to eat, he says:

အားမနှာနဲ့။   **Arh ma-nah nae.**   *Don't hold back / don't be shy.*

အားမနှာ	**arh ma-nah**	don't be shy / don't hold back (negative form of **Arh nah**)
နဲ့	**naet**	command particle

The command particle **naet** is the opposite of **pah / bah**. You use the particle **pah / bah** to urge someone to do someone, e.g., **sar bah** (please eat); **thauk pah** (please drink). **Naet** is for commands that *forbid* someone from doing certain things.

PATTERN PRACTICE 1: "DON'T DO THIS."

Practice these commands.

1. **Ma sar naet.**   Don't eat.
2. **Ma thauk naet.**   Don't drink.
3. **Ma thwar naet.**   Don't go.
4. **Ma lah naet.**   Don't come.
5. **Ma yu naet.**   Don't take.
6. **Ma wae naet.**   Don't buy it.
7. **Pout si ma sar naet.**   Don't eat a meat bun.
8. **Beer ma thauk naet.**   Don't drink beer.
9. **Yone ma thwar naet.**   Don't go to the office.
10. **Kyaung ma lah naet.**   Don't come to school.
11. **Khone ma yu naet.**   Don't take the chair.
12. **Cake mont ma wae naet.**   Don't buy cake.

PATTERN PRACTICE 2: TYPES OF MEAT

Practice these exchanges with a partner.

a) **Kyet thar sar lar.**   Do you eat chicken?
b) **Hote kaet. Kyet thar sar bah dae.**   Yes, I eat chicken.

a) **Ngar sar lar.**   Do you eat fish?
b) **Hote kaet. Ngar sar bah dae.**   Yes, I eat fish.

a) **Bazun sar lar.**   Do you eat shrimp?
b) **Hote kaet. Bazun sar bah dae.**   Yes, I eat shrimp.

a) **Amae thar sar lar.**   Do you eat beef?
b) **Hote kaet. A mae thar sar bah dae.**   Yes, I eat beef.

a) **Kyet thar ma sar naet.**   Don't eat chicken.
b) **Hote kaet. Kyet thar ma sar boo.**   OK, I won't eat chicken.

a) **Ngar ma sar naet.**   Don't eat fish.
b) **Hote kaet. Ngar ma sar boo.**   OK, I won't eat fish.

a) **Bazun ma sar naet.**   Don't eat shrimp.
b) **Hote kaet. Bazun ma sar boo.**   OK, I won't eat shrimp.

a)   **Amae thar ma sar naet.**   Don't eat beef.

b)   **Hote kaet. Amae thar ma sar boo.**   OK, I won't eat beef.

CULTURAL NOTE **A touch of Burmese politeness**

Naing Oo quips that Samantha is beginning to sound "a lot more Burmese" because she uses the polite sentence ending **shint**. For male speakers, it is **khamya**. (You'll also come across these words written and spoken as **shin** and **khamyar**.) You can try using these endings for some of the affirmative responses in Pattern Practice 2 above (**hote kaet shint** if you're a woman, **hote kaet khamyar** if you're a man). You don't have to do it for every response. If you do that, you might come across as too formal, too accommodating, or a bit of a pushover.

GRAMMAR NOTE **The verb "to like"—** *kyait*

In the dialog Win San asks Samantha if she likes fish curry:

ငါးဆီပြန်ကြိုက်လား။   **Ngar hsi byan kyait lar.**   *Do you like fish curry?*

ငါးဆီပြန်	**ngar hsi byan**	fish curry
ကြိုက်	**kyait**	to like
လား	**lar**	yes–no question particle

You can use the verb **kyait** with not only food but also with people and activities. For example:

ကျွန်မ သူ့ကို ကြိုက်တယ်။   **Kyama thu go kyait tae.**   *I like him / her.*

ကျွန်မ	**kyama**	I (formal, female speaker)
သူ့ကို	**thu go**	the pronoun for *he / she* with object particle **go**
ကြိုက်	**kyait**	to like
တယ်	**tae**	affirmative sentence ending

ကျွန်တော် ရေကူးတာ ကြိုက်တယ်။   **Kyanaw yay kuu dah kyait tae.**
I like swimming

ကျွန်တော်	**kyanaw**	I (formal, male)
ရေကူးတာ	**yay kuu dah**	swimming (the verb *to swim* in gerund form)
ကြိုက်	**kyait**	to like
တယ်	**tae**	affirmative sentence ending

PATTERN PRACTICE 3: "DO YOU LIKE THIS FLAVOR?"

The dialog in this chapter involves the use of some flavor-related words in the noun form. Practice the following exchanges:

a) **A sut sar naing lar.**   Can you eat spicy food? (Can you handle spicy food?)
b) **Hote kaet. Sar naing dae. A sut kyait tae.**   Yes, I can. I like spicy food.

a) **A ngan sar naing lar.**   Can you eat salty food?
b) **Hote kaet. Sar naing dae. A ngan kyait tae.**   Yes, I can. I like salty food.

a) **A khar sar naing lar.**   Can you eat bitter things?
b) **Hote kaet. Sar naing dae. A khar kyait tae.**   Yes, I can. I like bitter things.

a) **Acho sar naing lar.**   Can you eat sweet things?
b) **Hote kaet. Sar naing dae. Acho kyait tae.**   Yes, I can. I like sweet things.

a) **Achin sar naing lar.** Can you eat sour things?
b) **Hote kaet. Sar naing dae. Achin kyait tae.**   Yes, I can. I like sour things.

EXERCISE 1: FLAVOR MATCHING

Identify the correct flavors of these dishes.

1. **wet thar asut**
    a) sweet pork
    b) sour pork
    c) spicy pork

2. **kyet thar acho**
    a) sweet chicken
    b) spicy chicken
    c) sour chicken

3. **ngar achin**
    a) spicy fish
    b) sour fish
    c) sweet fish

4. **bazun achin**
    a) sweet shrimp
    b) sour shrimp
    c) spicy shrimp

PATTERN PRACTICE 4: "I DON'T REALLY EAT THAT."

To indicate she doesn't eat beef, Samantha says:

အမဲသားတော့ မစားဘူးရှင့်။   Amae thar dawt ma sar boo shint.
I don't really eat beef, though.

အမဲသား	amae thar	beef
တော့	dawt	however, though
မစားဘူး	ma sar boo	don't eat
ရှင့်	shint	politeness marker

The particle **dawt** is similar to *though* or *however* in the English "I don't really eat beef, though." It's one way to downplay the negative response "I don't eat beef." The addition of the polite **shint** (or **khamya** if you're male) also softens the negative response.

Practice these responses.
1. **Wet thar dawt ma sar boo khamya/shint.**   I don't really eat pork, though.
2. **Wet thar a sut tawt ma sar boo khamya/shint.**
   I don't really eat spicy pork, though.
3. **Ngar dawt ma sar boo khamya/shint.**   I don't really eat fish, though.

Aww, ngar hsee byan dawt ma sar boo shint. Sorry naw.
Hmm, I don't eat fish curry, though. Sorry!

4. **Ngar achin dawt ma sar boo khamya/shint.**
   I don't really eat sour fish, though.
5. **Bazun dawt ma sar boo khamya/shint.**   I don't really eat prawn, though.
6. **Bazun achin dawt ma sar boo khamya/shint.**
   I don't really eat sour prawn, though.

EXERCISE 2: "I DON'T REALLY EAT THAT."

Say the following in Burmese:
1. I don't really eat spicy fish, though.
2. I don't really eat pork, though.
3. I don't really eat sour fish, though.
4. I don't really eat fish curry, though.
5. I don't really eat beef, though.
6. I don't really eat spicy beef, though.

GRAMMAR NOTE "Because it's not agreeable ..."

Explaining why she won't eat beef, Samantha says:

ကျွန်မနဲ့ မတည့်လို့ပါ။   **Kyama nae ma taet lo bah.**   *It's not agreeable to me.*

ကျွန်မ	kyama	I (formal, female speaker)
နဲ့	naet	and, with
မတည့်	ma taet	not agreeable (negative form of the verb **taet**, *to be agreeable*)
လို့	lo	because, since (cause-indicator particle)
ပါ	bah	polite sentence ending

Note that, to say something is *not agreeable to* her, Samantha has to use the particle **naet** (with, and).

The verb involved, **taet** (to be agreeable), may also be used to describe getting along with people, or not. For example:

ကျွန်မ သူနဲ့ မတည့်ဘူး။   **Kyama thu naet ma taet boo.**
I don't get along with him / her.

ကျွန်မ	kyama	I (formal, female speaker)
သူနဲ့	thu naet	with him/her
မတည့်	ma taet	don't get along
ဘူး	boo	negative sentence ending

CULTURAL NOTE
On vegetarian meals and food-related allergies

There's really no direct equivalent for *vegetarian* in Burmese. The closest is **thet thut lute**, which literally translates to *killing-free*. That means the processing of that meal doesn't involve slaughtering or butchering, and implies it's made *without meat or fish*; however, it doesn't necessarily mean it's free of egg, cheese, or dairy products—animal products that can be acquired without killing the animal. Another useful phrase for vegetarians might be **athee aywet**, which literally translates to *fruit and vegetables*.

Due to a lack of understanding of food-related allergies and intolerance, terms like *gluten allergy, wheat allergy,* and *celiac* are not readily available in the Burmese language. One option to indicate something that you can't eat is this phrase:

   ... **naet ma taet boo.**   (... is not agreeable to me.)

For example:
   Jone naet ma taet boo.   Flour is not agreeable to me.
   Myay bae naet ma taet boo.   Peanuts are not agreeable to me.
   Paung mont naet ma taet boo.   Bread is not agreeable to me.

CHAPTER 15

Employment

 **DIALOGUE** EMPLOYMENT HISTORY

Today, Naing Oo interviews a local candidate who has come to apply for the job of general manager at his newly launched travel agency.

Naing Oo: *Are you Ko Kyaw Thu?*
Ko Kyaw Thu lar.
ကိုကျော်သူလား။

Kyaw Thu: *Yes.*
Hote par dae kha myar.
ဟုတ်ပါတယ် ခင်ဗျား။

Naing Oo: *A pleasure to meet you!*
Twaet ya dah wun thah bah dae.
တွေ့ရတာဝမ်းသာပါတယ်။

Kyaw Thu: *Yes, the pleasure is mine as well.*
Hote kaet. Kyanaw lae wun thah bah dae.
ဟုတ်ကဲ့။ ကျွန်တော်လည်း ဝမ်းသာပါတယ်။

Naing Oo: *Well, please tell me a bit about your work history.*
Kae, aloke yah zawin nae nae pyaw pya bah own.
ကဲ ... အလုပ်ရာဇဝင် နည်းနည်း ပြောပြပါဦး။

Kyaw Thu: *Yes, I graduated with an English major.*
Hote kaet. Kyanaw Ingalaik may jah naet kyaung pee gae dae.
ဟုတ်ကဲ့။ ကျွန်တော် အင်္ဂလိပ် မေဂျာနဲ့ ကျောင်းပြီးခဲ့ပါတယ်။
At the present time, I'm the manager of Yoh Ma Travel Agency.
Agu, Yoh Ma Kha Yee Thwar Loke Ngan hmah mun nay jah bah.
အခု ရိုးမ ခရီးသွားလုပ်ငန်းမှာ မန်နေဂျာပါ။
Previously, I was a staff member at Yadanah Inn.
Ayin ga dawt, Yadanah Tae Kho Gan hmah wun dan bah.
အရင်ကတော့ ရတနာတည်းခိုခန်းမှာ ဝန်ထမ်းပါ။

VOCABULARY

alote	work, job
yah zawin	history
alote yah zawin	employment history

kyaung pee	graduated (lit., finished school)
Ingalaik may jah	English major
kha yee thwar lote ngan	travel agency
agu	now, at the present
ayin ga	before, previously
wun dan	staff, employee
tae kho gan	inn, motel, guesthouse
balaut kyah	how long
akyaung pyan	respond, reply
hset thwae	contact
yauk	to arrive
pyan thwar	to go back

Supplementary Vocabulary

kyaung hsayah	school teacher
a soe ya wun dan	government employee
kha yee thwar lanbya	tourist guide
zay thae	street vendor
kone thae	merchant
hsayah wun	doctor
bajee hsayah	artist, painter
asodaw	singer
sah yay hsayah	writer (male or female)
sah yay hsayah ma	female writer
gabyar hsayah	poet (male or female)
gabyah hssayah ma	female poet
sayin gaing	accountant
sapho hmu	chef
Myanmar zah	Burmese language study
ban	bank
hsay yone	hospital
hsay yone ji	general hospital
Yangon Thet Gatho	Yangon University
Thet Gatho Hsay Yone	University Hospital
naing ngan yay thaik pan	political science
wait za	B.A. (bachelor of arts degree)
thaik pan	B.Sc. (bachelor of science degree)

GRAMMAR NOTE *"Also" — lae*

When Naing Oo and Kyaw Thu first meet, the following exchange occurs:

Naing Oo: တွေ့ရတာဝမ်းသာပါတယ်။ Twaet ya dah wun thah bah dae.
A pleasure to meet you!

Kyaw Thu: ကျွန်တော်လည်း ဝမ်းသာပါတယ်။ Kyanaw lae wun thah bah dae.
The pleasure's mine as well.

The combination of particle **lae** (as well, also) following the pronoun **kyanaw** (I, male speaker) means "me too" or "I as well." Here are some other examples of the use of this particle:

ကြက်သားကြိုက်တယ်။ ငါးလည်းကြိုက်တယ်။
Kyet thar kyait tae. Ngar lae kyait tae.   *I like chicken. I like fish* as well.

ကြက်သား	kyet thar	poultry, chicken
ကြိုက်တယ်။	kyait tae	like
ငါးလည်း	ngar lae	fish also

ကျွန်မလည်း ပုဂံသွားချင်တယ်။   **Kyama lae Bagan thwar jin dae.**
I also *want to go to Bagan.*

ကျွန်မလည်း	kyama lae	I also
ပုဂံ	Bagan	Bagan (city name)
သွားချင်တယ်။	thwar jin dae	want to go

 ## PATTERN PRACTICE 1: "I GRADUATED WITH ..."

When asked about his employment history, the applicant Kyaw Thu begins with:

ကျွန်တော် အင်္ဂလိပ် မေဂျာနဲ့, ကျောင်းပြီးခဲ့ပါတယ်။
Kyanaw Ingalaik may jah naet kyaung pee gaet dae.
I graduated with an English major.

ကျွန်တော်	kyanaw	I (formal, male speaker)
အင်္ဂလိပ် မေဂျာ	Ingalaik may jar	English major
နဲ့,	naet	with
ကျောင်းပြီးခဲ့	kyaung pee gaet	graduated (**gaet** is for past event)
ပါတယ်	bah dae	polite sentence ending

Practice these sentences which are based on the same structure.

1. **Kyanaw/Kyama Myanmar zar naet kyaung pee gaet bah dae.**
   I graduated with a Burmese language studies major.

2. **Kyanaw/Kyama sayin gaing naet kyaung pee gaet bah dae.**
   I graduated with an accounting major.

3. **Kyanaw/Kyama naing ngan yay thaik pan naet kyaung pee gaet bah dae.**
   I graduated with a political science major.

4. **Kyanaw/Kyama wait za naet kyaung pee gaet bah dae.**
   I graduated with a B.A.

5. **Kyanaw/Kyama thaik pan naet kyaung pee gaet bah dae.**
   I graduated with a B.Sc.

PATTERN PRACTICE 2: CURRENT WORK AND TITLE

Describing his current job, Kyaw Thu says:

အခု ရိုးမ ခရီးသွားလုပ်ငန်းမှာ မန်နေဂျာပါ။

Agu, Yoh Ma Kha Yee Thwar Loke Ngan hmah mun nay jar bah.

Right now, I'm the manager at Yoh Ma Travel Agency.

အခု	agu	right now, at the present
ရိုးမ	Yoma	Yoma (name of business)
ခရီးသွားလုပ်ငန်း	kha yee thwar loke ngan	travel business
မှာ	hmah	in, at
မန်နေဂျာ	mun nay jah	manager
ပါ	bah	polite sentence ending

A simpler variation of it would be:

အခု ကျွန်တော် ခရီးသွားလုပ်ငန်း မန်နေဂျာပါ။

Agu, kyanaw kha yee thwar loke ngan mun nay jar bah.

Right now, I'm a tour company manager.

အခု	agu	right now
ကျွန်တော်	kyanaw	I (male speaker, formal)
ခရီးသွားလုပ်ငန်း	kha yee thwar loke ngan	travel business
မန်နေဂျာ	mun nay jah	manager
ပါ	bah	polite sentence ending

Practice these sentences.

1. **Agu, Strand Hotel hmah mun nay jah bah.**
   Right now, I'm the manager at the Strand Hotel.
2. **Agu, International School hmah hsayah bah.**
   Right now, I'm a teacher at the International School.
3. **Agu, Shwedagon Phayar hmah zay thae bah.**
   Right now, I'm a vendor at Shwedagon Pagoda.
4. **Agu, KBZ Ban hmah sayin gaing bah.**
   Right now, I'm an accountant at KBZ Bank.
5. **Agu, Rangoon Teahouse hmah sapho hmu bah.**
   Right now, I'm a chef at Rangoon Teahouse.
6. **Agu, Hsay Yone Ji hmah hsayah wun bah.**
   Right now, I'm a doctor at the General Hospital.
7. **Agu, kyanaw/kyama bajee hsayah bah.**   Right now, I'm an artist.
8. **Agu, kyanaw/kyama kha yee thwar lan bya bah.**   Right now, I'm a tour guide.
9. **Agu, kyanaw/kyama zagabyan bar.**   Right now, I'm an interpreter.
10. **Agu, kyanaw/kyama Ingalaik sah hsayah bah.**
    Right now, I'm an English teacher.

PATTERN PRACTICE 3: PREVIOUS WORK / EMPLOYMENT

Applicant Kyaw Thu also continues:

> အရင်ကတော့ ရတနာတည်းခိုခန်းမှာ ဝန်ထမ်းပါ။
> **Ayin ga dawt, Yadanah Tae Kho Gan hmar wun dan bah.**
> *Previously, I was a staff member at Yadanah Guesthouse.*

အရင်ကတော့	ayin ga dawt	previously
ရတနာ	Yadanah	Yadanah (name of business)
တည်းခိုခန်း	tae kho gan	guesthouse
မှာ	hmah	in, at
ဝန်ထမ်း	wun dan	employee, staff
ပါ	bah	polite sentence ending

A simpler variation would be:

> အရင်က ကျွန်တော် တည်းခိုခန်း ဝန်ထမ်းပါ။
> **Ayin ga, kyanaw tae kho gan wun dan bah.**
> *Before, I was a guesthouse employee.*

အရင်က	ayin ga	before
ကျွန်တော်	kyanaw	I (male speaker, polite)
တည်းခိုခန်း	tae kho gan	guesthouse
ဝန်ထမ်း	wun dan	staff, employee
ပါ	bah	polite sentence ending

Practice the following:
1. **Ayin ga dawt, Yoh Ma Kah Yee Thwar Loke Ngan hmah mun nay jah bah.**
   Before, I was the manager at Yoh Ma Travel Agency.
2. **Ayin ga dawt, Bogalay Zay hmah zay thae bah.**
   Before, I was a vendor at Bogalay Market.
3. **Ayin ga dawt, Thek Gatho Hsay Yone hmah wun dan bah.**
   Before, I was a staff member at the University Hospital.
4. **Ayin ga dawt, Yangon Thek Gatho hmah Myanmar zah hsayah bah.**
   Before, I was a Burmese instructor at Yangon University.
5. **Ayin ga dawt, Strand Hotel hmar sapho hmu bah.**
   Before, I was a chef at the Strand Hotel.
6. **Ayin ga, kyanaw/kyama Myanmar zah hsayah bah.**
   Before, I was a Burmese teacher.
7. **Ayin ga, kyanaw/kyama ban sayin gaing bah.**
   Before, I was a bank accountant.
8. **Ayin ga, kyanaw/kyama a soe ya wun dan bah.**
   Before, I was a government employee.

EXERCISE 1:
"THIS IS WHAT I DO NOW / WHAT I DID THEN."
Say these sentences in Burmese:
1. Right now, I'm the manager at Rangoon Teahouse.
2. Before, I was a staff member at KBZ Bank.
3. Right now, I'm an accountant at the Strand Hotel.
4. Before, I was a doctor at the University Hospital.
5. Right now, I'm a writer.
6. Before, I was a teacher.
7. Right now, I'm a poet.
8. Before, I was a singer.
9. Right now, I'm a Burmese teacher at the International School.
10. Before, I was a tour guide at Shwedagon Pagoda.

DIALOGUE HOW LONG WERE YOU AT ...?

Naing Oo's interview of the job candidate Kyaw Thu continues:

Naing Oo: *How long have you been at Yoh Ma?*
Yoh Ma hmah bae laut kyah bee lae.
ရိုးမမှာ ဘယ်လောက်ကြာပြီလဲ။

Kyaw Thu: *One and a half years.*
Ta hnit khwae bah.
တစ်နှစ်ခွဲပါ။

Naing Oo: *How many years did you work at Yadanah?*
Yadahah hmah bae hna hnit lote khaet lae.
ရတနာမှာ ဘယ်နှစ်နှစ်လုပ်ခဲ့လဲ။

Kyaw Thu: *One year.*
Ta hnit pah.
တစ်နှစ်ပါ။

Naing Oo: *Very well. Thanks for your application.*
Kaung bi lay. Agu lo alote lah shaut taet a twet kyay zu bah.
ကောင်းပြီလေ။ အခုလိုအလုပ်လာလျှောက်တဲ့အတွက် ကျေးဇူးပါ။

Kyaw Thu: *Um, when will you get back to me?*
Ho, kyanawt go bae dawt akyaung pyan ma lae.
ဟို ... ကျွန်တော့်ကို ဘယ်တော့အကြောင်းပြန်မလဲ။

Naing Oo: *I'll get in touch next week.*
Naut apat hset thwae ba mae.
နောက်အပတ် ဆက်သွယ်ပါ့မယ်။

GRAMMAR NOTE
"How long have you been / How many years did you ...?"

When asking about Kyaw Thu's current job, Naing Oo's question is:

ရိုးမမှာ ဘယ်လောက်ကြာပြီလဲ။ **Yoh Ma hmar bae laut kyah bee lae.**
How long have you been at Yoh Ma?

ရိုးမ	**Yoma**	Yoma (name of business)
မှာ	**hmah**	in, at
ဘယ်လောက်	**bae lauk**	about how long (question word for duration)
ကြာပြီ	**kyah bi**	time has passed
လဲ	**lae**	question particle

Yoh Ma hmah bae laut kyah bee lae.
How long have you been at Yoh Ma?

Ta hnit khwae bah.
One and a half years.

Yadahah hmah bae hna hnit lote khaet lae.
How many years did you work at Yadanah?

Ta hnit pah.
One year.

Kaung bi lay. Agu lo alote lah shaut taet a twet kyay zu bah.
Very well. Thanks for your application.

Ho, Kyanawt go bae dawt akyaung pyan ma lae.
Um, when can you get back to me?

Naut apat hset thwae ba mae.
I'll get in touch in a week's time.

As a beginner, it's better to think of the phrase **bae lauk kyah bi lae** or **balauk kyah bi lae** as "How long has it been?" Other ways this phrase might be used include:

ဒီရောက်တာ ဘယ်လောက်ကြာပြီလဲ။
De yauk tah balauk kyah bi lae.
How long has it been since you arrived here?

ဒီ	**de**	here
ရောက်တာ	**yauk tah**	arriving (the verb **yauk** in gerund form)
ဘယ်လောက်ကြာပြီလဲ	**balauk kyah bi lae**	how long has it been?

သူ ပြန်သွားတာ ဘယ်လောက်ကြာပြီလဲ။
Thu pyan thwar dah balauk kyah bi lae.
How long has it been since he / she left?

သူ	**thu**	he / she
ပြန်သွားတာ	**pyan thwar dah**	going back (the verb **pyan thwar** in gerund form)
ဘယ်လောက်ကြာပြီလဲ	**balauk kyah bi lae**	how long has it been?

In contrast, when asking specifically about *the number of years* Kyaw Thu worked in his previous job, Naing Oo's question is:

ရတနာမှာ ဘယ်နှစ်နှစ်လုပ်ခဲ့လဲ။
Yadahah hmar bae hna hnit lote khaet lae.
How many years did you work at Yadanah?

ရတနာ	**Yadanah**	Yadanah (name of business)
မှာ	**hmah**	in, at
ဘယ်နှစ်နှစ်	**bae hna hnit**	how many years
လုပ်ခဲ့	**loke khaet**	did work (**khaet** emphasizes past action)
လဲ	**lae**	question particle

Here, the question word is **bae hna hnit**—**bae hna** (how many) + **hnit** (counting word for year). The following example sentences give the formula for talking about quantity, using an appropriate classifier word:

ပန်းသီး ဘယ်နှစ်လုံး ယူမလဲ။ Pan thee bae hna lone yu ma lae.
How many apples are you going to take?

Question word: **Bae hna** (how many) + **lone** (counting word for round objects) = **bae hna lone** (how many pieces of ...?)

ကော်ဖီ ဘယ်နှစ်ခွက် သောက်မလဲ။   Korphee bae hna khwet thauk ma lae.
How many cups of coffee are you going to drink?

Question word: **Bae hna** (how many) + **khwet** (counting word for cups of liquid) = **bae hna khwet** (how many cups of ...?)

ခရီးသည် ဘယ်နှစ်ယောက် ပါလဲ။   Kha yee thae bae hna yauk pah lae.
How many passengers are included/onboard?

Question word: **Bae hna** (how many) + **yauk** (counting word for people) = **bae hna yauk** (how many persons ...?)

PATTERN PRACTICE 4: "HOW LONG HAS IT BEEN?"

Practice these exchanges with a partner:
a) **Mandalay hmah balauk kyah be lae.**
    How long have you been / lived in Mandalay?
b) **Thone hnit khwae bah.** Three and a half years.

a) **Di hmah baluk kyah ma lae.**   How long will you be here?
b) **Lay yet pah.** Four days.

a) **Yangon hmah balauk kyah bi lae.**
    How long have you been / lived in Yangon?
b) **Hna hnit pah.**   Two years.

a) **Myanmar pyi hmah balauk kyah ma lae.**
    How long will you be in Myanmar?
b) **Ta hnit khwae bah.** A year and a half.

PATTERN PRACTICE 5: "HOW MANY UNITS OF THIS ... ?"

Practice the following exchanges with a partner:

a)   **Htamin bae hna pwe yu ma lae.**   How many servings of rice will you take?
b)   **Thone bwe bah.**   Three servings.

a)   **Beer bae hna palin thauk ma lae.**   How many bottles of beer will you drink?
b)   **Hna palin bah.**   Two bottles.

a)   **Di hmah bae hna hnit kyah ma lae.**   How many years will you be here?
b)   **Lay hnit khwae bah.**   Four and a half years.

a)   **Virgin Airlines hmah bae hna hnit loke khaet lae.**
     How many years did you work at Virgin Airlines?
b)   **Ngar hnit pah.**   Five years.

a)   **Chicago hmah bae hna hnit nay gaet lae.**
     How many years did you stay in Chicago?
b)   **Chauk hnit khwae bah.**   Six and a half years.

a)   **Di hotel hmah bae hna yet tae ma lae.**
     How many days will you stay at this hotel?
b)   **Thone yet pah.**   Three days.

CHAPTER 16

Getting Sick

 **DIALOGUE** **HOW DO YOU FEEL?**

Samantha is not feeling well, so she visits a local doctor, accompanied by Naing Oo.

In the waiting room of the clinic

Naing Oo: *OK, Sam, let the doctor know what's going on.*

          OK, Sam, daut ta go bah phyit nay lae pyaw pya lite.

          ကဲ ... Sam, ဒေါက်တာကို ဘာဖြစ်နေလဲပြောပြလိုက်။

Samantha and Naing Oo in the doctor's room.

Samantha: *I'm not feeling well.*

          Nay ma kaung boo shint.

          နေမကောင်းဘူးရှင့်။

          I'm coughing, and I also have a headache.

          Chaung hsoo dae. Gaung lae kait tae.

          ချောင်းဆိုးတယ်။ ခေါင်းလည်းကိုက်တယ်။

Doctor: *Do you have a stomachache? (Lit., Does your stomach hurt?)*

          Baik nah lar.

          ဗိုက်နာလား။

Samantha: *No stomachache though. (Lit., The stomach doesn't hurt that much.)*

          Baik thaik ma nah boo.

          ဗိုက်သိပ်မနာဘူး။

Doctor: *Is your throat sore?*

          Lae jaung nah lar.

          လည်ချောင်းနာလား။

Samantha: *My throat is a bit sore.*

          Lae jaung nae nae nah dae.

          လည်ချောင်းနည်းနည်းနာတယ်။

Doctor: *I'll take your temperature, OK?*

          Aphyar taing mae naw.

          အဖျားတိုင်းမယ်နော်။

Samantha: *OK.*

          Hote kaet.

          ဟုတ်ကဲ့။

VOCABULARY

chaung hsoo dae	cough
gaung kite tae	have a headache
bite nar dae	have a stomachache
lae jaung nah dae	have a sore throat
a phyar taing	take (someone's) temperature
a phyar shi dae	have a fever
hsay	medicine
pyaut	[sickness is] gone, recovered

Supplementary Vocabulary

aun jin dae	want to vomit
wun shaw dae	have diarrhea
chay dauk nah dae	legs hurting
let nah dae	arms hurting
yay ngat tae	thirsty
gaung moo dae	feel dizzy
hnar see dae	have a runny nose
nar ohn dae	have blocked ears
myet se nah dae	have sore eyes
yin kyat tae	have chest congestion

CULTURAL NOTE **The doctor is in**

When people talk about a doctor, they tend to use the Burmese word **hsayah wun**. But when addressing a doctor directly, they use the word **daut tah** (long tone), the English word *doctor* in Burmese pronunciation. When the word is the object of the sentence, it's usually used with a dropped tone or short tone, as **daut ta**.

GRAMMAR NOTE **"Tell him what's going on."**

To nudge Samantha to talk about her symptoms, Naing Oo says:

ဒေါက်တာကို ဘာဖြစ်နေလဲပြောပြလိုက်။

Daut ta go bah pyit nay lae pyaw pya lite.

Tell the doctor what's going on.

ဒေါက်တာကို	daut ta go	the doctor + object tag **go**
ဘာဖြစ်နေလဲ	bah pyit nay lae	what is happening?
ပြောပြလိုက်	pyaw pya like	tell him

The object tag **go** here is important. Without it, it's unclear if the doctor is supposed to tell someone what is happening, or if he should be told something. The object tag **go** makes it clear the doctor is supposed to be receiving the information, not conveying it.

This statement also involves a nested question—**bah phyit nay lae** (what's happening?). Take a look at some other examples of this approach:

> ဘာစားချင်လဲ ပြောပြပါ။ **Bah sar jin lae pyaw pya bah.**
> *Tell me what you'd like to eat.*

ဘာစားချင်လဲ	**Bah sar jin lae**	What do you want to eat?
ပြောပြပါ	**pyaw pya bah**	tell me

> ဘယ်သွားချင်လဲ ပြောပြပါ။ **Bae thwar jin lae pyaw pya like.**
> *Tell me where you'd like to go.*

ဘယ်သွားချင်လဲ	**Bae thwar jin lae.**	Where do you want to go?
ပြောပြပါ	**pyaw pya bah**	tell me

PATTERN PRACTICE 1: "THIS IS HOW I FEEL."

Practice these phrases for describing symptoms and discomfort.

1. **Chaung hsoo dae.** I'm coughing.
2. **Gaung kait tae.** I have a headache. (Lit., The head aches.)
3. **Bite nah dae.** I have a stomachache. (Lit., The stomach hurts.)
4. **Lae jaung nah dae.** I have a sore throat. (Lit., The throat is sore.)
5. **Wun shaw dae.** I have diarrhea.
6. **Chay dauk nah dae.** My legs hurt.
7. **Let nah dae.** My arms hurt.
8. **Arn jin dae.** I feel like vomiting.
9. **Gaung moo dae.** I feel dizzy.
10. **Yay ngat tae.** I'm thirsty.
11. **Hnah see dae.** I have a runny nose.
12. **Nar ohn dae.** My ears are blocked.
13. **Myet se nah dae.** My eyes are sore.
14. **Yin kyut tae.** My chest is congested.

PATTERN PRACTICE 2: "THIS IS *NOT* HOW I FEEL."

Practice saying the negative forms of these symptoms.

1. **Chaung ma hso boo.**   I don't have a cough.
2. **Bite ma nah boo.**
   I don't have a stomachache. (Lit., The stomach doesn't hurt.)
3. **Lae jaung ma nah boo.**   I don't have a sore throat. (Lit., The throat isn't sore.)
4. **Wun ma shaw boo.**   I don't have diarrhea.
5. **Chay dauk ma nah boo.**   My legs don't hurt.
6. **Let ma nah boo.**   My arms don't hurt.
7. **Ma aun jin boo.**   I don't feel like vomiting.
8. **Gaung ma moo boo.**   I don't feel dizzy.
9. **Yay ma ngat phoo.**   I don't feel thirsty.
10. **Yin ma kyut phoo.**   I don't have chest congestion.
11. **Hnar ma hsee boo.**   I don't have a runny nose.
12. **Nar ma ohn boo.**   My ears are not blocked.
13. **Myet se ma nah boo.**   My eyes are not sore.
14. **Yin ma kyut phoo.**   My chest is not congested.

EXERCISE 1: "TELL ME HOW YOU FEEL."

Describe the following in Burmese. (Remember to use **dah bae maet** *but* in your sentences.)

1. I have a stomachache. But I don't have a sore throat.
2. My legs hurt. But my arms don't hurt.
3. I have a runny nose. But I don't have blocked ears.
4. I don't feel thirsty. But my eyes are sore.
5. I don't feel dizzy. But I'm coughing.
6. I don't have a cough. But I don't feel like vomiting.

GRAMMAR NOTE "A little bit of this, not much of that"

Let's compare how Samantha talks about her stomachache and her sore throat.

ဗိုက်သိပ်မနာဘူး။ **Baik thaik ma nah boo.** *The stomach doesn't hurt that much.*

ဗိုက်	**baik**	the stomach
သိပ်	**thaik**	very much
မနာ	**ma nah**	doesn't hurt (negative form of the verb **nah**, to hurt)
ဘူး	**boo**	negative sentence ending

လည်ချောင်းနည်းနည်းနာတယ်။   Lae jaung nae nae nah dae.
My throat is a bit sore.

လည်ချောင်း	lae jaung	the throat
နည်းနည်း	nae nae	a bit
နာ	nah	hurt
တယ်	dae	affirmative sentence ending

PATTERN PRACTICE 3: "A LITTLE BIT OF THIS, NOT MUCH OF THAT"

Practice saying the following:

1. **Chaung nae nae hso dae.**   I'm coughing a little bit.
2. **Bite nae nae nah dae.**   I have a bit of a stomachache. (Lit., my stomach hurts a little bit.)
3. **Lae jaung nae nae nah dae.**   My throat is a little sore.
4. **Wun nae nae shaw dae.**   I have a little bit of diarrhea.
5. **Chay dauk thaik ma nah boo.**   My legs don't hurt that much.
6. **Let thaik ma nah boo.**   My arms don't hurt that much.
7. **Nae nae aun jin dae.**   I kind of feel like vomiting.
8. **Gaung thaik ma moo boo.**   I don't feel too dizzy.
9. **Yay nae nae ngat tae.**   I feel a bit thirsty.
10. **Hnah nae nae se dae.**   My nose is a bit runny.
11. **Nar nae nae ohn dae.**   My ears are a bit blocked.
12. **Myet se thaik ma nah boo.**   My eyes are not that sore.

EXERCISE 2: MIXED SYMPTOMS

Describe these in Burmese:

1. I don't have a cough. But I feel a little dizzy.
2. I feel a little dizzy. But I don't have a stomachache.
3. My nose is not too runny. But my ears are a bit blocked.
4. I have a stomachache. But I don't have diarrhea.
5. My throat is a bit sore. But I'm not coughing.
6. My arms hurt. My legs hurt.

DIALOGUE FREQUENCY OF TAKING MEDICINE

Doctor:	*Umm, you have a tiny bit of fever.*
	Inn, a phyar nae nae shi dae.
	အင်း ... အဖျားနည်းနည်းရှိတယ်။
	I think you caught a cold.
	A aye mi dah htin dae.
	အအေးမိတာ ထင်တယ်။
Samantha:	*Oh, I see.*
	Aww, hote kaet.
	ဪ ... ဟုတ်ကဲ့။
Doctor:	*I'll give you some medicine.*
	Kyanaw hsay pay lite mae.
	ကျွန်တော် ဆေး ပေးလိုက်မယ်။
Samantha:	*OK.*
	Hote kaet bah shint.
	ဟုတ်ကဲ့ပါရှင့်။
Doctor:	*Take it twice a day.*
	Ta yet ko hna khah thauk pah.
	တစ်ရက်ကို နှစ်ခါသောက်ပါ။
Samantha:	*Yes.*
	Hote.
	ဟုတ်။
Doctor:	*Once in the morning, once in the evening.*
	Manet ta khah, nya ta khah thaut pah.
	မနက်တစ်ခါ ညတစ်ခါ သောက်ပါ။
Samantha:	*Yes.*
	Hote.
	ဟုတ်။
Doctor:	*If you're still not feeling well after five days, please come back.*
	Naut ngah yet kyah lo ma pyaut thae yin pyan lah gae bah.
	နောက် ငါးရက်ကြာလို့ မပျောက်သေးရင် ပြန်လာခဲ့ပါ။
Samantha:	*Yes, thanks! Please excuse me.*
	Hote kaet. Kyay zu bah shint. Khwint pyu bah ohn.
	ဟုတ်ကဲ့၊ ကျေးဇူးပါရှင့် ၊ ခွင့်ပြုပါဦး။
Doctor:	*Very well.*
	Kaung bah bi.
	ကောင်းပါပြီ။

GRAMMAR NOTE Conditional particle *yin*

The doctor's instruction to Samantha is:

မပျောက်သေးရင် ပြန်လာခဲ့ပါ။ Ma pyaut thae yin pyan lah gae bah.
If you're still not well, come back.

မပျောက်သေး	ma pyauk thay	still not well (Lit., symptoms still not gone)
ရင်	yin	if, in case of
ပြန်လာခဲ့	pyan lah gaet	come back
ပါ	bah	command particle

You can use the particle **yin** to make conditional statements using the pattern "If ... then ..." Here are some more examples:

ရေငတ်ရင် Coca Cola သောက်ပါ။   Yay ngyat yin Coca Cola thauk pah.
If you're thirsty, drink Coca Cola.

ရေငတ်	yay ngat	thirsty
ရင်	yin	if, in that case
Coca Cola	Coca Cola	Coca Cola
သောက်	thauk	drink
ပါ	bah	command particle

မုန့်ဟင်းခါးမရှိရင် ရှမ်းခေါက်ဆွဲယူမယ်။ Moke hingar ma shi yin, shan khauk swae yu mae. *If there's no moke hingar, I'll take Shan noodles.*

မုန့်ဟင်းခါး	moke hingar	catfish chowder and noodles
မရှိ	ma shi	not available (negative form of the verb **shi**, to exist)
ရင်	yin	if, in case of
ရှမ်းခေါက်ဆွဲ	shan khauk swae	Shan noodles
ယူ	yu	take
မယ်	mae	future sentence ending

PATTERN PRACTICE 4:
"HOW OFTEN SHOULD I TAKE THIS?"

To specify how often Samantha must take a particular medicine, the doctor says:

တစ်ရက်ကို နှစ်ခါသောက်ပါ။ Ta yet ko hna khah thauk pah.
Take it twice a day.

တစ်ရက်	ta yet	one day
ကို	ko	for, in
နှစ်ခါ	hna khah	twice
သောက်	thauk	drink
ပါ	pah	command particle

Practice these frequency expressions:

1. **Ta nah yi go ta khah.**   Once an hour.
2. **Ta yet ko hna khah.**   Twice a day.
3. **Da but ko thone gah.**   Three times a week.
4. **Ta la ko lay gah.**   Four times a month.
5. **Ta hnit ko ngar gah.**   Five times a year.
6. **Ta yet ko chauk khah.**   Six times a day.
7. **Da but ko kho-na khah.**   Seven times a week.
8. **Ta la ko shiq khah.**   Eight times a month.
9. **Ta hnit ko koe gah.**   Nine times a year.
10. **Ta hnit ko hsae gah.**   Ten times a year.

ta yet ko hna khah
twice a day

Da but ko kho-na khah.
Seven times a week.

CHAPTER 17
Pagoda Fair

 **DIALOGUE** LET'S EAT, DRINK, PLAY.

A week later, Samantha feels better, so she and Naing Oo go to visit a Pagoda Fair.

Samantha:	*Naing, so many people! Really fun!*
	Naing, lu dway amyar ji. Pyaw zayah ji!
	နိုင် ... လူတွေအများကြီး။ ပျော်စရာကြီး။
Naing Oo:	*Hmm, yeah.*
	Inn, hote tae.
	အင်း ဟုတ်တယ်။
	Where do you want to go, Sam?
	Bae thwar jin lae, Sam.
	ဘယ်သွားချင်လဲ Sam။
Samantha:	*Let's go up to the pagoda walkway.*
	Phayar zaung dan paw thwar ya aung.
	ဘုရားစောင်းတန်းပေါ် သွားရအောင်။
Naing Oo:	*That's good. Let's go.*
	Kaung dae. Thwar ja zo.
	ကောင်းတယ်၊ သွားကြစို့။
	And then?
	Pi dawt.
	ပြီးတော့ ...
Samantha:	*After that, let's go to the night market.*
	Pi dawt, nya zay dan thwar ja zo.
	ပြီးတော့ ညဈေးတန်းကိုသွားကြစို့။
Naing Oo:	*And then?*
	Pi yin.
	ပြီးရင် ...
Samantha:	*Then we'll go have fried squash.*
	Pi yin boo thee jaw thwar sar ja so.
	ပြီးရင် ဘူးသီးကြော်သွားစားကြစို့။

Naing Oo: *That plan sounds good.*
Di asi azin kaung dae.
ဒီအစီအစဉ်ကောင်းတယ်။
Come, let's go.
Lah, thwar ja zo.
လာ ... သွားကြစို့။

VOCABULARY

a myar ji	a lot
pyaw za yah ji	so much fun!
nya zay dan	night market
asi azin	plan, program
pe dawt	after that, then
pe yin	after that, then

Supplementary Vocabulary

sar jin zayah ji	looks so delicious (lit., makes me want to eat!)
thauk chin za yah ji	looks so delicious (lit., makes me want to drink!)
mote saing	snack shop
laphet yay zaing	teashop
kor phee zaing	coffee shop
zay	market
sah kyi taik	library
pan jan	park
yote shin	cinema, movie
ohn no khaut swe	coconut noodle soup
lephet thoke	tea leaf salad
Shan khauk swe	Shan noodle salad
kimar palata	*keema paratha* (pan-fried paratha stuffed with meat)
kyet thon kyaw	onion fritter
be yar	beer

 **GRAMMAR NOTE** "Let's do something"—*ja zo, ya aung*

When describing what they should do together, Samantha says:

ဘုရားစောင်းတန်းပေါ် သွားရအောင်။   Phayar zaung dan paw thwar ya aung.
Let's go up to the pagoda walkway.

ဘုရားစောင်းတန်း	pyayar zaung dan	pagoda walkway
ပေါ်	baw	on, above
သွား	thwar	to go
ရအောင်	ya aung	let's

ညစျေးတန်းကိုသွားကြစို့။   Nya zay dan thwar ja zo.
Let's go to the night market.

ညစျေးတန်း	nya zay dan	night market
ကို	go	to
သွား	thwar	to go
ကြစို့	ja zo	let's

The phrases **ja zo** and **ya aung** are almost interchangeable. When they follow a verb, they function like the English phrase *let's*—urging others to join you in an action. Here are more examples:

ဗိုလ်ချုပ်ဈေး သွားရအောင်။   Bogyoke zay thwar ya aung.
Let's go to Bogyoke Market.

ဗိုလ်ချုပ်ဈေး	Bogyoke zay	Bogyoke Market
သွား	thwar	to go
ရအောင်	ya aung	let's

သီချင်း နားထောင်ကြစို့။   Thachin nar htaung ja zo.   *Let's listen to music.*

သီချင်း	thachin	songs, music
နားထောင်	nar htaung	to listen
ကြစို့	ja zo	let's

PATTERN PRACTICE 1: "LET'S DO SOMETHING."

Practice the following sentences:

1. **Mote saing thwar ya aung.**   Let's go to a snack shop.
2. **Laphet yay zaing thwar ya aung.**   Let's go to a teashop.
3. **Kor phee zaing thwar ja zo.**   Let's go to a coffee shop.
4. **Zay thwar ja zo.**   Let's go to the market.
5. **Sah kyi daik thwar ya aung.**   Let's go to the library.
6. **Pan jan thwar ya aung.**   Let's go to the park.
7. **Yote shin thwar kyi ja zo.**   Let's go watch a movie.

8. **Moke hingar thwar sar ya aung.**
   Let's go eat *moke hingar* (catfish chowder with noodles).
9. **Ohn no khauk swe thwar sar ya aung.** Let's go eat *ohn no khaut swe* (coconut noodle soup).
10. **Lephet thoke thwar sar ja zo.** Let's go eat tea leaf salad.
11. **Shan khauk swe thwar sar ja zo.** Let's go eat Shan noodle salad.
12. **Kimar palata thwar sar ya aung.** Let's go eat *keema paratha.*
13. **Kyet thon kyaw thwar sar ja zo.** Let's go eat onion fritters.
14. **Beer thwar thauk kya zo.** Let's go drink beer.
15. **Wine thwar thauk kya zo.** Let's go drink wine.
16. **Laphet yay thwar thauk ya aung.** Let's go drink tea.
17. **Korphe thwar thauk ya aung.** Let's go drink coffee.

GRAMMAR NOTE "Then, after that"

To talk about a series of activities, Samantha uses two transition words to loosely link them:

ပြီးတော့ ညဈေးတန်းကိုသွားကြစို့။ **Pi dawt, Nya Zay dan thwar ja zo.**
After that, let's go to the night market.

ပြီးတော့ **pi dawt** after that

ညဈေးတန်းသွားကြစို့ **Nya zay dan thwar ja zo**
Let's go to the night market.

ပြီးရင် ဘူးသီးကြော်သွားစားကြစို့။ **Pi yin boo thee jaw thway sar ja zo.**
Then we'll go have fried squash.

ပြီးရင် **pi yin** after that

ဘူးသီးကြော်သွားစားကြစို့ **Bo thi jaw thwar sar ja zo.**
Let's go eat fried squash.

The phrases **pi dawt** and **pi yin** (also pronounced **pyi dawt** and **pyi yin**) roughly means, *after that*, *next*, or *then*.

PATTERN PRACTICE 2: "AFTER THAT ..."

Practice using the two phrases with the following:

1. **Pi dawt, zay thwar ja zo.** And then, let's go to the market.
2. **Pi yin, yote shin thwar ja zo.** After that, let's go to the movie.

3. **Pi dawt, pan jan thwar ya aung.**   And then, let's go to the park.
4. **Pi yin, laphet yay zaing thwar ya aung.**   After that, let's go to a teashop.
5. **Pi dawt, sar kyi daik thwar ja zo.**   And then, let's go to the library.
6. **Pi yin, Bogyoke zay thwar ya aung.**   After that, let's go to Bogyoke market.

EXERCISE 1: A SERIES OF ACTIVITIES

Say these sentences in Burmese:

1. Let's go to a teashop. After that, let's go to the movie.
2. Let's go to the library. And then, let's go to the market.
3. Let's go to Shwedagon Pagoda. After that, let's go to Bogyoke Market.
4. Let's go eat *moke hingar*. And then, let's go drink tea.
5. Let's go eat *ohn no khaut swe*. After that, let's go drink coffee.
6. Let's go to the park. And then, let's go eat fried squash.
7. Let's go to the Strand Hotel. And then, let's go drink beer.

PATTERN PRACTICE 3: MORE EXCLAMATIONS

Seeing the large crowd at the pagoda fair, Samantha exclaimed:

Pyaw za yah ji!   *Looks so much fun!*

In Chapter 7: Sightseeing, you learn a number of useful exclamations constructed with the suffix **kyi** or **ji** (to emphasize largeness) and **lay** (to emphasize smallness). Here are some more useful expressions for you to practice and learn:

1. **Sar jin zayah ji**   Makes me want to eat it! (if the food item is big)
2. **Sar jin zayah lay**   Makes me want to eat it! (if the food item is small)
3. **Thauk chin zayah ji**   Makes me want to drink it! (if the drink is big)
4. **Thauk chin zayah lay**   Makes me want to drink it! (if the drink is small)
5. **Chit sayah ji**   Looks so lovely! (if the item, person, or creature is big)
6. **Chit sayah lay**   Looks so lovely! (if the item, person, or creature is small)
7. **Pyaw zayah ji!**   Looks so much fun!
8. **Pyin zayah ji!**   Looks so boring!

EXERCISE 2: FINDING THE RIGHT EXCLAMATION

Give an appropriate exclamation in Burmese for each of these:

1. a tiny poodle
2. a small child
3. an oversize mug of beer
4. a large plate of Shan noodles
5. a lively pagoda fair
6. a small cupcake
7. an uninteresting movie

CHAPTER 18
Talking to Monks

 **DIALOGUE** MONASTIC BURMESE

With just a few days left before they depart, Samantha and Naing Oo visit a monastery to donate some robes to the monks, a traditional offering to acquire merit.

Abbot: *Hm, the name of the travel agency is Shwe Hintha, is it?*

                 Aww, kha yee thwar lote ngan yaet namae ga Shwe Hintha daet lar.

                 ဪ ... ခရီးသွားလုပ်ငန်းရဲ့ နာမည်က ရွှေဟင်္သာ့တဲ့လား။

Naing Oo: *Yes.*

                 Tin bah, phayar.

                 တင်ပါ ဘုရား။

Abbot: *And your name is?*

                 Dagah lay namae ga aw.

                 ဒကာလေး နာမည်ကရော။

Naing Oo: *I'm Naing Oo, Phone Phone.*

                 Da baet daw Naing Oo bah, Phone Phone.

                 တပည့်တော် နိုင်ဦးပါ ဘုန်းဘုန်း။

Abbot: *And you, young lady?*

                 Dagama lay ga aw.

                 ဒကာမလေးကရော။

Samantha: *It's Samantha, Phone Phone.*

                 Samantha bah, Phone Phone.

                 Samantha ပါ ဘုန်းဘုန်း။

Abbot: *Well, well, thanks for visiting the monastery.*

                 Aye, aye, kyaung go la lae dah kyay zu tin bah dae.

                 အေး ... အေး ... ကျောင်းကို လာလည်တာကျေးဇူးတင်ပါတယ်။

Naing Oo: *Of course.*

                 Tin bah.

                 တင်ပါ။

Abbot: *Also, thanks for donating robes.*

                 Thin-gan hlu dah go lae kyay zu tin bah dae.

                 သင်္ကန်းလှူတာကိုလည်း ကျေးဇူးတင်ပါတယ်။

Naing Oo: *Certainly. Please excuse us.*

                 Tin bah, Phone Phone. Da baet daw do go khwint pyu bah ohn.

                 တင်ပါ ဘုန်းဘုန်း။ တပည့်တော်တို့ကို ခွင့်ပြုပါဦး။

Abbot:	*May the great Shwe Hintha Agency be successful!*
	Shwe Hintha lote ngan ji aung myin bah zay.
	ရွှေဟင်္သာလုပ်ငန်းကြီး အောင်မြင်ပါစေ။
Naing Oo:	*May your blessings come true!*
	Pay dae hsu naet pyaet bah zay.
	ပေးတဲ့ဆုနဲ့ပြည့်ပါစေ။

VOCABULARY

kha yee thwar lote ngan	travel agency
Shwe Hintha	Golden Bird
tin bah	yes (only used in conversations with monks and nuns)
dagah lay	great patron (only used by monks, to address younger men)
dagah ji	great patron (only used by monks, to address older men)
dagama lay	great patron (only used by monks, to address younger women)
dagama ji	great patron (only used by monks, to address older women)
da baet daw	your disciple (used by people to refer to themselves when speaking to monks)
da baet daw ma	your disciple (used specifically by female speakers to refer to themselves when speaking to monks)
thin gan	a monk's robe
hlu	to donate
aung myin	to be successful
Phone Phone	form of address for a monk

Supplementary Vocabulary

hsayah daw	abbot, head monk of monastery
hsyah lay	nun
hsayah ji	head nun of a nunnery
koyin	novice (a young boy who's chosen monkhood for a brief period)
Kyan mah bah zay.	May you be healthy.
Chan thar bah zay.	May you be wealthy.
Aung myin bah zay.	May you be successful.
Bay kin bah zay.	May you be safe / free from harm.
Khayi phyaungt bah zay.	May your journey be smooth.

CULTURAL NOTE An extra layer of politeness for monks and nuns

In Burmese culture, monks, nuns, and members of religious orders are considered sacred. Therefore, when ordinary people speak to them, they use a different set of pronouns to show respect. Even polite, formal pronouns like **shin** and **khamyar** are not suitable for addressing monks and nuns. Even if you know the monk well, or if you consider him your friend, or he happens to be younger than you, you still should not use the casual *you* form **min** or **nin**.

Similarly, when referring to yourself in a conversation with monks and nuns, the usual formal pronouns **kyanaw** and **kyama** are not suitable. Instead, you should use **da baet daw**, which literally means *disciple*.

Women *may* use **da baet daw ma**, the feminine form of **da baet daw**, when speaking to monks and nuns. But it's entirely optional. **Da baet daw** can be used by both men and women.

With lay people, you say **hote tae**, **hote pah dae**, or **hote kaet** to say *yes*. But when speaking to members of the religious orders, you use **tin bah** instead.

 **PATTERN PRACTICE 1:
SELF–INTRODUCTION, THE MONASTIC VERSION**

When he introduces himself to the head monk of the monastery, Naing Oo says:

တပည့်တော် နိုင်ဦးပါ ဘုန်းဘုန်း။ Da baet daw Naing Oo bah, Phone Phone.
I'm Naing Oo, Phone Phone.

တပည့်တော်	da baet daw	the disciple (substitute for *I*, male)
နိုင်ဦး	Naing Oo	Naing Oo
ပါ	bah	polite sentence ending
ဘုန်းဘုန်း	Phone Phone	monk (polite way to address a monk)

In the same conversation, Samantha uses a shortened sentence to announce her name. The full version would be:

တပည့်တော်မ Samantha ပါ ဘုန်းဘုန်း။
Da baet daw ma Samantha bah, Phone Phone.
I'm Samantha, Phone Phone.

တပည့်တော်မ	da baet daw ma	the disciple (substitute for *I*, female)
Samantha	Samantha	Samantha
ပါ	bah	polite sentence ending
ဘုန်းဘုန်း	Phone Phone	monk (polite way to address a monk)

Practice these special self-introductions:

1. **Da baet daw Naing Oo bah, Hsayah lay.** (Man, speaking to a nun)
2. **Da baet daw ma Samantha bah, Hsayah lay.** (Woman, speaking to a nun)
3. **Da baet daw Naing Oo bah, Hsayah ji.** (Man, speaking to a head nun)
4. **Da baet daw ma Samantha bah, Hsayah ji.** (Woman, speaking to a head nun)
5. **Da baet daw Naing Oo bah, Hsayah daw.** (Man, speaking to an abbot)
6. **Da baet daw ma Samantha bah, Hsayah daw.** (Woman, speaking to an abbot)
7. **Da baet daw Naing Oo bah, Koyin.** (Man, speaking to a novice)
8. **Da baet daw ma Samantha bah, Koyin.** (Woman, speaking to a novice)

EXERCISE 1:
INTRODUCING YOURSELF TO SOMEONE HOLY.

1. Your name is Jonathan. Introduce yourself to **an abbot**.
2. Your name is Kelly. Introduce yourself to **a nun**.
3. Your name is Win San. Introduce yourself to **a monk**.
4. Your name is Thida [woman's name]. Introduce yourself to **a head nun**.
5. Your name is Brendon. Introduce yourself to **a novice**.

PATTERN PRACTICE 2:
SAYING "YES," THE MONASTIC VERSION

When Naing Oo says *yes* to the monk, he doesn't say **hote kaet, hote tae,** or **hote pah dae,** all acceptable and respectful ways to say *yes* to ordinary people. Instead, he says **tin bah,** the special word used by ordinary people to express agreement to monks and nuns.

Practice the following:

1. **Tin bah, Phone Phone.**   Yes, respected monk.
2. **Tin bah, Hsayah daw**   Yes, abbot.
3. **Tin bah, Hsayah lay.**   Yes, respected nun.
4. **Tin bah, Hsayah ji.**   Yes, head nun.
5. **Tin bah, Koyin.**   Yes, novice.

EXERCISE 2: SAYING "YES" TO SOMEONE HOLY.

1. How would you say "Yes" to **a head nun**?
2. How would you say "Yes" to **a monk**?
3. How would you say "Yes" to **a novice**?
4. How would you say "Yes" to **a nun**?
5. How would you say "Yes" to **an abbot**?

CULTURAL NOTE   Novicehood—a link to the Buddhist past

A *novice* is a young boy who enters the monkhood temporarily, usually for a few days or several weeks. Many Burmese boys in Buddhist households go through this as a rite of passage. The ceremony in which a boy is ordained as a novice is called **shinbyu**. As part of the ceremony, the young boy may wear a princely outfit and ride a white horse to the monastery, followed by family members and musicians. This procession is a reenactment of Prince Siddhartha renouncing his royal life to seek spiritual enlightenment—the decision that led him to become Gautama Buddha.

CULTURAL NOTE   Receiving blessings

When the monk gives him a blessing, Naing Oo says, **pay dae hsu nae pyaet bah zay** (May your blessings come true!). This is a set phrase, a common way to respond when a monk or a nun wishes you well or says a prayer for your benefits. You may also use it when an older person wishes you well or gives you a blessing. Blessings are easy to recognize when you hear them. They usually end with the phrase **bah zay** or **pah zay**.

Here are common Burmese blessings. Practice them so you'll recognize them when you hear them.
1. **Kyan mah bah zay.**   May you be healthy!
2. **Chan thah bah zay.**   May you be wealthy!
3. **Kyan mah, chan thah bah zay.**   May you be healthy and wealthy!
4. **Aung myin bah zay.**   May you be successful!
5. **Bay kin bah zay.**   May you be safe / free from harm!

CULTURAL NOTE   Making offerings to the monks

Since becoming a Buddhist monk means renouncing worldly goods and luxuries, then strictly speaking, monks are not supposed to receive cash donations directly from their patrons. Monasteries usually have designated laypeople who oversee the monks' financial transactions. If you'd like to make a cash donation, you should ask the monk or abbot to identify that person for you.

The more customary offerings include the **swan offering** (to prepare and serve midday meals to a number of monks) or the **thin gan offering** (to donate robes to the monks). While anyone is welcome to make such offerings, the rituals involved—how to invite the monks, how to prepare for the monks' arrival, how to behave during the event, and so on—could be a challenge to those without a Buddhist upbringing. Therefore, if you choose to make such an offering, you should seek help from a local person to guide you through the process.

CHAPTER 19
Farewell

 **DIALOGUE** TIME TO SAY GOODBYE

It's time for Naing Oo and Samantha to return to San Francisco. At Yangon International Airport, they say goodbye to Win San.

Naing Oo: *Well, my friend, I'll get going now.*
Kae, thwar ohn mae naw, tha nge jin.
ကဲ ... သွားဦးမယ်နော်၊ သူငယ်ချင်း။

Win San: *Sure, sure, very well then.*
Aye aye, kaung bi kwah.
အေးအေး ... ကောင်းပြီကွာ။

Naing Oo: *We'll be back.*
Pyan lah ohn mae.
ပြန်လာဦးမယ်။

Win San: *About when?*
Bae dawt laut lae.
ဘယ်တော့ လောက်လဲ။

Naing Oo: *In about four, five months from now.*
Naut lay ngah la laut kyah yin pawt.
နောက် လေး ငါးလလောက်ကြာရင်ပေါ့။

Win San: *I'll be waiting.*
Hmyaw nay mae naw.
မျှော်နေမယ်နော်။

Samantha: *Ko Win San, I'll be going too.*
Ko Win San, kyama lae pyan dawt mae.
ကိုဝင်းဆန်း၊ ကျွန်မလည်း ပြန်တော့မယ်။
Please excuse me.
Khwint pyu bah ohn shint.
ခွင့်ပြုပါဦးရှင်။

Win San: *All right, very well then.*
Hote kaet, kaung bah bi byah.
ဟုတ်ကဲ့၊ ကောင်းပါပြီဗျာ။

Vocabulary

thwar	to go
naut	later, at a later time
lah	to come
bae dawt laut	roughly when, about when
la	month
hmyaw	to wait, to hope for
pyan	to go back (to one's home or point of origin)
yone	office
kyaung	school
ain	home

Supplementary Vocabulary

yet	day
nah yi	hour
manit	minute
pat, bat	week
hnit	year
saunt	to wait
tae kho gan	guesthouse, inn, motel

GRAMMAR NOTE *"About to do something"—dawt, tawt*

Bidding farewell to Win San, Samantha says:

ကျွန်မလည်း ပြန်တော့မယ်॥   **Kyama lae pyan dawt mae.**
I, too, shall be going [home].

ကျွန်မ	kyama	I (female speaker, formal)
လည်း	lae	also, as well
ပြန်	pyan	go back
တော့	dawt	about to
မယ်	mae	future sentence ending

Here, the particle **dawt** indicates Samantha is **about** to leave. Here are other ways this particle can be used:

ညနေစာ စားတော့မယ်॥   **Nya nay zah sar dawt mae.**
I'm about to have dinner.

ညနေစာ	nya nay zah	dinner
စား	sar	to eat
တော့	dawt	about to
မယ်	mae	future sentence ending

အလုပ် သွားတော့မယ်။   **Aloke thwar dawt mae.**   *I'm about to go to work.*

အလုပ်	aloke	to work
သွား	thwar	to go
တော့	dawt	about to
မယ်	mae	future sentence ending

USAGE NOTE *Thwar vs pyan*

You can use **thwar** to talk about going to any place or destination. But you should only use **pyan** to talk about going back to the place you have come from, or going back to your point of origin. For example:

- **Kyaung thwar mae.** I'm going to school.
- **Zay thwar mae.** I'm going to the market.
- **Yone thwar mae.** I'm going to the office.

- **Ain pyan mae.** I'm going back home.
- **Hotel pyan mae.** I'm going back to the hotel.
- **Tae kho gan pyan mae.** I'm going back to the motel/inn/guesthouse.

If you say **yone pyan mae** or **kyaung pyan mae**, it suggests you came from the office or from school; therefore, you're now going *back* to the office or to school. If you say **pyan mae** while you're visiting someone's home, it implies you're ready to go home, or go back to the hotel.

GRAMMAR NOTE "In about X months ... "

When Win San asks Naing Oo roughly when he plans to come back for another visit, Naing Oo says:

နောက် လေး ငါးလလောက်ကြာရင်ပေါ့။   **Naut lay, ngah la laut kyah yin pawt.**
In about four, five months from now.

နောက်	naut	next
လေး ငါးလ	lay ngar la	four, five months
လောက်	laut	about
ကြာရင်	kyah yin	have passed
ပေ့ါ	pawt	casual, emphatic sentence ending

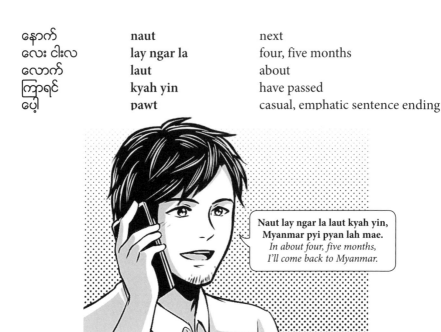

Naut lay ngar la laut kyah yin,
Myanmar pyi pyan lah mae.
*In about four, five months,
I'll come back to Myanmar.*

PATTERN PRACTICE 1: "WHEN WILL YOU BE BACK?"

Practice the following responses:

1. **Naut lay, ngah *yet* laut kyah yin pawt.**   In about four, five *days* from now.
2. **Naut lay, ngah *but* laut kyah yin pawt.**   In about four, five *weeks* from now.
1. **Naut lay, ngah *nah yi* laut kyah yin pawt.**   In about four, five *hours* from now.
4. **Naut lay, ngah *ma nit* laut kyar yin pawt.**
   In about four, five *minutes* from now.
5. **Naut lay, ngah *hnit* laut kyar yin pawt.**   In about four, five *years* from now.
6. **Naut *ta la* laut kyah yin pawt.**   In about *a month* from now.
7. **Naut *hna yet* laut kyah yin pawt.**   In about *two days* from now.
8. **Naut *thone but* laut kyah yin pawt.**   In about *three weeks* from now.
9. **Naut *lay nah yi* laut kyah yin pawt.**   In about *four hours* from now.
10. **Naut *ngar ma nit* laut kyah yin pawt.**   In about *five minutes* from now.
11. **Naut *chauk yet* laut kyah yin pawt.**   In about *six days* from now.
12. **Naut *khon na hnit* laut kyah yin pawt.**   In about *seven years* from now.
13. **Naut *shiq yet* laut kyah yin pawt.**   In about *eight days* from now.
14. **Naut *koe la* laut kyah yin pawt.**   In about *nine months* from now.
15. **Naut *hsae nah yi* laut kyah yin pawt.**   In about *ten hours* from now.

GRAMMAR NOTE Place, time, action

Suppose Naing Oo includes the place he plans to return to, using the appropriate verb, he will then say:

နောက် လေး ငါးလလောက်ကြာရင် မြန်မာပြည် ပြန်လာမယ်။
Naut lay ngar la laut kyah yin, Myanmar pyi pyan lah mae.
In about four, five months, I'll come back to Myanmar.

နောက်	naut	next
လေး ငါးလ	lay, ngar la	four, five months
လောက်	laut	about
ကြာရင်	kyah yin	have gone by
မြန်မာပြည်	Myanmar pyi	Myanmar (country of Myanmar)
ပြန်လာ	pyan lah	to return, to come back
မယ်။	mae	future sentence ending

PATTERN PRACTICE 2: PLACE, TIME, ACTION

Let's add some place indicators and proper verbs to complete the sentence above. Practice saying these:

1. Naut *ta nah yi* laut kyah yin, *yone* lah mae.
   I'll *come to the office* in about *an hour* from now.
2. Naut *hna nah yi* laut kyah yin, *kyaung thwar* mae.
   I'll *go to school* in about *two hours* from now.
3. Naut *thone nah yi* laut kyah yin, *ain pyan* mae.
   I'll *go home* in about *three hours* from now.
4. Naut *lay yet* kyah yin, *Mandalay thwar* mae.
   I'll *go to Mandalay* in about *four days* from now.
5. Naut *ngar yet* laut kyah yin, *Bagan thwar* mae.
   I'll *go to Bagan* in about *five days* from now.
6. Naut *chauk yet* laut kyah yin, *San Francisco pyan* mae.
   I'll *go back to San Francisco* in about *six days* from now.
7. Naut *khonna ma nit* laut kyah yin, *lay zait lah* mae.
   I'll *come to the airport* in about *seven minutes* from now.

EXERCISE 1: COMING AND GOING

Translate the following into English:

1. Naut thone la laut kyah yin <u>pyan mae</u>.
2. Naut da but laut kyah yin <u>thwar mae</u>.
3. Naut hna nar yi laut kyah yin <u>lah mae</u>.
4. Naut lay, ngar la laut kyah yin <u>thwar mae</u>.
5. Naut thone, lay nar yi laut kyah yin <u>pyan mae</u>.
6. Naut hsae ma nit laut kyah yin <u>thwar mae</u>.
7. Naut shiq la laut kyah yin <u>lah mae</u>.
8. Naut koe nah yi laut kyah yin <u>thwar mae</u>.

EXERCISE 2: "I'LL LEAVE IN ABOUT ..."

Say the following in Burmese:

1. I'll leave in about four, five minutes from now.
2. I'll go in about a year from now
3. I'll come in about six months from now.
4. I'll go in about two days from now.
5. I'll leave in about ten minutes from now.
6. I'll come in about nine days from now.
7. I'll go in about a week from now.
8. I'll come in about seven hours from now.
9. I'll leave in about three years from now.

USAGE NOTE Asking for permission to leave

Samantha's final words to Win San are:

ခွင့်ပြုပါဦးရှင်။ **Khwint pyu bah ohn shin.**
Please excuse me. (Lit., Please give me permission to leave.)

ခွင့်ပြုပါဦး	khwint pyu bah ohn	please give permission
ရှင်	shin	polite sentence ending (used by a female speaker)

The male version would be:

ခွင့်ပြုပါဦး ခင်ဗျား။ **Khwint pyu bah ohn khamyar.** *Please excuse me.*

It wouldn't make much sense to dissect **khwint pyu bah ohn** into verbs and command particles, even though that's what they are. Better to think of the whole expression as a set phrase for saying goodbye courteously.

CULTURAL NOTE In the digital era, *goodbye* is not *goodbye*.

Since Myanmar began its transition from military to civilian rule in 2011, many Burmese citizens—especially the young people—have flocked to the web, to Facebook in particular. These days, when you become friends with someone in Burmese, you'll most likely hear them say:

Facebook ရှိလား။ **Facebook shi lar.**
Do you have Facebook (a Facebook profile)?

Facebook မှာ add လိုက်မယ်နော်။ **Facebook hmah add like mae naw.**
I'll add you on Facebook, OK?

Answers to Exercises

CHAPTER 3

Exercise 1: Yes–no questions

1. Hote tae.
2. Hote tae naw.
3. Kaung dae.
4. Kaung dae naw.
5. Nay kaung dae.
6. Pu lar.
7. Khar lar.
8. Aye dae naw.

Exercise 2: Introducing someone

1. Dah nga amyo thamee Samantha bah.
2. Dah kyanawt / kyama amyo thar bah.
3. Dah kyanawt / kyama kyaung nay bet tha nge jin James bah.
4. Dah nga nge tha nge jin Kelly bah.
5. Dah kyanawt / kyama loke phor kaing bet Ba Toe bah.
6. Dah nga hsayah bah.
7. Dah kyanawt / kyama ahtet ayarshi bah.
8. Dah kyanawt / kyama aphae bah.
9. Dah gha amae bah.
10. Dah kyanawt nyi bah (male speaker) / Dah kyama maung bah (female speaker).

CHAPTER 4

Exercise 1: Stating what's available

1. Di hmar pout si shi dae. Moke hingar shi dae. Kyet oo jaw lae shi dae.
2. Di hmar lephet thoke shi dae. Pout si shi dae. Ohn no khauk swe lae shi dae.
3. Di hmar hsi htamin shi dae. Lephet thoke shi dae. Cake mont lae shi dae.

Note: Using **ya** (to be available) instead of **shi** (to exist) is also an option. For example:
1. Di hmar pout si ya dae. Moke hingar ya dae. Kyet oo jaw lae ya dae.

Exercise 2: "I'll take this and that."

1. Pout si yu mae. Laphet thoke yu mae. Moke hingar lae yu mae.
2. Hsi htamin yu mae. Pout si yu mae. Pae byote naet naan byar lae yu mae.
3. Laphet yay yu mae. Paung mote htaw but thoke yu mae. Cake mont lae yu mae.

CHAPTER 5

Exercise 1: Current work, previous work

1. Nyi lay ayin ga bae hmah aloke loke lae. (Male speaker) / Maung lay, bae hmah aloke loke lae. (Female speaker)
2. Ama agu bae hmah aloke loke lae.
3. Nyi ma agu bae hmah aloke loke lae.
4. Nyi ma ayin ga bae hmah aloke loke lae.
5. Ko Chan Aye agu bae hmah aloke loke lae.
6. Ma Lwin Lwin ayin ga bae hmah aloke loke lae.
7. U Kan Paw ayin ga bae hmah aloke loke lae.
8. Daw Khin Oo agu bae hmah aloke loke lae.

Exercise 2: "Where I teach a certain language."

1. Mandalay hmah Myanmar zah thin dae.
2. Maymyo hmah Pyinthit sah thin dae.
3. A may ri ka hmah Jar man zah thin dae.
4. Yangon hmah Japan zah thin dae.
5. Mandalay hmah Ingalaik sah thin dae.
6. In-tah-nay-shin-nae kyaung hmah Myanmar zah thin dae.
7. In-tah-nay-shin-nae kyaung hmah Ko ree yan zar thin dae.

Exercise 3: Turning statements into questions

1. Tayoke sah thin lar.   Do you teach Chinese?
2. Ingalake sah thin lar.   Do you teach English?
3. Japan zah thin lar.   Do you teach Japanese?
4. Amay ri ka hmah Myanmar zah thin lar.   Do you teach Burmese in America?
5. Mandalay hmah Tayoke sah thin lar.   Do you teach Chinese in Mandalay?
6. Maymyo hmah Ingalake sah thin lar.   Do you teach English in Maymyo?

Exercise 4: "Is this your job?"

1. Korphee zaing wun dan lar.   Are you a cafe employee?
2. Yadanah zaing man nay jar lar.   Are you a jewelry shop owner?
3. Sar thauk hsaing wun dan lar.   Are you a restaurant staffer (waiter or waitress)?
4. Sar thauk hsaing paing shin lar   Are you a restaurant owner?
5. Lephet yay zaing paing shin lar.   Are you a teashop owner?
6. Awut hsaing paing shin lar.   Are you a clothing shop owner?
7. Sah oak hsaing man nay jah lar.   Are you a bookstore manager?

CHAPTER 6

Exercise 1: How to say "Don't want to ..."

1. ma sar jin boo   don't want to eat
2. ma thauk chin boo   don't want to drink
3. ma lah jin boo   don't want to come
4. ma ait chin boo   don't want to sleep
5. ma nar jin boo   don't want to rest
6. ma twaet jin boo   don't want to meet
7. ma htaing jin boo   don't want to sit
8. ma pyan jin boo.   don't want to go home, don't want to leave

Exercise 2: Directions

1. Mee point hmah bae choe.
2. Hmut taing hmah nyah choe.
3. Hmut taing hmah bae choe.
4. Sah oak saing hmah bae choe.
5. Lephet yay zaing hmah nyah choe.
6. Akyaw zaing hmar bae choe.
7. Mee point hmar nyar choe.

Exercise 3: "After eight stops, you're there."

1. Shiq hmut taing hso yauk pe.
2. Hna hmut taing hso yauk pe.
3. Chauk hmut taing hso yauk pe.
4. Thone hmut taing hso hauk pe.
5. Koe hmut taing hso hauk pe.

Exercise 4: "After three blocks, you're there."
1. Thone ba-lauk hso yauk pe.
2. Chauk ba-lauk hso yauk pe.
3. Lay ba-lauk hso yauk pe.
4. Hna ba-lauk hso yauk pe.
5. Koe ba-lauk hso yauk pe.

CHAPTER 7

Pattern Practice 1: "What's it called?"
1. *Museum* go bamah lo bah khaw lae.
2. *Nunnery* go bamah lo bah khaw lae.
3. *Shop* ko bamah lo bah khaw lae.
4. *Market* ko bamah lo bah khaw lae.
5. *School* go bamah lo bah khaw lae.
6. *River* go bamah lo bah khaw lae.
7. *Bridge* ko bamah lo bah khaw lae.
8. *Library* go bamah lo bah khaw lae.

Pattern Practice 2: "What's it called?" (shorter form)
1. *Shop* ko bah khaw lae.
2. *School* go bah khaw lae.
3. *Vendors* go bah khaw lae.
4. *Market* ko bah khaw lae.
5. *Gate* ko bah khaw lae.

Pattern Practice 3: "It's called ..."
1. Monastery go phone ji kyaung lo khaw dae.
2. Nunnery go thi la shin kyaung lo khaw dae.
3. Market ko zay lo khaw dae.
4. School go kyaung lo khaw dae.
5. Shop ko hsaing lo khaw dae.
6. River go myit lo khaw dae.
7. Bridge ko da dar lo khaw dae.
8. Library go sah kyi daik lo khaw dae.

Exercise 1: Cardinal directions
1. a shayt moke   is the eastern gate
2. taung bet zaung dan   is the southern corridor
3. myauk phet da-dar   is the northern bridge
4. a nauk phet win baut   is the west entrance

Exercise 2: Learning to exclaim
1. a myint ji (really tall!)
2. a shay ji (really long!)
3. a kyi ji (really big!)
4. pu bu lay (so short!)
5. thay thay lay (so small!)
6. to do lay (so short!)

CHAPTER 8

Exercise 1: Learning to count
1. Coca Cola ta khwet
2. keyboard hna khu
3. lu thone yauk
4. panthee lay lone
5. zabae ngar gone
6. khway chauk kaung.
7. aung thabyay khon-na hsee
8. T-shirt shiq htae
9. yay koe balin
10. htamin hsae bwae

Exercise 2:   Counting large numbers

1. Hna htaungt koe yah
2. Thone daungt shiq yah
3. Lay ya khona hsae
4. Thone ya chauk hsae
5. Hna thaung chauk htaung
6. Thone thaung khona htaung
7. Lay daungt hna yah
8. Ngar daungt ta yah

Exercise 3: Counters and counter-offers

1. Coke chauk palin
2. yay khona khwet
3. T-shirt thone dae
4. panthee hna lone
5. thone daungt ngar yah
6. koe ya hna hsae
7. ngar thaung ta htaung
8. zabae chauk kone lay daung naet ya malar.
9. htamin hna pwe hna htaungt ngar yah naet ya malar.
10. aung thabyay hsae zee shiq htaungt ngar yah naet ya malar.

CHAPTER 9

Exercise 1:   "I want to go there."

1. Bogyoke Panjan thwar jin dae.
2. Bandoola Panjan thwar jin dae.
3. Mingalah Zay thwar jin dae.
4. Inya Kan thwar jin dae.
5. Kandaw Ji thwar jin dae.

Exercise 2: "How much to go to ...?"

1. Botataung balauk lae.
2. Bondoola Panjan balauk lae.
3. Kandaw Ji balauk lae.
4. Inya Kan balauk lae.
5. Bogyoke Panjan balauk lae.

Exercise 3:   Negotiating a cab fare

1. Hna htaung htar like pah.
2. Lay daungt hna yah htar like pah.
3. Chauk htaungt lay yah htar like pah.
4. Khonna htaungt ta yah htar like pah.
5. Shiq htaung htar like pah.

CHAPTER 10

Exercise 1:   "I want this object."

1. Minthar yoke thay lo hin dae.
2. Balu yoke thay lo jhin dae.
3. Myin yoke thay lo jin dae.
4. Zaw gyi yoke thay lo hin dae.
5. Kor phee lo jin dae.
6. Nar yi lo jin dae.
7. Lephet yay lo jin dae.
8. Sar oak lo jin dae.
9. Phone lo jin dae.
10. Beer lo jin dae.

Exercise 2:   Talking about size

1. Nae nae to dah shi lar.
2. Nae nae shay dah shi lar.
3. Nae nay myint dah shi lar.
4. Nae nae pu dah shi lar.
5. Nae nae lay dah shi lar.
6. Nae nae paut dah shi lar.

Exercise 3:   Talking about attributes

1. A wah yaung shi lar.
2. A net yaung shi lar.
3. A sein yaung shi lar.
4. Nae nae kyi dah shi lar.
5. Nae nae myint dah shi lar.
6. Nae nae to dah shi lar.
7. Nae nae paut dah shi lar.

Exercise 4:   More colors

1. Blue
2. Red
3. Yellow
4. Black
5. White
6. Green
7. Orange
8. Purple
9. Pink

CHAPTER 11

Exercise 1:   "For me, it's …"

1. Kyanawt/kyama a twet tawt sut lun tae.
2. Kyanawt/kyama a twet tawt nae nae cho dae.
3. Kyanawt/kyama a twet tawt ma cho boo.
4. Kyanawt/kyama a twet tawt nae nae chin dae.
5. Kyanawt/kyama a twet tawt thaik chin dae.
6. Kyanawt/kyama a twet tawt ma khar boo.
7. Kyanawt/kyama a twet tawt khar lun dae.
8. Kyanawt/kyama a twet tawt nae nae mar dae.
9. Kyanawt/kyama a twet tawt thaik pyawt dae.
10. Kyanawt/kyama a twet tawt pyit lun tae.

For simplicity or preference, the particle **tawt** may be omitted.

Exercise 2:   Using "but" to show contrasting ideas

For simplicity, the particle **tawt** is omitted, but you can include it if desired.

1. Kyanawt/kyama a twet a taw bae. Dah bae maet, thu a twet khar lun dae.
2. Kyanawt/kyama a twet a taw bae. Dah bae maet, thu a twet thaik cho dae.
3. Kyanawt/kyama a twet a taw bae. Dah bae maet, thu a twet chin lun dae.
4. Kyanawt/kyama a twet pyawt dae. Dah bae maet, thu a twet mar dae.
5. Kyanawt/kyama a twet cho dae. Dah bae maet, thu a twet khar dae.
6. Kyanawt/kyama a twet khar dae. Dah bae maet, thu a twet ma khar boo.
7. Kyanawt/kyama a twet ma sut phoo. Dah bae maet, thu a twet nae nae sut tae.
8. Kyawt/kyama a twet ma mar boo. Dah bae maet, thu a twet nae nae mar dae.
9. Thu atwet a taw bae. Dah bae maet, kyanawt/kyama a twet thaik chin dae.
10. Thu atwet a taw bae. Dah bae maet, kyanawt/kyama a twet nae nae sut tae.

Exercise 3:   "Is there [something] in this dish?"

1. Di hmah sait thar pah lar.
2. Di hmah kyet thar pah lar.
3. Di hmah amae thar pah lar.
4. Di hmah thoe thar pah lar.
5. Di hmah nga yoke thee pah lar.
6. Di hmah thajar pah lar.
7. Di hmah thajar atu pah lar.
8. Di hmah acho hmont pah lar.
9. Di hmah bazun pah lar.
10. Di hmah ngar pah lar.

Exercise 4: "Only this"

1. Ngar bae pah dae.
2. Thoe thar bae pah dae.
3. Wet thar bae pah dae.
4. Bazun bae pah dae.
5. Amae thar bae pah dae.
6. Sait thar bae pah dae.

CHAPTER 12

Exercise 1: Classroom vocabulary check

1. *Vocabulary* go *waw hah ra* lo khaw dae. Vocabulary is called *waw hah ra.*
2. *Window* go *badin bauk* lo khaw dae. A window is called *nadin bauk.*
3. *Lesson* go *thin gan zah* lo khaw dae. A lesson is called *thin gan zar.*
4. *Student* go *kyaung thar* lo khaw dae. A student is called *kyaung thar.*
5. *Homework* ko *ain zah* lo khaw dae. Homework is called *ain zar.*
6. *Teacher* go *hsayah* lo khaw dae. A teacher is called *hsayah.*

Exercise 2: Sorting out the possessives

1. kyanawt/kyama yaet kyaung thar
2. thu yaet kyaung
3. tha nge jin yaet phat sah oak.
4. tha nge jin yaet sah thin gan.
5. kyanawt/kyama yaet thin gan zah.
6. kyaung thar yaet kala-htaing.
7. hsaya yaet phat sah oak.
8. hsaya yaet ain zah.

CHAPTER 13

Exercise 1: Price each

1. 2) 900 per guest
2. 1) 800 per cup of coffee
2. 1) 30,000 per sculpture
4. 3) 4,000 per day

Exercise 2: A classifier for each occasion

1. c) Ta khwet ko chauk yah.
2. a) Ta yauk ko koe thaung.
3. c) Ta nya go chauk thaung
4. a) Da bwe go koe yah

Exercise 3: "How do we get there?"

1. Bus sakar naet lar.
2. Ya htar naet lar.
3. Thimmaw naet lar.
4. A hngar kar naet lar.
5. Ko baing kar naet lar.

Exercise 4: "This is how we'll go."

1. Lay yin naet bah khamyar / shint.
2. Ya htar naet bah khamyar / shint.
3. Ko baing kar naet bah khamyar / shint.
4. A hngar kar naet bah khamyar / shint.
5. Thimmaw naet bah khamyar / shint.

Exercise 5: Join these nouns, using *naet*

1. Nay lae zah naet nya nay zah pah dae.
2. Lan bya naet zagabyan pah dae.
3. Kar hsayah naet zagabyan pah dae.
4. Akyo apo naet thant shin yay pah dae.
5. Win jan naet awar athauk pah dae.

Exercise 6: "This and this, but not that."

1. Nay lae zah naet nya nay zah pah dae. Dah bae maet kar hsayah ma pah boo.
2. Lan bya pah dae. Dah bae maet zagabyan ma pah boo.
3. Akyo apo pah dae. Dah bae maet thant shin yay ma pah boo.

4. Asar athauk pah dae. Dah bae maet akyo apo ma pah boo.
5. Tae dah pah dae. Dah bae maet asar athauk ma pah boo.
6. Manet sah naet nya nay zah pah dae. Dah bae maet tae dah ma pah boo.

CHAPTER 14

Exercise 1:   Flavor matching

3) spicy pork
1) sweet poultry
2) sour fish
2) sour shrimp

Exercise 2:   "I really don't eat that."

1. Ngar asut tawt ma sar boo khamya/shint.
2. Wet thar dawt ma sar boo khamya/shint.
3. Ngar achin dawt ma sar boo khamya/shint.
4. Ngar hsi byan dawt ma sar boo khamya/shint.
5. Amae thar dawt ma sar boo khamya/shint.
6. Amae thar asut tawt ma sar boo khamya/shint.

CHAPTER 15

Exercise 1:   "This is what I do now / what I did then."

1. Agu, kyanaw/kyama Rangoon Teahouse hmah mun nay jah bah.
2. Agu, kyanaw/kyama KBZ Ban hmah wun dan bah.
3. Agu, kyanaw/kyama Strang Hotel hmah sayin gaing bah.
4. Ayin ga, kyanaw/kyama Thet Gatho Hsay Yone hmah hsayah wun bah.
5. Agu, kyanaw/kyama sah yay hsayah bah.
6. Ayin ga, kyanaw/kyama kyaung hsayah bah.

CHAPTER 16

Exercise 1:   "Tell me how you feel."

1. Bike nah dae. Dah bae maet lae jaung ma nah boo.
2. Chay dauk nah dae. Dah bae maet let ma nah boo.
3. Hnah see dae. Dah bae maet nar ma ohn boo.
4. Yay ma ngat phoo. Dah bae maet myet see nah dae.
5. Ma moo boo. Dah bae maet chaung hsoe dae.
6. Chaung ma hsoe boo. Dah bae maet aun jin dae.

Exercise 2:   Mixed symptoms

1. Chaung ma hsoe boo. Bah bae maet gaung nae nae moo dae.
2. Gaung nae nae moo dae. Dah bae maet bite ma nah boo.
3. Hnar thaik ma se boo. Dah bae maet nar nae nae ohn dae.
4. Bike nah dae. Dah bae maet wun ma shaw boo.
5. Lae jaung nae nae nah dae. Dah bae maet chaung ma hso boo.
6. Let nah dae. Dah bae maet chay dauk nah dae.

CHAPER 17

Exercise 1:   A series of activities

1. Let phet yay zaing thwar ya aung. Pe dawt, yoke shin thwar ja zo.
2. Sah kyi daik thwar ya aung. Pe dawt, zay thwar ja zo.
3. Shwedagon Phayar thwar ya aung. Pe dawt, Bogyoke Zay thwar ja zo.
4. Moke hingar thwar sar ya aung. Pe dawt, lephet yay thwar thauk kya zo.
5. Ohn no khauk swe thwar sar ya aung. Pe dawt, kaw phe thwar thauk kya zo.
6. Pan jan thwar ya aung. Pe dawt, boo thee yaw thwar sar ja zo.
7. Strand Hotel thwar ya aung. Pe dawt, be yar thwar thauk kya zo.

Exercise 2:   Finding the right exclamation

1. Chit sayah lay
2. Chit sayah lay
3. Thauk chin zayah ji
4. Sar jin zayah ji
5. Pyaw zayah ji
6. Sar jin zayah lay
7. Pyin zayah ji

CHAPTER 18

Exercise 1:   Introducing yourself to someone holy

1. Da baet daw Jonathan bah, Hsayah daw.
2. Da baet daw ma Kelly bah, Hsayah lay.
3. Da baet daw Win San bah, Phone Phone.
4. Da baet daw ma Thidar bah, Hsayah ji.
5. Da baet daw Brendon bah, Koyin.

Exercise 2:   Saying "yes" to someone holy

1. Tin bah, Hsayah ji.
2. Thin bah, Phone Phone.
3. Tin bah, Koyin.
4. Tin bah, Hsayah lay.
5. Tin bah, Hsayah daw.

CHAPTER 19

Exercise 1:   Coming and going

1. I'll go back in about three months from now.
2. I'll go in about a week from now.
3. I'll come in about two hours from now.
4. I'll go in about four, five months from now.
5. I'll go back in about three, four hours from now.
6. I'll go in about ten minutes from now.
7. I'll come in about eight months from now.
8. I'll go in about nine hours from now.

Exercise 2:   "I'll leave in about ..."

1. Naut lay, ngar manit laut kyah yin pyan mae.
2. Naut ta hnit laut kyah yin thwar mae.
3. Naut chauk la laut kyah yin lah mae.
4. Naut hna yet laut kyah yin thwar mae.
5. Naut hsae manit laut kyah yin pya mae.
6. Naut koe yet laut kyah yin lah mae.
7. Naut da but laut kyah yin thwar mae.
8. Naut khona nah yi laut kyah yin lah mae.
9. Naut thone hnit laut kyah yin pyan mae.

ENGLISH–BURMESE
COMMON WORDS AND PHRASES

Words associated with time

day   nayt   နေ့
week   put   ပတ်
month   la   လ
year   hnit   နှစ်
today   de nayt   နေ့
this week   de aput   ဒီအပတ်
this month   de la   ဒီလ
this year   de hnit   ဒီနှစ်
yesterday   manayt ga   မနေ့က
last week   ayin aput   အရင်အပတ်
last month   ayin la   အရင်လ
last year   ayin hnit   အရင်နှစ်
tomorrow   manet phyan   မနက်ဖြန်
the next day, tomorrow   nauk
    nayt   နောက်နေ့
next week   nauk aput   နောက်အပတ်
next month   nauk la   နောက်လ
next year   nauk hnit   နောက်နှစ်
always   amyae   အမြဲ
often, every once in a while   khana khana
    ခဏခဏ
sometimes   takhah talay   တစ်ခါတစ်လေ

Words associated with nature

cloud   tain   တိမ်
creek   chaung   ချောင်း
earth   myay jee   မြေကြီး
fire   mee   မီး
flower   pan   ပန်း
forest   taw   တော
mountain   taung   တောင်
ocean, sea   pin lae   ပင်လယ်
river   myit   မြစ်
sky   kaung kin   ကောင်းကင်
tree   thit pin   သစ်ပင်
water   yay   ရေ
wind   lay   လေ
world   gabah   ကမ္ဘာ

Words associated with food

beef   amae thar   အမဲသား

bitter   khar   ခါး
bowl, goblet   phalar   ဖလား
chopsticks   tu   တူ
cup   khwet   ခွက်
[it's] delicious   ayathah shi dae
    အရသာရှိတယ်
[not] delicious   ayathah ma shi boo
    အရသာမရှိဘူး
drink (v)   thauk   သောက်
eat   sar   စား   fish   ngah   ငါး
fork   khayin   ခက်ရင်း
fruit and vegetables   athee
    aywet   အသီးအရွက်
I'd like, I want   Lo jin dae   လိုချင်တယ်
I'd like to place an order   Hmah jin dae
    မှာချင်တယ်
I'd like to settle the bill   Ngway chay jin dae
    ငွေချေချင်တယ်
I'm full (can't eat anymore)   Wa bi   ဝပြီ
I'm not full yet   Ma wa thay boo
    မဝသေးဘူး
I'm thirsty   Yay ngat tae   ရေငတ်တယ်။
I want to drink   Thauk chin dae
    သောက်ချင်တယ်
I want to eat   Sar jin dae   စားချင်တယ်
meatless (lit., killing-free)   thet thut lute
    သက်သတ်လွတ်
plate   bagan   ပန်းကန်
pork   wet thar   ဝက်သား
poultry   kyet thar   ကြက်သား
rich in flavor, umami   hsaint   ဆိမ့်
salty   ngan   ငံ
sour   chin   ချဉ်
spicy   sut   စပ်
spoon   zoon   ဇွန်း
sweet   cho   ချို

Words associated with transport

airport   lay zait   လေဆိပ်
arrive   yauk   ရောက်
bus   bus sakar   ဘတ်စ်ကား
bus stop   hmut taing   မှတ်တိုင်

bus terminal **kar gate** ကားဂိတ်
car **kar** ကား
dock (v) (ships) **hsait** ဆိုက်
gate **gate** ဂိတ်
harbor **thin maw zait** or **thin baw
zait** သင်္ဘောဆိပ်
I don't know how to get there **Ma thwar dat
phoo** မသွားတတ်ဘူး
I want to go **Thwar jin dae** သွားချင်တယ်
land (v) (planes) **hsait** ဆိုက်
long-distance bus **away byay
kar** အဝေးပြေးကား
plane **lay yin** လေယာဉ်
ride **see** စီး
ticket **let hmut** လက်မှတ်

train **ya htar** ရထား
train station **bu dah** ဘူတာ

Common counting words

for liquid in number of cups **khwet** ခွက်
for number of days **yet** ရက်
for number of inanimate objects (like
sculpture and toys) **khu** ခု
for number of nights/evenings **nya** ည
for number of people **yauk** ယောက်
for number of pieces of clothing **htae**
ထည်
for number of food servings **bwe** ပွဲ
for number of animals **kaung** ကောင်
for number of fruits **lone** လုံး

ENGLISH–BURMESE GLOSSARY

A

a lot, very much **amyar ji** အများကြီး
abbot **hsayah daw** ဆရာတော်
ability **ayay achin** အရည်အချင်း
about (something) **akyaung** အကြောင်း
about when (used in asking questions)
bae dawt laut ဘယ်တော့လောက်
accept **let khan** လက်ခံ
acceptable **ya dae** ရတယ်
accident, not mean to do something
Mataw lo မတော်လို့
accidentally **akhant mathint** အခန့်မသင့်
actor **minthar** မင်းသား
actress **minthamee** မင်းသမီး
add **paung** ပေါင်း
address **lait sah** လိပ်စာ
admire, look up to **a htin kyi** အထင်ကြီး
admission fee **win jay** ဝင်ကြေး
admonish, teach (matters of morality)
hsone ma ဆုံးမ
adopt **mway zar** မွေးစား
adult **lu ji** လူကြီး
afraid (of something or someone) **kyauk**
ကြောက်
after that, then **pe dawt** ပြီးတော့

after that, then **pe yin** ပြီးရင်
again, more **htut** ထပ်
age; life **athet** အသက်
agent, broker (for business negotiation)
akyoe zaung အကျိုးဆောင်
agree **tha baw tu** သဘောတူ
air **lay** လေ
air-conditioning **air kon** or **lay aye set**
အဲယားကွန်း or လေအေးစက်
airplane **lay yin byan** လေယာဉ်ပျံ
airport **lay zait** လေဆိပ်
all right, OK **kaung bi** ကောင်းပြီ
alley **lan jar** လမ်းကြား
alphabet **ek khayah** အက္ခရာ
altar, shrine (indoor) **phayar zin** ဘုရားစင်
altogether, all, everything **arh lone** အားလုံး
always **amyae** အမြဲ
America **Amay yi ka** အမေရိက
ancestry, heritage **myoe yoe** မျိုးရိုး
anchor (for ship) **kyauk hsu** ကျောက်ဆူး
anger **daw tha** ဒေါသ
angry **daw tha htwet** ဒေါသထွက်
answer (n) **aphyay** အဖြေ
answer (v) **phyay** ဖြေ

antique   shay haung pyitsee
ရှေးဟောင်းပစ္စည်း
anytime   achain ma ywae   အချိန်မရွေး
apologize   taung ban or taung
man   တောင်းပန်
appeal   (n) ayu gan /   အယူခံ /
appeal (v)   ayu gan tin   အယူခံတင်
appetizer, cocktail snack   amyee   အမြည်း
applaud (v)   let khote tee   လက်ခုပ်တီး
apple   pan thee   ပန်းသီး
appointment, to have   chain htar dae
ချိန်းထားတယ်
areca nut   kwune thee   ကွမ်းသီး
argue   nyin   ငြင်း
arm, hand   let   လက်
arrange, plan   si zin   စီစဉ်
arrest (v)   phan   ဖမ်း
arrive   yauk   ရောက်
arrogant, aloof   bawin myint   ဘဝင်မြင့်
art, creative arts   anu pyinyah   အနုပညာ
article (news, magazine)   hsaung bar
ဆောင်းပါး
artificial sweetener   thaghar atu   သကြားအတု
artist   anu pyinyah thae   အနုပညာသည်
ash   pyah   ပြာ
ashtray   pyah gwet   ပြာခွက်
Asia   Ah sha   အာရှ
ask   may   မေး
ask for, request   taung   တောင်း
attack (v)   taik khaik   တိုက်ခိုက်
aunt   aunty   အန်တီ
avenge   let sar chay   လက်စားချေ
aw (exclamation, interjection)   aw   ဩော်
ax   pa hsain   ပုဆိန်

B

bad (at something)   nyant   ညံ့
bad (not good)   Ma kaung boo
မကောင်းဘူး
bag   ait   အိတ်
ball   baw lone   ဘောလုံး
ballpoint pen   baw la pin   ဘောလ်ပင်
bamboo   war   ဝါး
ban, banish (v)   hnin htote   နှင်ထုတ်
banana   ngapyaw thee   ငှက်ပျောသီး

bandage   put tee   ပတ်တီး
bank   ban   ဘဏ်
bank account   ngway sayin or ban
sayin   ငွေစာရင်း or ဘဏ်စာရင်း
bar, place that serves alcohol   ayet hsaing
အရက်ဆိုင်
basket   taung or chindaung   တောင်း or
ခြင်းတောင်း
bath, take a   yay choe   ရေချိုး
be careful   thadi htar   သတိထား
beach   kan nar   ကမ်းနား
beauty salon   a hla pyin hsaing
အလှပြင်ဆိုင်
bedroom   ait khan   အိပ်ခန်း
beef   amae thar   အမဲသား
beer   be yar   ဘီယာ
before, previously   ayin ga   အရင်က
believe   yone   ယုံ
best, the   a kaung zone   အကောင်းဆုံး
betel quid   kune yah   ကွမ်းယာ
bible   thama kyan   သမ္မာကျမ်း
bicycle   set bain   စက်ဘီး
bicycle is broken   set bain pyet
စက်ဘီးပျက်
big   kyee   ကြီး
bite (v)   kait   ကိုက်
bitter   khar   ခါး
black color   a net yaung   အနက်ရောင်
blanket   saung   စောင်
block (city street)   balauk   ဘလောက်
blood   thway   သွေး
blood pressure, to have high   thway doe shi
သွေးတိုးရှိ
blue color   a pyah yaung   အပြာရောင်
boat, ship   thin maw   သင်္ဘော
boil (cooking)   pyote   ပြုတ်
boiled beans   pae byote   ပဲပြုတ်
boiled egg   kyet oo byote   ကြက်ဥပြုတ်
bone   a yoe   အရိုး
bookshop   sah oak hsaing   စာအုပ်ဆိုင်
bored   pyin dae   ပျင်းတယ်။
boss, teacher, master, mentor   hsayah   ဆရာ
bowl, goblet   phalar   ဖလား
boyfriend, fiancé   amyo thar   အမျိုးသား
bread   paung mont   ပေါင်မုန့်

break (v) **choe** ချိုး

break time **anar yu jain** အနားယူချိန်

breakfast (lit., morning meal) **manet sah** မနက်စာ

breed, give birth to **mway** မွေး

bright **lin** လင်း

broad, wide **kyae** ကျယ်

broker (for business negotiations), agent, go-between **pwae zar** ပွဲစား

broom **dabyet see** တံမြက်စည်း

brush one's teeth **thwar tike** သွားတိုက်

build **hsaut** ဆောက်

build (a home) **ain hsaut** အိမ်ဆောက်

build (a school) **kyaung hsaut** ကျောင်းဆောက်

bullock cart **nwar hlae** နွားလှည်း

bundle up, pack **htote** ထုပ်

Burmese cuisine **Myanmah asar asah** မြန်မာအစားအစာ

Burmese language **Myanmah zar** မြန်မာစာ

Burmese language (spoken only) **Bamah zagar** ဗမာစကား

Burmese style sticky rice **hsi htamin** ဆီထမင်း

Burmese tea **laphet yae** လက်ဖက်ရည်

bus **bus sakar** ဘတ်စ်ကား

bus fare **kar ga** ကားခ

bus is crowded **kar kyut** ကားကြပ်

bus is not crowded **kar chaung** ကားချောင်

bus stop **kar hmut taing** ကားမှတ်တိုင်

bus stop, train stop **hmut taing** မှတ်တိုင်

bus terminal **kar gate** ကားဂိတ်

bus ticket **kar let hmut** ကားလက်မှတ်

business **loke ngan** လုပ်ငန်း

busy **alote myar** အလုပ်များ

busy; I'm busy **ma ar boo** မအားဘူး

buttered bread **paung mote htaw but thoke** ပေါင်မုန့်ထောပတ်သုပ်

buttock **tinbar** တင်ပါး

buy **wae** ဝယ်

C

cabinet, closet **bido** ဘီရို

cake **cake mote** ကိတ်မုန့်

calendar **pyet gadain** ပြက္ခဒိန်

call **khaw** ခေါ်

camp **sakhan** စခန်း

Can I get it? Is it doable? [informal] **Ya ma lar** ရမလား

can speak (a certain language) **pyaw dat** ပြောတတ်

candle **phayaung daing** ဖယောင်းတိုင်

candy **thajar lone** သကြားလုံး

capital **myo daw** မြို့တော်

car broke down **kar pyet** ကားပျက်

car tire **kar bain** ကားဘီး

car was late, bus was late **kar nauk kya dae** ကားနောက်ကျတယ်

carry (objects) **thae** သယ်

carry (people) **chi** ချီ

carry umbrella **htee hsaung** ထီးဆောင်း

cart (drawn by animal) **hlae** လှည်း

cat **kyaung** ကြောင်

catch a cold **a aye mi** အအေးမိ

catfish chowder with noodles **moke hinghar** မုန့်ဟင်းခါး

cemetery **thin jaing** သချႄႝင်း

ceremonious, festive **khan nar** ခမ်းနား

ceremony **akhan anar** အခမ်းအနား

chair **kala htaing** ကုလားထိုင်

chairman, chief **oak ka hta** ဥက္ကဋ္ဌ

change (v) **pyaung** ပြောင်း

charitable spirit, goodwill **say danah** စေတနာ

cheek **par** ပါး

chef **saphoh hmuu** စားဖိုမှူး

cheroot **hsay bawt lait** ဆေးပေါ့လိပ်

chew **war** ဝါး

chicken **kyet** ကြက်

child **kha lay** ကလေး

childhood friend **ngae tha ngae jin** ငယ်သူငယ်ချင်း

chili **nga yoke thee** ငရုတ်သီး

chin (anatomy) **may zi** မေးစေ့

Chin (ethnic nationality) **Chin** ချင်း

Chinese cuisine **Tayote asar asah** တရုတ်အစားအစာ

Chinese language **Tayoke sar** တရုတ်စာ

chop **khote** ခုတ်

chopsticks **tu** တူ

chubby **toat** တုတ်

church, temple, place of worship   **phayar jaung** ဘုရားကျောင်း

cigar **hsay byin lait** ဆေးပြင်းလိပ်

cigarette **hsay lait** ဆေးလိပ်

cinema, movies **yote shin** ရုပ်ရှင်

city **myo** မြို့

city hall **myo daw khan ma** မြို့တော်ခန်းမ

clarify **shin lin** ရှင်းလင်း

clean **thant shinn** သန့်ရှင်း

clean up, tidy up **shin** ရှင်း

cleaning, cleanup **thant shin yay** သန့်ရှင်းရေး

cleaver, butchering knife **dama** ဓါးမ

clever, smart, good [at something]   **taw** တော်

close the door **dagar pait** တံခါးပိတ်

close the window **badin bauk pait** ပြတင်းပေါက်ပိတ်

close, near **nee** နီး

close, turn off **pait** ပိတ်

closing hour (business, shop)   **hsaing pait chaing** ဆိုင်ပိတ်ချိန်

clothes shop **awut hsaing** အဝတ်ဆိုင်

coal **mee thway** မီးသွေး

coconut **one thee** အုန်းသီး

coconut juice **one yay** အုန်းရည်

coconut milk **one no** အုန်းနို့

coconut noodle soup **ohn no khauk swe** အုန်းနို့ခေါက်ဆွဲ

coffee **kaw phe** ကော်ဖီ

coffee shop **kor phe zaing** ကော်ဖီဆိုင်

cold season **hsaung yah thi** ဆောင်းရာသီ

collect **su** စု

comb hair **zabin phee** ဆံပင်ဖီး

come **lah** လာ

come up **tet** တက်

computer **kon pyu tah** ကွန်ပျူတာ

concert **thachin hsoh bwae** သီချင်းဆိုပွဲ

content **tin tain** တင်းတိမ်

contract, treaty **sah jote** စာချုပ်

cook (n) **htamin jet** ထမင်းချက်

cook (v) **chet** ချက်

cool, to be [slang] **mite tae** မိုက်တယ်

correct, right, true **hman** မှန်

corridor, walkway **zin gyan** စင်္ကြန်

corridor, walkway (of a religious site)   **zaung dan** စောင်းတန်း

cost, expense **kon kya zayait** ကုန်ကျစားရိတ်

cotton **chi** ချည်

cough **chaung hsoe** ချောင်းဆိုး

country **taing pyi** တိုင်းပြည်

courage **thatti** သတ္တိ

court (judiciary) **tayar yone** တရားရုံး

cover (v) **kah** ကာ

cow **nwar** နွား

coworker **loke phaw kaing bet** လုပ်ဖော်ကိုင်ဘက်

crazy, insane **yoo** ရှူး

crooked **kauk** ကောက်

cross (v) **kuu** ကူး

crowded, to be **lu myar dae** လူများတယ်

crunchy **kyute** ကြွပ်

culture **yin kyay hmu** ယဉ်ကျေးမှု

cup **khwet** ခွက်

current price, market price   **pauk zay** ပေါက်စျေး

curse, cuss **hsae** ဆဲ

curtain, partition **like kah** လိုက်ကာ

D

dance **ka** က

danger **andayae** အန္တရာယ်

dangerous **andayae shi** အန္တရာယ်ရှိ

dark **hmaung** မှောင်

dawn **ah yone** အာရုဏ်

day **yet** ရက်

debt **akyway** အကြွေး

deflated, to feel [slang] **sait pain dae** စိတ်ပိန်တယ်

delicious, to be **ayathah shi dae** အရသာရှိတယ်

delivery fee **po ga** ပို့ခ

demand **taung** တောင်း

democracy **di mo kray si** ဒီမိုကရေစီ

demon **baluu** ဘီလူး

dense **kyit** ကျစ်

deposit money **ngway thwin** ငွေသွင်း

depressed **sait nyit** စိတ်ညစ်

desk **khone** ခုံ

dessert, sweet dishes **acho bwae** အချိုပွဲ

destroy **phyet** ဖျက်

destroyed, ruined, fallen apart **pyet** ပျက်

dharma hall, prayer hall **damah yone** ဓမ္မာရုံ

die (blunt, not polite) **thay** သေ

difficult **khet khae** ခက်ခဲ

difficulty **akhet akhae** အခက်အခဲ

diner, restaurant customer **sar thone thu** စားသုံးသူ

dining room **htamin sar gan** ထမင်းစားခန်း

dinner **nya nay zah** ညနေစာ

dirty **nyit pat** ညစ်ပတ်

disappointed, feel let down **Sait dut kya dae** စိတ်ဓါတ်ကျတယ်

discounted price **shawt zay** လျှော့စျေး

disdainful **makhant lay zar** မခန့်လေးစား

disease **yaw gah** ရောဂါ

dishonest **kaut kyit** ကောက်ကျစ်

distinct **htoo jar** ထူးခြား

dizzy, drunk **moo dae** မူးတယ်။

doctor **hsayah wun** ဆရာဝန်

dog **khwae** ခွေး

donate **hlu** လှူ

donation **a hlu** အလှူ

door **dagah** တံခါး

door **dagar** တံခါး

draw **an zwae** အံဆွဲ

drink (v) **thauk** သောက်

drinks, refreshment **thauk sayah** သောက်စရာ

drive (a vehicle) **maung** မောင်း

drive a car **kar maung** ကားမောင်း

driver **kar hsayah** ကားဆရာ

drizzle (as in rain) **moe phwa bwae kya** မိုးဖွဲဖွဲကျ

dry **chauk** ခြောက်

dusty **phon htu** ဖုံထူ

duty, obligation **tah won** တာဝန်

E

early **saw** စော

earth (the ground) **myay jee** မြေကြီး

Earth (planet) **Gabah** ကမ္ဘာ

earthquake **ngalyin** ငလျင်

east, eastern **ashayt** အရှေ့

easygoing **aye aye say zay** အေးအေးဆေးဆေး

eat **ar** စား

economy **see bwar yay** စီးပွားရေး

education **pyan nyah yay** ပညာရေး

egg (generic term) **u/oo** ဥ

elderly home, old folks' home **boe bwar yait thah** ဘိုးဘွားရိပ်သာ

eloquent **zagar kywae** စကားကြွယ်

embassy **than yone** သံရုံး

end of the line **lan zone** လမ်းဆုံး

engaged (to be married) **sayt zut** စေ့စပ်

English language **Ingalake sah** အင်္ဂလိပ်စ

English language (spoken only) **Ingalake zagar** အင်္ဂလိပ်စကား

enlarge, cause something to expand **chaet** ချဲ့

entrance **win baut** ဝင်ပေါက်

envious **manah loh** မနာလို

escape **lute** လွတ်

essential **mashi maphyit** မရှိမဖြစ်

establish **ti htaung** တည်ထောင်

eugenia **aung thabay** အောင်သပြေ

Europe **Urawpa** ဥရောပ

evening **nya nay** ညနေ

exceed **poh** ပို

excited **sait hlote shar** စိတ်လှုပ်ရှား

excited (lit, my heart is jumping) **yin khone dae** ရင်ခုန်တယ်

exclusive **thee thant** သီးသန့်

excuse **hsin jay** ဆင်ခြေ

expense (lit., money spent) **htwet ngway** ထွက်ငွေ

expensive **zay kyi** စျေးကြီး

explain **shin pya** ရှင်းပြ

express train **a myan ya htar** အမြန်ရထား

extra, excess **apoh** အပို

eye **myet lone** မျက်လုံး

F

fable **pon byin** ပုံပြင်
face **myet hnah** မျက်နှာ
face towel **myet hna thote pawah** မျက်နှာသုတ်ပဝါ
fall asleep **ait pyaw** အိပ်ပျော်
family **mi thar zu** မိသားစု
far **way** ဝေး
farm (n) **lae** လယ်
farm (v) **lae htune** လယ်ထွန်
farmer **lae thamar** လယ်သမား
fast **myan** မြန်
fat **wa** ဝ
father **aphay** အဖေ
favor, help, assistance **aku anyi** အကူအညီ
feed (n) **nah** နာ
feed (v) **kywae** ကျွေး
ferry fare **gado ga** ကူးတို့ခ
fever, have a **aphyar shi** အဖျားရှိ
fill **phyaet** ဖြည့်
find, look for **shah** ရှာ
fine (punitive fee) **dan ngway** ဒဏ်ငွေ
fine, good, well **kaung** ကောင်း
fine; I'm fine **Nay kaung dae** နေကောင်းတယ်
fire, light **mee** မီး
firefighter **mee thut thamar** မီးသတ်သမား
fireworks **mee ban** မီးပန်း
first, foremost (in a series) **pa hta ma zone** ပထမဆုံး
first sale for the day **zay oo bauk** ဈေးဦးပေါက်
fish **ngar** ငါး
fist **let thee** လက်သီး
flashlight **let hnate dut mee** လက်နှိပ်ဓါတ်မီး
flat tire, have a **bain pout** ဘီးပေါက်
flavor, taste **ayathah** အရသာ
flavorful, rich in taste **hsaint** ဆိမ့်
flea **jaboe** ကြမ်းပိုး
flight attendant, female **lay yin mae** လေယာဉ်မယ်
flight attendant, male **lay yin maung** လေယာဉ်မောင်

flour **jone** ဂျုံ
fluent, skillful **kywon kyin** ကျွမ်းကျင်
fly (v) **pyan** ပျံ
fog, mist **myu** မြူ
follow, chase **lite** လိုက်
food and drinks **asar athauk** အစားအသောက်
food, edibles **sar zayah** စားစရာ
footwear **phanut** ဖိနပ်
for **atwet** အတွက်
forbid **tar myit** တားမြစ်
foreigner **naing ngan jar thar** နိုင်ငံခြားသား
forget **mayt** မေ့
fork **khayin** ခက်ရင်း
fortune teller **bay din hsayah** ဗေဒင်ဆရာ
fragrant, aromatic **hmway** မွှေး
free (someone or something) **hlute** လွှတ်
free; I'm free **Ar dae** အားတယ်
free, at no cost **akha maet** အခမဲ့
French language **Pyinthit sah** ပြင်သစ်စာ
French language (spoken only) **Pyinthit zagar** ပြင်သစ်စကား
fresh, vitalized **lan zan** လန်းဆန်း
Friday **thauk kya nayt** သောကြာနေ့
fried egg **kyet oo jaw** ကြက်ဥကြော်
friend [casual word] **tha ngae jin** သူငယ်ချင်း
friend [formal word] **mait sway** မိတ်ဆွေ
friendly **khin min** ခင်မင်
fritter shop **akyaw zaing** အကြော်ဆိုင်
front of, in **shayt hmah** ရှေ့မှာ
fruit **athee** အသီး
fruit and vegetables **athee aywet** အသီးအရွက်
fry **kyaw** ကြော်
full moon day **la pyayt nayt** လပြည့်နေ့
full moon night **la pyayt nya** လပြည့်ည
full, filled **pyaet** ပြည့်
funeral **a thu ba** အသုဘ
funeral [formal] **zah pana** ဈာပန
futile, unproductive (lit., time and effort wasted) **achain kon lu pin ban** အချိန်ကုန်လူပင်ပန်း
future (n) **anar gat** အနာဂတ်

G

garbage **a hmite** အမှိုက်

garbage bin / can **a hmite pone** အမှိုက်ပုံး

garbage truck **a hmite kar** အမှိုက်ကား

garden, park **pan jan** ပန်းခြံ

gasoline **dut hsee** ဓါတ်ဆီ

gate (of a religious place) **moke** မုဒ်

gaze at **ngay** ငေး

generation **myoe zet** မျိုးဆက်

German language **Jarmun sah** ဂျာမန်စာ

German language (spoken) **Jarmun zagar** ဂျာမန်စကား

get married **min galah hsaung** မင်္ဂလာဆောင်

gift items **let hsaung pyitsee** လက်ဆောင်ပစ္စည်း

give **pay** ပေး

give a speech **maint gun pyaw** မိန့်ခွန်းပြော

give an excuse **hsin jay pay** ဆင်ခြေပေး

give up **let shawt** လက်လျှော့

globetrotter, world traveler **gabah hlaet khayee thae** ကမ္ဘာလှည့်ခရီးသည်

gloves **let ait** လက်အိတ်

glue (n) **kaw** ကော်

glue (verb) (v) **kaw naet kaat** ကော်နဲ့ကပ်

go **thwar** သွား

go, let's go **thwar zo** သွားစို့

go back, return **pyan** ပြန်

go on a trip **kha yee htwet** ခရီးထွက်

go shopping **zay wae** စျေးဝယ်

go to the restroom **ain thah tet** အိမ်သာတက်

goat **hsait** ဆိတ်

goat meat **hsait thar** ဆိတ်သား

God **Phayar** ဘုရား

going well, convenient **a sin pyay** အဆင်ပြေ

gold **shway** ရွှေ

golf (n) **gaut** ဂေါက်

golf (v) **gaut yaik** ဂေါက်ရိုက်

golf ball **gaut thee** ဂေါက်သီး

gong (musical instrument) **maung** မောင်း

good-natured **thabaw kaung** သဘောကောင်း

gossip (v) **atin pyaw** အတင်းပြော

gossip, rumor **kawla hala** ကောလာဟလ

govern, administrate **oak choke** အုပ်ချုပ်

government **a soe ya** အစိုးရ

Great Patron (only used by monks, to address older men) **Dagah ji** ဒကာကြီး

Great Patron (only used by monks, to address older women) **Dagama ji** ဒကာမကြီး

Great Patron (only used by monks, to address younger men) **Dagah lay** ဒကာလေး

Great Patron (only used by monks, to address younger women) **Dagama lay** ဒကာမလေး

green (adj) **a sein yaung** အစိမ်းရောင်

grill (v) **kin** ကင်

grocery store, general goods store **kone zone zaing** ကုန်စုံဆိုင်

guard, take care of **saungt shaut** စောင့်ရှောက်

guest **ae thae** ဧည့်သည်

guesthouse, inn, motel **tae kho gan** တည်းခိုခန်း

guilt **apyit** အပြစ်

guilty **apyit shi** အပြစ်ရှိ

guitar **gitah** ဂီတာ

H

habit **akyint** အကျင့်

hair **zabin** ဆံပင်

hairdresser's shop **zabin hnyut hsaing** ဆံပင်ညှပ်ဆိုင်

hall **khan ma** ခန်းမ

hand towel **let thote pawah** လက်သုတ်ပဝါ

handicraft (the art of making) **let hmu pyin nyah** လက်မှုပညာ

handkerchief **let kaing pawah** လက်ကိုင်ပဝါ

handsome **khant** ခန့်

happen, occur **phyit** ဖြစ်

happy **pyaw** ပျော်

happy; I'm happy **Wun thah dae** ဝမ်းသာတယ်

harbor, pier **sait kaan** ဆိပ်ကမ်း

harbor, pier **thinbaw zait** သင်္ဘောဆိပ်

hard **mah** မာ

harp **saung** စောင်း

hate (n) **a mone** အမုန်း

hate (v)   **mone**   မုန်း
have, exist   **shi**   ရှိ
head nun of a nunnery   **sayah ji**   ဆရာကြီး
headmaster, principal   **kyaung oak**   ကျောင်းအုပ်
headmistress, female principal   **kyaung oak hsayah ma**   ကျောင်းအုပ်ဆရာမ
heal, cure   **ku**   ကု
heart   **athae**   အသည်း
heartbeat   **yin khone than**   ရင်ခုန်သံ
heartbroken   **athae kwae**   အသည်းကွဲ
heavy   **lay**   လေး
help   **ku**   ကု
here   **di hmah**   ဒီမှာ
Here we are! We've arrived!   **Yauk pe**   ရောက်ပြီ
hereditary   **mi yoe phalah**   မိရိုးဖလာ
hide (from people)   **pone**   ပုန်း
hide (something)   **phwet**   ဖွက်
high   **myint**   မြင့်
history   **thamaing**   သမိုင်း
history [formal word]   **yah zawin**   ရာဇဝင်
hobby   **wah thanah**   ဝါသနာ
hold   **kaing**   ကိုင်
holiday   **aloke pait yet**   အလုပ်ပိတ်ရက်
home   **ain**   အိမ်
home address   **ain lait sah**   အိမ်လိပ်စာ
honest   **yoe thar**   ရိုးသား
honey   **pyar yay**   ပျားရည်
horizon   **moe gote set wain**   မိုးကုပ်စက်ဝိုင်း
horse   **myin**   မြင်း
horse-drawn cart   **myin hlae**   မြင်းလှည်း
hospital   **hsay yon**   ဆေးရုံ
host, master or mistress of the house   **ain shin**   အိမ်ရှင်
hot air balloon   **mee bone pyan**   မီးပုံးပျံ
hot season   **nway yah thi**   နွေရာသီ
hotel   **haw tae**   ဟော်တယ်
hotel address   **haw tae lait sah**   ဟော်တယ်လိပ်စာ
hour   **nah yi**   နာရီ
housewarming   **ain tet mingalah**   အိမ်တက်မင်္ဂလာ
how   **bae lo** or **balo**   ဘယ်လို
How is it?   **bae lo nay lae**   ဘယ်လိုနေလဲ

however   **dah bay maet**   ဒါပေမယ့်
hug, embrace (v)   **phet**   ဖက်
human   **lu thar**   လူသား
hungry   **hsah**   ဆာ
hunt   **amae lite**   အမဲလိုက်
hunter   **mote hsoe**   မုဆိုး
hurry, in a   **law**   လော
husband   **lin**   လင်
husband [formal]   **khin boon**   ခင်ပွန်း

I

I [formal, female speaker]   **kyama**   ကျွန်မ
I [formal, male speaker]   **kyanaw**   ကျွန်တော်
ice   **yay khae**   ရေခဲ
ice cream   **yay khae mont**   ရေခဲမုန့်
ice water   **yay khae yay**   ရေခဲရေ
idea   **akyan**   အကြံ
idea, to have   **akyan shi dae**   အကြံရှိတယ်
ill-tempered, malicious   **sait pote**   စိတ်ပုပ်
imagination   **sait koo**   စိတ်ကူး
immature, childlike   **khalay hsan**   ကလေးဆန်
immediately, right away   **chet chin**   ချက်ချင်း
import-export   **yhwin kon htote kon**   သွင်းကုန်ထုတ်ကုန်
important   **ayay kyee**   အရေးကြီး
improve   **toe tet**   တိုးတက်
inch   **let ma**   လက်မ
incidentally, unintentionally   **a hmat tamaet**   အမှတ်တမဲ့
include   **pah**   ပါ
income   **win ngway**   ဝင်ငွေ
increase   **toe**   တိုး
Indian cuisine   **kalar asar asah**   ကုလားအစားအစာ
inexpensive, cheap, abundant   **paw**   ပေါ
influence   **awe zah**   သြဇာ
innocent, guiltless   **apyit ma shi**   အပြစ်မရှိ
insect   **poe**   ပိုး
inside   **a htae**   အထဲ
interested (in something)   **wah thanah pah**   ဝါသနာပါ
introduce   **mait hset**   မိတ်ဆက်
investigate   **sone zan**   စုံစမ်း

invite **phait** ဖိတ်
Islam **Isalam** အစ္စလမ်
itchy **yar** ယား

J

jade **kyaut saine** ကျောက်စိမ်း
Japanese cuisine **Japan asar asah**
  ဂျပန်အစားအစာ
Japanese language **Japan zah** ဂျပန်စာ
Japanese language (spoken only) **Japan**
  zagar ဂျပန်စကား
jar **oh** အိုး
jasmine **zabae** စပယ်
jealous **thawun to** သဝန်တို
jeans **jin** ဂျင်း
jewelry shop **yadanah zaing** ရတနာဆိုင်
job, work, occupation **aloke** အလုပ်
jostle, shove, push **toe** တိုး
journal **jah nae** ဂျာနယ်
judge **tayar thu jee** တရားသူကြီး
jump, leap **khone** ခုန်
just right **ataw bae** အတော်ပဲ
just, fair **hmya ta** မျှတ

K

Kachin (ethnic nationality) **Kachin** ကချင်
Karen (ethnic nationality) **Kayin** ကရင်
Kayah (ethnic nationality) **Kayar** ကယား
keep, confiscate **thain** သိမ်း
keep, put something in a certain
  place **htar** ထား
kettle **khayar** ကရား
key **yhawt** သော့
kick **kan** ကန်
kill **thut** သတ်
kindhearted, sympathetic **thanar dut**
  သနားတတ်
king **shin bayin** ရှင်ဘုရင်
kitchen **mee bo jaung** မီးဖိုချောင်
knee **doo** ဒူး
knife, sword **dar** ဓါး
Korean language **Ko ree yan sah**
  ကိုရီးယန်းစာ
Korean language (spoken) **Ko ree yan zagar**
  ကိုရီးယန်းစကား

kyat (Burmese currency denomination)
  kyut ကျပ်

L

lake **yay kan** ရေကန်
lamb (meat) **thoe thar** သိုးသား
lamp **mee bone** မီးပုံး
land travel, land route **kone lan** ကုန်းလမ်း
last, final (in a series) **nauk hsone**
  နောက်ဆုံး
last offer, final price **nauk hsone zay**
  နောက်ဆုံးဈေး
last stop, end of the line **gate hsone**
  ဂိတ်ဆုံး
late **nauk kya** နောက်ကျ
late, not on time **achain ma hman**
  အချိန်မမှန်
late afternoon **mon lwae** မွန်းလွဲ
laundry detergent **hsut pyah hmont**
  ဆပ်ပြာမှုန့်
law **u baday** ဥပဒေ
lawyer **shayt nay** ရှေ့နေ
leave, depart **htwet** ထွက်
lemon, lime **than ma yah** သံပရာ
library **sah kyi taik** စာကြည့်တိုက်
lie, deceive **lain** လိမ်
lie, recline horizontally **hlae** လှဲ
life, existence **bawa** ဘဝ
light (in weight, in flavor) **pawt** ပေါ့
light festival **mee htun bwae** မီးထွန်းပွဲ
lighter **mee jit** မီးခြစ်
like **kyait** ကြိုက်
lion **chin thaet** ခြင်္သေ့
liquid soap **hsut pyah yay** ဆပ်ပြာရည်
little, a **nae nae** နည်းနည်း
little brother **nyi lay** ညီလေး
little sister **nyi ma lay** ညီမလေး
live **nay** နေ
liver **thae chay** သည်းခြေ
living room **aet gan** ဧည့်ခန်း
living standard **lu nay hmu ahsint atan**
  လူနေမှုအဆင့်အတန်း
lobby, reception area **aet jo khan ma**
  ဧည့်ကြိုခန်းမ
local people **day tha gan** ဒေသခံ

long   shay   ရှည်
long-distance bus   away byay kar
အဝေးပြေးကား
long-distance travel   khayee way   ခရီးဝေး
long for   taan ta   တမ်းတ
long-winded   shah shay   လျှာရှည်
look, watch (v)   kyi   ကြည့်
looks so delicious! (for drinks)   thauk chin
za yar ji   သောက်ချင်စရာကြီး
looks so delicious! (for food)   sar jin za yar
ji   စားချင်စရာကြီး
loose   chaung   ချောင်
lose (something)   pyaut   ပျောက်
loss   asone a shone   အဆုံးအရှုံး
loud   kyae   ကျယ်
lovable   chit sayah kaung
ချစ်စရာကောင်း
love (n)   achit   အချစ်
love (v)   chit   ချစ်
lover, boyfriend, girlfriend   chit thu
ချစ်သူ
low   naint   နိမ့်
lumber   pyin   ပျဉ်
lunar eclipse   la kyut   လကြတ်
lunch   nayt lae zah   နေ့လည်စာ

M

magic   myet hlaet   မျက်လှည့်
magician   myet hlaet hsayah
မျက်လှည့်ဆရာ
magnifier, magnifying glass   hman baloo
မှန်ဘီလူး
mail, letter   sah   စာ
main road   lan ma jee   လမ်းမကြီး
man, male   yauk kyar   ယောက်ျား
man's sarong shop   pasoe hsaing   ပုဆိုးဆိုင်
mango   thayet thee   သရက်သီး
manufacturing business   set hmu loke
ngan   စက်မှုလုပ်ငန်း
many, much, a lot   myar   များ
marionette, puppet   yoke thay   ရုပ်သေး
market   zay   ဈေး
marriage   ain daung   အိမ်ထောင်
married couple, husband and wife
lin mayar   လင်မယား
married, got married   ain daung
kya   အိမ်ထောင်ကျ
mat   phyah   ဖျာ
mature, adult-like   lu jee hsan   လူကြီးဆန်
May you be healthy! (blessing)   Kyan mar
bah zay   ကျန်းမာပါစေ
May you be safe! (blessing)   Bay kin bah
zay   ဘေးကင်းပါစေ
May you be successful! (blessing)   Aung
myin bah zay   အောင်မြင်ပါစေ
May you be wealthy! (blessing)   Chan thar
bah zay   ချမ်းသာပါစေ
May your journey be safe!
(blessing)   Khayee phyaungt bah zay
ခရီးဖြောင့်ပါစေ
meat bun   pout si   ပေါက်စီ
meat, flesh   athar   အသား
medicine   hsay   ဆေး
medicine, to take   hsay thauk   ဆေးသောက်
medicine man, healer   hsay hsayah
ဆေးဆရာ
meditate   tayar htaing   တရားထိုင်
meet   hson   ဆုံ
meet with someone, want to   twayt jin dae
တွေ့ချင်တယ်
meet with someone, don't want to   ma twayt
jin boo   မတွေ့ချင်ဘူး
memorize   hmat   မှတ်
mentally ill [polite]   sait ma hman
စိတ်မမှန်
merchant   kon thae   ကုန်သည်
merit   ku thoh   ကုသိုလ်
mermaid   yay thu ma   ရေသူမ
messy, confusing   shote   ရှုပ်
meteor   oak kah gae   ဥက္ကာခဲ
midday, noon   nayt lae   နေ့လည်
middle   alae   အလယ်
midnight   thagaung or than gaung
သန်းခေါင်
milk (from cow)   nwar no   နွားနို့
milk (n)   no   နို့
mind   sait   စိတ်
minute   ma nit   မိနစ်
mirror   hman   မှန်
misery, trouble   dote kha   ဒုက္ခ

miss (to miss someone) **lwan** လွမ်း

miss the mark **chaw** ချော်

mobile phone **let kaing phone** လက်ကိုင်ဖုန်း

mock, satirize **thayaw** သရော်

monastery **phone ji kyaung** ဘုန်းကြီးကျောင်း

Monday **tanin lah nayt** တနင်္လာနေ့

money **pat hsan** or **pite hsan** ပိုက်ဆံ

money [formal] **ngway** ငွေ

monk ([formal way to address] **U Zin** ဦးဇင်း

monk [less formal way to address] **Phone Phone** ဘုန်းဘုန်း

monsoon season **mote thone yah thi** မုတ်သုန်ရာသီ

month **la** လ

moonlight **la yaung** လရောင်

morning **manet** မနက်

mother **amay** အမေ

mountain **taung** တောင်

move, relocate **shwayt pyaung** ရွှေ့ပြောင်း

MSG, artificial flavor **acho hmont** အချိုမှုန့်

muscle stiffness, to have **akyaw tet** အကြောတက်

museum **pya dike** ပြတိုက်

mushroom **hmoh** မှို

my [familiar, intimate] **nga** ငါ့

my [formal, used by female speaker] **kyama** ကျွန်မ

my [formal, used by male speaker] **kyanawt** ကျွန်တော့်

N

naan bread **nan byah** နံပြား

nanny, babysitter **khalay daine** ကလေးထိန်း

narrow, cramped **kyin** ကျဉ်း

nation **naing ngan** နိုင်ငံ

nationalism **amyoe thar yay** အမျိုးသားရေး

nationality **lu myoe** လူမျိုး

neat, tidy **thut yut** သပ်ရပ်

neck **lae bin** လည်ပင်း

need, necessary **lo aut** လိုအပ်

needle **ut** အပ်

neighborhood **yut kwet** ရပ်ကွက်

news **thadin** သတင်း

newspaper **thadin zah** သတင်းစာ

next, later, after that, then **naut** နောက်

night **nya** ည

night market **nya zay dan** ညစျေးတန်း

no [casual way to say No] **hin in** ဟင့်အင်း

no deal [slang; literally, "It doesn't add up"] **ma kait phoo** မကိုက်ဘူး

noisy, to be **hsu dae** ဆူတယ်

nonprofit **para hita** ပရဟိတ

north, northern **myaut phet** မြောက်ဘက်

not at all **lone wa** လုံးဝ

noun **nun** နာမ်

novice **koyin** ကိုရင်

novitiation, ordination to become monk **shin pyu** ရှင်ပြု

now **agu** အခု

nun **sayah lay** ဆရာလေး

nunnery **thi la shin kyaung** သီလရှင်ကျောင်း

nurse (n) **thu nah byu** သူနာပြု

nurse (v) **pyu zu** ပြုစု

nurture **pyoe htaung** ပျိုးထောင်

O

ocean **pin lae** ပင်လယ်

octopus **yay bawae** ရေဘဝဲ

office **yone** ရုံး

offspring, children **thar thamee** သားသမီး

oil **hsi** ဆီ

old **oh** အို

older brother **ako** အကို

on time **achain hman** အချိန်မှန်

onion fritter **kyet thon kyaw** ကြက်သွန်ကြော်

open the door **dagar phwint** တံခါးဖွင့်

open the window **badin bauk phwint** ပြတင်းပေါက်ဖွင့်

open (turn on) **phwint** ဖွင့်

opening hours (business, shop) **hsaing phwint jain** ဆိုင်ဖွင့်ချိန်

order, give a message   hmar   မှာ
orphan   mi ba maet   မိဘမဲ့
outlaw, fugitive   wayan byay   ဝရမ်းပြေး
outside   apyin   အပြင်
oven   mee boh   မီးဖို
overcast   moe oak   မိုးအုံ့
owe (a debt)   akyway tin   အကြွေးတင်
owner   paing shin   ပိုင်ရှင်
ox-drawn cart   nwar hlae   နွားလှည်း

P

paddy (rice grain with husk)   zabar   စပါး
pagoda   phayar   ဘုရား
painting   baji kar   ပန်းချီ
palace   nan daw   နန်းတော်
palm   let war   လက်ဝါး
paper (writing material)   set ku   စက္ကူ
paper bag   set ku ait   စက္ကူအိတ်
parachute   lay htee   လေထီး
parasite   than gaung   သန်ကောင်
paratha (Indian bread)   palata   ပလာတာ
park   pan jan   ပန်းခြံ
parliament   hlute taw   လွှတ်တော်
part ways   khwae khwah   ခွဲခွာ
part ways, be separated   kwae kwah   ကွဲကွာ
pass away [die]   kwae lun   ကွယ်လွန်
passenger   khayee thae   ခရီးသည်
past (n)   atate   အတိတ်
patient   sait shay   စိတ်ရှည်
patron, regular customer   phauk thae   ဖောက်သည်
pay tax   akhon hsaung   အခွန်ဆောင်
peace   nyain jan yay   ငြိမ်းချမ်းရေး
pearl   palae   ပုလဲ
pen name   kalaung nam mae   ကလောင်နာမည်
pencil   khae dan   ခဲတံ
perfume   yay hmway   ရေမွှေး
person   lu   လူ
personal affairs   ko yay ko dah   ကိုယ်ရေးကိုယ်တာ
pharmacy, medicine shop   hsay zaing   ဆေးဆိုင်
phone, make a phone call   phone hset or phone khaw   ဖုန်းဆက် or ဖုန်းခေါ်

photograph (n)   dut pone   ဓါတ်ပုံ
photograph (v)   dut pone yite   ဓါတ်ပုံရိုက်
pickpocket   gabite hnite   ခါးပိုက်နှိုက်
pickup and drop-off, transportation   akyo apo   အကြိုအပို့
pig   wet   ဝက်
pilgrimage, visiting shrines and temples   phayar boo   ဘုရားဖူး
pill   hsay lone   ဆေးလုံး
pilot   lay yin hmoo   လေယာဉ်မှူး
pine   htin yuu or htin shoo   ထင်းရှူး
plain tea   yay nway jan   ရေနွေးကြမ်း
plan, program   asi azin   အစီအစဉ်
plane ticket   lay yin let hmut   လေယာဉ်လက်မှတ်
plant (n)   apin   အပင်
plant (v)   site   စိုက်
plant, factory   set yone   စက်ရုံ
plastic bag   palat satit ait   ပလတ်စတစ်အိတ်
plate   bagan   ပန်းကန်
play   gazar   ကစား
play (theatrical [n])   pya zut   ပြဇာတ်
play guitar   gitah tee   ဂီတာတီး
playground   gazar gwin   ကစားကွင်း
playing card   phae   ဖဲ
please excuse me! Please don't mind me   sait mashi bah naet   စိတ်မရှိပါနဲ့
please fix it for me   pyin pay bah   ပြင်ပေးပါ
polite   yin kyay   ယဉ်ကျေး
politics   naing ngan yay   နိုင်ငံရေး
pool   aing   အိုင်
poor   hsin yae   ဆင်းရဲ
poor thing!   thanar zayah lay   သနားစရာလေး
popsicle   yay gae jaung   ရေခဲချောင်း
pork   wet thar   ဝက်သား
postman   sah po thamar   စာပို့သမား
poultry, chicken meat   kyet thar   ကြက်သား
pout, brood (v)   sait kauk   စိတ်ကောက်
power outage, have a   mee pyet   မီးပျက်
prayer bead string   sait badee   စိပ်ပုတီး
predawn, early morning, wee hours   way li way lin   ဝေလီဝေလင်း
prefix for adult male   Ko   ကို
prefix for mature man   U   ဦး
prefix for mature woman   Daw   ဒေါ်

prefix for young male   **Maung**   မောင်
prefix for young woman   **Ma**   မ
pregnant woman   **mee nay thae**   မီးနေသည်
present (time) (n)   **pyit sote pan**   ပစ္စုပွန်
pressure   **phi ar**   ဖိအား
pretty   **hla**   လှ
prevent   **tar**   တား
prince, actor   **minthar**   မင်းသား
princess, actress   **minthamee**   မင်းသမီး
printer, press   **pone hnate set**   ပုံနှိပ်စက်
prison   **htaung**   ထောင်
private car   **ko baing kar**   ကိုယ်ပိုင်ကား
private, self-owned   **ko baing**   ကိုယ်ပိုင်
problem   **pyet thanah**   ပြဿနာ
procrastinate   **achain hswae**   အချိန်ဆွဲ
profit   **amyat**   အမြတ်
project   **simun gain**   စီမံကိန်း
promise (n)   **gadi**   ကတိ
promise (v)   **gadi pay**   ကတိပေး
pronounce   **athun htwet**   အသံထွက်
pronunciation   **athan dwet**   အသံထွက်
prophesize, predict someone's fortune
  bay din haw   ဗေဒင်ဟော
proverb   **zagabone**   စကားပုံ
put pressure on   **phi ar pay**   ဖိအားပေး

Q

quake (v)   **ngalyin hlote**   ငလျင်လှုပ်
quarrel   **zagar myar**   စကားများ
queen   **bayin ma**   ဘုရင်မ
question   **may gun**   မေးခွန်း
quickly   **myan myan**   မြန်မြန်
quiet   **tait sait**   တိတ်ဆိတ်
quiet, to be   **nar aye dae**   နားအေးတယ်
quiet, [a person] of few words   **zagar nae**
  စကားနည်း
quietly   **tait tait sait sait**   တိတ်တိတ်ဆိတ်ဆိတ်

R

racism   **lu myoe khwae jar yay**
  လူမျိုးခွဲခြားရေး
radio   **ray diyoh**   ရေဒီယို
rain   **moe**   မိုး
raincoat   **moe gah ain ji**   မိုးကာအင်္ကျီ
raining heavily   **moe thae**   မိုးသည်း

rainy season   **moe yah thi**   မိုးရာသီ
raise, erect   **htaung**   ထောင်
rat   **kywet**   ကြွက်
razor blade   **mote hsait yait dar**
  မုတ်ဆိတ်ရိတ်ဓါး
read   **phat**   ဖတ်
read someone's future, tell someone's
  fortune   **bay din kyi**   ဗေဒင်ကြည့်
reading glasses   **myet hman**   မျက်မှန်
really big!   **a kyi ji**   အကြီးကြီး
really long!   **a shay ji**   အရှည်ကြီး
really short (in length)   **to to lay**   တိုတိုလေး
really short! (in height)   **pu pu lay**   ပုပုလေး
really small!   **thay thay lay**   သေးသေးလေး
really tall!   **a myint ji**   အမြင့်ကြီး
really, truly   **dagae**   တကယ်
reception   **aet gan bwae**   ဧည့်ခံပွဲ
receptionist   **aet jo sayay**   ဧည့်ကြိုစာရေး
reclining chair   **palet kala htaing**
  ပက်လက်ကုလားထိုင်
red color   **a ni yaung**   အနီရောင်
refrigerator   **yaygae thit tah**   ရေခဲသတ္တာ
refugee   **dote kha thae**   ဒုက္ခသည်
religion   **bah thah yay**   ဘာသာရေး
remember   **thadi ya**   သတိရ
remember   **hmat mi**   မှတ်မိ
remorse, regret   **naung da**   နောင်တ
remove one's footwear   **phanut chute**
  ဖိနပ်ချွတ်
rent   **hngar**   ငှား
repair, to fix   **pyin**   ပြင်
reporter   **thadin dauk**   သတင်းထောက်
respect   **lay zar**   လေးစား
rest   **nar**   နား
restaurant   **sar thauk hsaing**
  စားသောက်ဆိုင်
rice (uncooked)   **hsan**   ဆန်
rich   **chan thah**   ချမ်းသာ
rich person   **tha htay**   သူဌေး
richly flavored   **lay**   လေး
ride (a vehicle)   **see**   စီး
ride a bicycle   **set bain see**   စက်ဘီးစီး
ride a car   **kar see**   ကားစီး
ring   **let soot**   လက်စွပ်
ripe   **hmaet**   မှည့်

road, street **lan** လမ်း
rob **lu** လု
robe (a monk's) **thin gan** သင်္ကန်း
rock **kyauk** ကျောက်
room **akhan** အခန်း
roomy, loose, relaxed fit **chaung** ချောင်
root, origin **zit myit** ဇစ်မြစ်
rose **hnin ze** နှင်းဆီ
rough **kyan** ကြမ်း
rubber band **thayay gwin** သားရေကွင်း
ruby **badamyar** ပတ္တမြား
rude **yaing** ရိုင်း
rules **see kan** စည်းကမ်း
rumor **kawlah hala** ကောလာဟလ
run **pyay** ပြေး
run out of (gas) **dut hsee kon** ဓါတ်ဆီကုန်

S

sad **wun nae** ဝမ်းနည်း
safebox **mee gan thit tah** မီးခံသေတ္တာ
sailor, seaman **thin maw thar** သင်္ဘောသား
salt **hsar** ဆား
salty **ngan** ငံ
Saturday **sanay nayt** စနေနေ့
scale (for weighing) **chain gwin** ချိန်ခွင်
scary **kyauk sayah kaung** ကြောက်စရာကောင်း
scatter, sprinkle **kyae** ကြဲ
school teacher **kyaung hsayah** ကျောင်းဆရာ
school, monastery **kyaung** ကျောင်း
schoolmate, classmate **kyaung nay bet tha nge jin** ကျောင်းနေဘက်သူငယ်ချင်း
scratch **kote** ကုတ်
sculpture, carved figurines **babu yoke** ပန်းပု
sea travel, sea route **yay lan** ရေလမ်း
season **yah thi** ရာသီ
see, witness, meet **twayt** တွေ့
selfish **dagoh gaung san** တစ်ကိုယ်ကောင်းဆန်
sell **yaung** ရောင်း
send **po** ပို့
send a letter **sah po** စာပို့
sentence **wut kya** ဝါကျ
set up camp **sakhan cha** စခန်းချ

settle the bill **ngway chay** ငွေချေ
sew **chote** ချုပ်
sex **lain** လိင်
shade, shadow **a yait** အရိပ်
shame **ashet** အရှက်
shampoo **gaung shaw yay** ခေါင်းလျှော်ရည်
Shan (ethnic nationality) **Shan** ရှမ်း
Shan noodle salad **Shan khauk swe** ရှမ်းခေါက်ဆွဲ
shawl **chone pawah** ခြုံပဝါ
shirt **ainji** အင်္ကျီ
shirt shop **ain jee hsaing** အင်္ကျီဆိုင်
shoe **shuu phanut** ရှူးဖိနပ်
shoot a movie **yoke shin yite** ရုပ်ရှင်ရိုက်
shoot video **bwi diyo yite** ဗီဒီယိုရိုက်
shop **zay hsaing** စျေးဆိုင်
shore, beach **kan jay** ကမ်းခြေ
short (for objects) **to** တို
short (for people) **pu** ပု
short-tempered, angry **sait to** စိတ်တို
shoulder **pakhone** ပုခုံး
shout, scream (v) **aw** အော်
show (v) **pya** ပြ
shower (v) **yay choe** ရေချိုး
shower room **yay choe gan** ရေချိုးခန်း
shrimp **bazun** ပုဇွန်
shrine, pagoda **zedi** စေတီ
sick **phyar** ဖျား
sidecar (trishaw) **sike kar** ဆိုက်ကား
silver **ngway** ငွေ
simple **yoe** ရိုး
sing **thachin hsoe** သီချင်းဆို
singer **a hsoh daw** အဆိုတော်
single man, bachelor **lu byoh** လူပျို
single woman, bachelorette **apyoh** အပျို
sister **nyi ma** ညီမ
sister (older) **ama** အမ
ait **htaing** ထိုင်
skirt **gah wune** ဂါဝန်
sky **kaung kin** ကောင်းကင်
sleepy **ait ngite** အိပ်ငိုက်
slim, willowy **thwae** သွယ်
slow **hnay** နှေး
slowly **phyae phyae** ဖြေးဖြေး
small **thay** သေး

smile (v) **pyone** ပြုံး
smile (n) **apyone** အပြုံး
smoking pipe **hsay dan** ဆေးတံ
smooth **chaw** ချော
snack **mont** မုန့်
snack shop **mont zaing** မုန့်ဆိုင်
snow **hnin** နှင်း
So much fun! **pyaw za yar ji**
ပျော်စရာကြီး
soap **hsut pyah** ဆပ်ပြာ
social **lu hmu yay** လူမှုရေး
sock **chay zoot** ခြေစွပ်
soft **pyawt** ပျော့
solar eclipse **nay kyut** နေကြတ်
soldier **sit thar** စစ်သား
something a bit bigger **nae nae kyi dah**
နည်းနည်းကြီးတာ
something a bit longer **nae nae shay dah**
နည်းနည်းရှည်တာ
something a bit shorter **nae nae to dah**
နည်းနည်းတိုတာ
something a bit smaller **nae nae thay dah**
နည်းနည်းသေးတာ
sometimes **takhah talay** တစ်ခါတစ်လေ
song **thachin** သီချင်း
sour **chin** ချဉ်
south, southern **taung bet** တောင်ဘက်
speak **pyaw** ပြော
specialist (medical) **thamar daw**
သမားတော်
speech **maint gon** မိန့်ခွန်း
spelling **sah lone baung** စာလုံးပေါင်း
spicy **sut** စပ်
spirit medium **nat gadaw** နတ်ကတော်
spirits, angels **nut** နတ်
spit out **htway** ထွေး
split apart, separate **khwae** ခွဲ
spoken word, language **zagar** စကား
spoon **zune** ဇွန်း
sports **ar gazar** အားကစား
squander, waste **phyone** ဖြုန်း
staff, clerk **wun dan** ဝန်ထမ်း
stand **yut** ရပ်
star **kyae** ကြယ်
star flower **khayay** ခရေ

stay (v) **tae** တည်း
steal **khoe** ခိုး
steam cook (v) **paung** ပေါင်း
sticky **see** စေး
stinky **nun** နံ
stocky **htwar** ထွား
stomach **bait** ဗိုက်
stop **yut** ရပ်
store, shop **hsaing** ဆိုင်
story, plot **zut lan** ဇာတ်လမ်း
straight ahead **shae tae tae** ရှေ့တည့်တည့်
strange **htoo zan** ထူးဆန်း
stranger **lu zain** or **thazain** လူစိမ်း or သူစိမ်း
strike, hit **yait** ရိုက်
stroll, take a **lan shauk** လမ်းလျှောက်
stubborn **gaung mah** ခေါင်းမာ
student **kyaung thar** ကျောင်းသား
student (female) **kyaung thu** ကျောင်းသူ
successful **aung myin** အောင်မြင်
sue, file a suit against someone **tayar swae**
တရားစွဲ
suffer from jet lag (lit., travel fatigue) **kha
yee pan** ခရီးပန်း
sugar **thajar** သကြား
sunflower **nay jar ban** နေကြာပန်း
sunburn **nay laung** နေလောင်
Sunday **tanin ga nway nayt** တနင်္ဂနွေနေ့
sunglasses **nay gah myet hman**
နေကာမျက်မှန်
sunlight **nay yaung** နေရောင်
sunrise **nay htwet chaing** နေထွက်ချိန်
sunset **nay win jain** နေဝင်ချိန်
supervisor **a htet ayar shi** အထက်အရာရှိ
support **htaut pant** ထောက်ပံ့
sure, certain **thay jah** သေချာ
sure; I'm sure of it **thay jah dae**
သေချာတယ်
surprised, amazed **aut awe** အံ့သြ
surroundings, environment **put wun kyin**
ပတ်ဝန်းကျင်
sweat (n) **chway** ချွေး
sweat (v) **chway htwet** ချွေးထွက်
sweet **cho** ချို
sweet tea **let phet yay** လက်ဖက်ရည်
swim **yay koo** ရေကူး

swimming pool **yay koo kan** ရေကူးကန်
sympathize **thanar** သနား
sympathy, to have for someone **kyin nah** ကြင်နာ

T

table **zabwae** စားပွဲ
tailoring shop **aat chote hsaing** အပ်ချုပ်ဆိုင်
take **yu** ယူ
take out, bring out **htote** ထုတ်
talkative **zagar myar** စကားများ
tall **myint** မြင့်
taste, flavor **ayathah** အရသာ
tattoo (n) **say hmin jaung** ဆေးမင်ကြောင်
tax **akhon** အခွန်
taxi, cab **a hngar kar** အငှားကား
teach **thin** သင်
tea leaf salad **laphet thoke** လက်ဖက်သုပ်
tease (v) **nauk** နောက်
teashop **laphet yay zaing** လက်ဖက်ရည်ဆိုင်
technology **nee pyin nyah** နည်းပညာ
technology business **nee pyin nyah loke ngan** နည်းပညာလုပ်ငန်း
teeth **thwar** သွား
temporary address **yah ye lait sah** ယာရီလိပ်စာ
tender, soft **nu** နု
testy, reactionary **a hti makhan** အထိမခံ
tha na kha (aromatic wood paste used as cosmetic) **tha-na-khar** သနပ်ခါး
that **dah** ဒါ
that object, that thing **ho hah** ဟိုဟာ
theatrical play **pya zat** ပြဇတ်
there **ho hmah** ဟိုမှာ
therefore **dah jaunt** ဒါကြောင့်
thick (as in books) **htuh** ထူ
thief **thakhoe** သူခိုး
thin **pain** ပိန်
thin, flimsy **par** ပါး
this object, this thing **di hah** ဒီဟာ
thorn **hsu** ဆူး
thousand **htaung or daung** ထောင်
thumb **let ma** လက်မ

thunder **moe joe** မိုးကြိုး
thunder strikes **moe joe pyit** မိုးကြိုးပစ်
Thursday **kyah thah baday nayt** ကြာသပတေးနေ့
ticket **let hmut** လက်မှတ်
tide **di yay** ဒီရေ
tie, fasten **chi** ချည်
tiger **kyar** ကျား
tight **kyut** ကျပ်
time **achain** အချိန်
time, to have **achain shi dae** အချိန်ရှိတယ်
time, don't have **achain mashi boo** အချိန်မရှိဘူး
time to go to work (also time to go to work/ time to shut down work/timetable) **aloke thwar jain** အလုပ်သွားချိန်
time to shut down work **aloke hsin jain** အလုပ်ဆင်းချိန်
timetable **achain zayar** အချိန်ဇယား
tired, weary **pin ban** ပင်ပန်း
title, headline **gaung zin** ခေါင်းစဉ်
tofu **to hoo** or **to foo** တိုဟူး
toilet paper **ain thah set ku** အိမ်သာစက္ကူ
toilet, restroom **ain thah** အိမ်သာ
tolerate **thee khan** သည်းခံ
tongue **shah** လျာ
toothbrush **thaboot tan** သွားပွတ်တံ
toothpaste **shwar dite hsay** သွားတိုက်ဆေး
toothpick **thwaa jaa htoo dan** သွားကြားထိုးတံ
top (choice, selection) **let yway zin** လက်ရွေးစင်
touch (v) **hti** ထိ
towel **pawah** ပဝါ
toy shop **ayoke hsaing** အရုပ်ဆိုင်
traditional **yoe yah** ရိုးရာ
traffic light **mi point** မီးပွိုင့်
train **ya htar** ရထား
train ticket **ya htar let hmut** ရထားလက်မှတ်
translator **zagabyan** စကားပြန်
transportation **thae yu po hsaung yay** သယ်ယူပို့ဆောင်ရေး
trap **htaung jaut** ထောင်ချောက်
travel **kha yee thwar** ခရီးသွား

travel agency **kha yee thwar loke ngan** ခရီးသွားလုပ်ငန်း

travel guide, tour guide **lan bya** လမ်းပြ

traveler **kha yee thae** ခရီးသည်

tray **lin ban** လင်ပန်း

treasure, jewel **yadanah** ရတနာ

tree **thit pin** သစ်ပင်

trip and fall **chaw lae** ချော်လဲ

trip, journey **kha yee** ခရီး

truck **kone tin kar** ကုန်တင်ကား

Tuesday **inga nayt** အင်္ဂါနေ့

turn around, turn back **naut hlae** နောက်လှည့်

turn left **bae choe** ဘယ်ချိုး

turn off the light **mee pait** မီးပိတ်

turn on the light **mee phwint** မီးဖွင့်

turn right **nyar choe** ညာချိုး

TV **TV** တီဗွီ

twin **a hmwah** အမွှာ

U

ugly **yote hsoe** ရုပ်ဆိုး

umbrella **khauk htee** ခေါက်ထီး

umbrella **htee** ထီး

uncle **oo lay** ဦးလေး

understand **nar lae dae** နားလည်တယ်

understand, don't **nar ma lae boo** နားမလည်ဘူး

understanding **nar lae hmu** နားလည်မှု

underwear **a twin gan awute** အတွင်းခံအဝတ်

uninterested, half-hearted **sait mapah boo** စိတ်မပါဘူး

unnecessary **ma lo boo** မလိုဘူး

unsure about something **ma thay jah boo** မသေချာဘူး

untrue **ma hote** မဟုတ်

urinate **thay pauk** သေးပေါက်

use **thone** သုံး

useful **a thone kya** အသုံးကျ

V

vegetarian **thet thut lwut** သက်သတ်လွတ်

vendors, merchants **zay thae** စျေးသည်

verb **kari yah** ကြိယာ

very **thaik** သိပ်

village **ywah** ရွာ

visit **thwar lae** သွားလည်

vocabulary **waw hah ra** ဝေါဟာရ

voice **athan** အသံ

volunteer (v) **loke ar pay** လုပ်အားပေး

volunteer (n) **loke ar bay** လုပ်အားပေး

W

wait **saungt** စောင့်

wait, to hope for, to anticipate **hmyaw** မျှော်

waiter, waitress **zabwae doe** စားပွဲထိုး

wake up **noe lah** နိုးလာ

walk **shauk** လျှောက်

walk fast **myan myan shauk** မြန်မြန်လျှောက်

walk slowly **phyae phyae shauk** ဖြေးဖြေးလျှောက်

wall **nan yan** နံရံ

want to come **lah chin dae** လာချင်တယ်

want to rest **nar jin dae** နားချင်တယ်

want to sleep **ait chin dae** အိပ်ချင်တယ်

war **sit** စစ်

wash **hsay** ဆေး

wash clothes **awut shaw** အဝတ်လျှော်

wash one's face **myet hnah thit** မျက်နှာသစ်

wash one's feet **chay hsay** ခြေဆေး

wash one's hands **let hsay** လက်ဆေး

washing machine **awute shaw zet** အဝတ်လျှော်စက်

waste money **pa hsan phyone** or **pite hsan phyone** ပိုက်ဆံဖြုန်း

waste time **achain phyone** အချိန်ဖြုန်း

watch TV **TV kyi** တီဗွီကြည့်

waterfall **yay dagon** ရေတံခွန်

watermelon **phayae the** ဖရဲသီး

wealthy **chan thah** ချမ်းသာ

weapon **let net** လက်နက်

wear (clothing, jewelry) **wute** ဝတ်

wedding **min galah hsaung** မင်္ဂလာဆောင်

Wednesday **boke da hoo nayt** ဗုဒ္ဓဟူးနေ့

week **pat, bat** ပတ်

well-behaved **lain mah** လိမ္မာ

west, western **anaut** အနောက်

Western cuisine **anauk taing asar asah** အနောက်တိုင်းအစားအစာ

Westerner, foreigner [slang] **boh** ဘို

Westerners' cuisine [slang] **bo zah** ဘိုစာ

wet **soh** စို

what **bah** ဘာ

where **bae** ဘယ်

Where is it? **Bae hmah lae** ဘယ်မှာလဲ

while, been a; it's been too long **kyah be** ကြာပြီ

white color **a phyu yaung** အဖြူရောင်

who **bae thu** or **bathu** ဘယ်သူ

wife **mayar** မယား

wife [formal] **zanee** ဇနီး

win, defeat (v) **naing** နိုင်

window **badin bauk** ပြတင်းပေါက်

wish comes true **hsu taung pyaet** ဆုတောင်းပြည့်

withdraw money **ngway htote** ငွေထုတ်

wizard **zawgyi** ဇော်ဂျီ

woman, female **main ma** မိန်းမ

woman, girlfriend, fiancée **amyo thamee** အမျိုးသမီး

woman's sarong shop **htamain hsaing** ထဘီဆိုင်

wood **thit thar** သစ်သား

wood (forest) **taw** တော

work **a loke** အလုပ်

worker **a loke thamar** အလုပ်သမား

working hours **alote lote chain** အလုပ်ချိန်

worry (v) **sait pu** စိတ်ပူ

worst, the **a hsoe zone** အဆိုးဆုံး

wristwatch **let pat nah yi** လက်ပတ်နာရီ

write **yay** ရေး

wrong **hmar** မှား

x-ray (n) **dut hman** ဓါတ်မှန်

x-ray (v) **dut hmaan yite** ဓါတ်မှန်ရိုက်

Y

year **hnit** နှစ်

yellow color **a wah yaung** အဝါရောင်

yes (only used in conversations with monks and nuns) **tin bah** တင်ပါ

you [familiar, intimate] **min** မင်း

you [formal, used by female speaker] **shin** ရှင်

you [formal, used by male speaker] **khamyar** ခင်ဗျား

young **ngae** ငယ်

young people **lu ngae** လူငယ်

younger brother (if you're a man) **nyi** ညီ

younger brother (if you're a woman) **maung** မောင်

your disciple (used by men as first-person pronoun in conversation with monks) **da baet daw** တပည့်တော်

your disciple (used by women as first-person pronoun in conversation with monks) **da baet daw ma** တပည့်တော်မ

youth **lu ngae** လူငယ်

youthful **nu** နု

Z

zoo **tarait hsan yone** တိရိစ္ဆာန်ရုံ

BURMESE–ENGLISH COMMON WORDS AND PHRASES

Words associated with time

amyae အမြဲ always

ayin aput အရင်အပတ် last week

ayin hnit အရင်နှစ် last year

ayin la အရင်လ last month

de aput ဒီအပတ် this week

de hnit ဒီနှစ် this year

de la ဒီလ this month

de nayt ဒီနေ့ today

hnit နှစ် year

khana khana ခဏခဏ often, every once in a while

la လ month
manayt ga မနေ့က yesterday
manet phyan မနက်ဖြန် tomorrow
nauk aput နောက်အပတ် next week
nauk hnit နောက်နှစ် next year
nauk la နောက်လ next month
nauk nayt နောက်နေ့ the next day, tomorrow
nayt နေ့ day
put ပတ် week
takhah talay တစ်ခါတစ်လေ sometimes

Words associated with nature

chaung ချောင်း creek
gabah ကမ္ဘာ world
kaung kin ကောင်းကင် sky
lay လေ wind
myay jee မြေကြီး earth
mee မီး fire
myit မြစ် river
pan ပန်း flower
pin lae ပင်လယ် ocean, sea
tain တိမ် cloud
taung တောင် mountain
taw တော forest
thin pin သစ်ပင် tree
yay ရေ water

Words associated with food

amae thar အမဲသား beef
athee aywet အသီးအရွက် fruit and
  vegetables
ayatha ma shi boo အရသာမရှိဘူး it's not
  delicious
ayathar shi dae အရသာရှိတယ် it's delicious
bagan ပန်းကန် plate
chin ချဉ် sour
cho ချို sweet
hsaint ဆိမ့် rich in flavor, umami
khar ခါး bitter
khayin ခက်ရင်း fork
khwet ခွက် cup
kyet thar ကြက်သား poultry
ngah ငါး fish

ngan ငံ salty
sar စား to eat
sut စပ် spicy
thauk သောက် to drink
thet that lute သက်သတ်လွတ် meatless
  (lit., killing-free)
tu တူ chopsticks
wet thar ဝက်သား pork
zoon ဇွန်း spoon

Common counting words

htae ထည် counting word for pieces of
  clothing
kaung ကောင် counting word for animals
khu ခု counting word for item (inanimate
  objects like sculpture and toys)
khwet ခွက် counting word for cups of liquid
lone လုံး counting word for fruits and round
  objects
nya ည counting word for number of
  nights/evenings
yauk ယောက် counting word for number
  of persons
yet ရက် counting word for number of days

Words associated with transport

away pyay kar အဝေးပြေးကား long-
  distance bus
bu dah ဘူတာ train station
but sakar ဘတ်စ်ကား bus
gate ဂိတ် gate
hmut taing မှတ်တိုင် bus stop
hsait ဆိုက် to land (planes and ships only)
kar ကား car
kar gate ကားဂိတ် bus terminal
lay yin လေယာဉ် plane
lay zait လေဆိပ် airport
let hmut လက်မှတ် ticket
see စီး to ride
thin maw zait or thin baw zait
  သင်္ဘောဆိပ် harbor
ya htar ရထား train
yauk ရောက် to arrive

BURMESE–ENGLISH GLOSSARY

A

a aye mi   အအေးမိ   to catch a cold

a hla pyin hsaing   အလှပြင်ဆိုင်   beauty salon

a hlu   အလှူ   donation

a hmat tamaet   အမှတ်တမဲ့   incidentally, unintentionally

a hmwah   အမွှာ   twin

a hmite   အမှိုက်   garbage

a hmite kar   အမှိုက်ကား   garbage truck

a hmite pone   အမှိုက်ပုံး   garbage bin / can

a hngar kar   အငှားကား   taxi, cab

a hsoe zone   အဆိုးဆုံး   the worst

a hsoh daw   အဆိုတော်   singer

a htae   အထဲ   inside

a htet ayar shi   အထက်အရာရှိ   supervisor

a hti makhan   အထိမခံ   untouchable, testy, reactionary

a htin kyi   အထင်ကြီး   to look up to, to admire

a kaung zone   အကောင်းဆုံး   the best

a kyi ji   အကြီးကြီး   really big!

a loke   အလုပ်   work

a myan ya htar   အမြန်ရထား   express train

a myar ji   အများကြီး   a lot

a myint ji   အမြင့်ကြီး   really tall

a net yaung   အနက်ရောင်   black color

a ni yaung   အနီရောင်   red color

a nu pyin nyah   အနုပညာ   art, creative arts

a nu pyin nyah loke ngan   အနုပညာလုပ်ငန်း   art business

a phyu yaung   အဖြူရောင်   white color

a pyah yaung   အပြာရောင်   blue color

a sein yaung   အစိမ်းရောင်   green color

a shay ji   အရှည်ကြီး   really long

a sin pyay   အဆင်ပြေ   going well, convenient

a soe ya   အစိုးရ   government

a thone kya   အသုံးကျ   useful

a thu ba   အသုဘ   funeral

a twin gan awute   အတွင်းခံအဝတ်   underwear

a wah yaung   အဝါရောင်   yellow color

a yait   အရိပ်   shade, shadow

a yoe   အရိုး   bone

aat chote hsaing   အပ်ချုပ်ဆိုင်   tailoring shop

achain   အချိန်   time

achain hman   အချိန်မှန်   to be on time

achain hswae   အချိန်ဆွဲ   to procrastinate

achain kon lu pin ban   အချိန်ကုန်လူပင်ပန်း   futile, unproductive (lit., time and effort wasted)

achain ma hman   အချိန်မမှန်   not on time

achain ma ywae   အချိန်မရွေး   anytime

achain mashi boo   အချိန်မရှိဘူး   I don't have time

achain phyone   အချိန်ဖြုန်း   to waste time

achain shi dae   အချိန်ရှိတယ်   I have time

achain zayar   အချိန်ဇယား   timetable

achit   အချစ်   love (n)

acho bwae   အချိုပွဲ   dessert, sweet dishes

acho hmont   အချိုမှုန့်   MSG, artificial flavor

aet gan   ဧည့်ခန်း   living room

aet gan bwae   ဧည့်ခံပွဲ   reception

aet jo khan ma   ဧည့်ကြိုခန်းမ   lobby, reception area

aet jo sayay   ဧည့်ကြိုစာရေး   receptionist

aet thae   ဧည့်သည်   guest

agu   အခု   now

ain   အိမ်   home

ain daung   အိမ်ထောင်   marriage

ain daung kya   အိမ်ထောင်ကျ   to be married, to get married

ain hsaut   အိမ်ဆောက်   to build a home

ain jee hsaing   အင်္ကျီဆိုင်   shirt shop

ain lait sah   အိမ်လိပ်စာ   home address

ain shin   အိမ်ရှင်   host, master or mistress of the house

ain tet mingalah   အိမ်တက်မင်္ဂလာ   housewarming

ain thah   အိမ်သာ   toilet, restroom

ain thah set ku   အိမ်သာစက္ကူ   toilet paper

ain thah tet   အိမ်သာတက်   to use the restroom

aing   အိုင်   pool

ainji chaung   အင်္ကျီချောင်   shirt is loose

ainji kyut   အင်္ကျီကြပ်   shirt is tight

ainji mataw အင်္ကျီမတော် shirt doesn't fit

ainji pwa အင်္ကျီပွ shirt is oversize, baggy

air kon အဲယားကွန်း air-conditioning

ait အိတ် bag

ait chin dae အိပ်ချင်တယ် want to sleep

ait khaan အိပ်ခန်း bedroom

ait ngite tae အိပ်ငိုက်တယ်။ feeling sleepy

ait pyaw အိပ်ပျော် to fall asleep

akha maet အခမဲ့ free, at no cost

akhan အခန်း room

akhan anar အခမ်းအနား ceremony

akhant mathint အခန့်မသင့် accidentally

akhet akhae အခက်အခဲ difficulty

akhon အခွန် tax

akhon hsaung အခွန်ဆောင် to pay tax

ako အကို older brother

aku anyi အကူအညီ favor, help, assistance

akwyay tin အကြွေးတင် to owe a debt

akyan အကြံ idea

akyan shi dae အကြံရှိတယ် I have an idea

akyaung အကြောင်း about (something)

akyaw tet အကြောတက် to have muscle stiffness

akyaw zaing အကြော်ဆိုင် fritter shop

akyint အကျင့် habit

akyo apo အကြိုအပို့ pickup and drop-off, transportation

akyoe zaung အကျိုးဆောင် agent, broker (for business negotiations)

akyway အကြွေး debt

alae အလယ် middle

aloke အလုပ် job, work, occupation

aloke hsin jain အလုပ်ဆင်းချိန် time to shut down work

aloke pait yet အလုပ်ပိတ်ရက် holiday

aloke thamar အလုပ်သမား worker

aloke thwar jain အလုပ်သွားချိန် time to go to work

alote lote chain အလုပ်ချိန် working hours

alote myar အလုပ်များ busy

ama အမ big sister

amae lite အမဲလိုက် to go hunting

amae thar အမဲသား beef

amay အမေ mother

Amay yi ka အမေရိက America

amyae အမြဲ always

amyat အမြတ် profit

amyee အမြည်း appetizer, cocktail snack

amyo thamee အမျိုးသမီး woman, girlfriend, fiancée

amyo thar အမျိုးသား boyfriend, fiancé

amyoe thar yay အမျိုးသားရေး nationalism

an zwae အံဆွဲ draw

anar gat အနာဂတ် the future

anar yu jain အနားယူချိန် break time

anauk taing asar asah အနောက်တိုင်းအစားအစာ Western cuisine

anaut အနောက် the west, western

andayae အန္တရာယ် danger

andayae shi အန္တရာယ်ရှိ dangerous

ant awe အံ့သြ to be surprised, amazed

aphay အဖေ father

aphyar shi အဖျားရှိ to have a fever

aphyay အဖြေ answer

apin အပင် plant (n)

apoh အပို extra, excess

apyin အပြင် outside

apyit အပြစ် guilt

apyit ma shi အပြစ်မရှိ to be guiltless

apyit shi အပြစ်ရှိ to be guilty

apyoh အပျို single woman, bachelorette

apyone အပြုံး smile (n)

ar dae အားတယ် I'm free

ar gazar အားကစား sports

ar lone အားလုံး altogether, all, everything

Ar sha အာရှ Asia

ar yone အာရုဏ် dawn

asar athauk အစားအသောက် food and drink

ashayt အရှေ့ the east, eastern

ashet အရှက် shame

asi azin အစီအစဉ် plan, program

asone a shone အဆုံးအရှုံး loss

atate အတိတ် the past

ataw bae အတော်ပဲ just right

athae အသည်း heart

athae kwae အသည်းကွဲ heartbroken

athar အသား meat, flesh

athee အသီး fruit

athee aywet အသီးအရွက် fruit and vegetables

athet အသက် age; life

athan အသံ voice

athan dwet အသံထွက် pronunciation

atin pyaw အတင်းပြော to gossip

atwet အတွက် for (particle)

aung myin အောင်မြင် to be successful

Aung myin bah zay. အောင်မြင်ပါစေ May you be successful! (blessing)

aung thabay အောင်သပြေ eugenia

aunty အန့်တီ aunt

aut awe dae အံ့ဩတယ်။ surprised, amazed

aw အော် to shout, to scream

aw ကြော် aw (exclamation, interjection)

away byay kar အဝေးပြေးကား long distance bus

awe zah ဩဇာ influence

awut hsaing အဝတ်ဆိုင် clothing shop

awut shaw အဝတ်လျှော် to wash clothes

awute shaw zet အဝတ်လျှော်စက် washing machine

ayathah အရသာ taste, flavor

ayathah shi dae အရသာရှိတယ် It's delicious!

ayay achin အရည်အချင်း ability

ayay kyee အရေးကြီး important

aye aye say zay အေးအေးဆေးဆေး easygoing

ayet hsaing အရက်ဆိုင် bar, places that serves alcohol

ayin ga အရင်က before, previously

ayoke hsaing အရုပ်ဆိုင် toy shop

ayu gan အယူခံ appeal, plea (n)

ayu gan tin အယူခံတင် to appeal, to plead for

B

babu yoke ပန်းပု sculpture, carved figurines

badamyar ပတ္တမြား ruby

badin bauk ပြတင်းပေါက် window

badin bauk pait ပြတင်းပေါက်ပိတ် to close the window

badin bauk phwint ပြတင်းပေါက်ဖွင့် to open the window

bae ဘယ် where

bae choe ဘယ်ချိုး turn left

bae dawt laut ဘယ်တော့လောက် about when?

bae hmah lae ဘယ်မှာလဲ Where is it?

bae lo or balo ဘယ်လို how

bae lo nay lae ဘယ်လိုနေလဲ How is it?

bae thu or bathu ဘယ်သူ who

bagan ပန်းကန် plate

bah ဘာ what

bah thah yay ဘာသာရေး religion

bain pout ဘီးပေါက် had a flat tire

bait ဗိုက် stomach

baji kar ပန်းချီ painting

balauk ဘလောက် block (city street)

baluu ဘီလူး demon

Bamah zagar ဗမာစကား Burmese language (spoken only)

ban ဘဏ် bank

baw la pin ဘောလ်ပင် ballpoint pen

baw lone ဘောလုံး ball

bawa ဘဝ life, existence

bawin myint ဘဝင်မြင့် arrogant, aloof

bay din hsayah ဗေဒင်ဆရာ fortune teller

bay din kyi ဗေဒင်ကြည့် to have one's future read, to see a fortune teller

bay kin bah zay ဘေးကင်းပါစေ May you be safe! (blessing)

bayin ma ဘုရင်မ queen

bazun ပုဇွန် shrimp

be yar ဘီယာ beer

bido ဘီရို cabinet, closet

bo zah ဘိုစာ Westerners' cuisine [slang]

boe bwar yait thah ဘိုးဘွားရိပ်သာ elderly home, old folks' home

boh ဘို Westerner, foreigner [slang]

boke da hoo nayt ဗုဒ္ဓဟူးနေ့ Wednesday

bus sakar ဘတ်စ်ကား bus

bwi diyo yite ဗီဒီယိုရိုက် to shoot video

C

cake mote ကိတ်မုန့် cake

chaet ချဲ့ to cause (something) to expand

chain ချိန်း to make an appointment
chain gwin ချိန်ခွင် scale (for weighing)
chain htar dae ချိန်းထားတယ် I have an appointment.
chan thah ချမ်းသာ wealthy
chan thar bah zay ချမ်းသာပါစေ May you be wealthy! (blessing)
chauk ခြောက် dry
chaung ချောင် loose
chaung ချောင် roomy, loose, relaxed fit
chaung hsoe ချောင်းဆိုး to cough
chaw ချော smooth
chaw ချော် to miss the mark
chaw lae ချော်လဲ to trip and fall
chay hsay ခြေဆေး to wash one's feet
chay zoot ခြေစွပ် sock
chet ချက် to cook
chet chin ချက်ချင်း immediately, right away
chi ချီ to carry
chi ချည် to faster, to tie
chi ချည် cotton
Chin ချင်း Chin (ethnic nationality)
chin ချဉ် sour
chindaung ခြင်းတောင်း basket
chin thaet ခြင်္သေ့ lion
chit ချစ် to love
chit sayah kaung ချစ်စရာကောင်း lovable
chit thu ချစ်သူ lover, boyfriend, girlfriend
cho ချို sweet
choe ချိုး to break
chone pawah ချိုပဝါ shawl
chote ချုပ် to sew
chway ချွေး sweat (n)
chway htwet ချွေးထွက် to sweat

D

da baet daw တပည့်တော် your disciple (used by men as first-person pronoun in conversation with monks)
da baet daw ma တပည့်တော်မ your disciple (used by women as first-person pronoun in conversation with monks)
dabyet see တံမြက်စည်း broom
dagae တကယ် really, truly

Dagah ji ဒကာကြီး Great patron (only used by monks, to address older men)
Dagah lay ဒကာလေး Great patron (only used by monks, to address younger men)
Dagama ji ဒကာမကြီး Great patron (only used by monks, to address older women)
Dagama lay ဒကာမလေး Great patron (only used by monks, to address younger women)
dagar တံခါး door
dagar pait တံခါးပိတ် to close the door
dagar phwint တံခါးဖွင့် to open the door
dagoh gaung san တစ်ကိုယ်ကောင်းဆန် selfish
dah ဒါ that
dah bay maet ဒါပေမယ့် however
dah jaunt ဒါကြောင့် therefore
dama ဓါးမ cleaver, butchering knife
damah yone ဓမ္မရုံ Dharma hall
dan ngway ဒက်ငွေ fine (punitive fee [n])
dar ဓါး knife, sword
daw ဒေါ် rrefix for mature woman
daw tha ဒေါသ anger
daw tha htwet ဒေါသထွက် to be angry
day tha gan ဒေသခံ local people
di hah ဒီဟာ this object, this thing
di hmah ဒီမှာ here
di mo kray si ဒီမိုကရေစီ democracy
di yay ဒီရေ tide
doo ဒူး knee
dote kha thae ဒုက္ခသည် refugee
dut hman ဓါတ်မှန် x-ray (n)
dut hman yite ဓါတ်မှန်ရိုက် x-ray (v)
dut hsee ဓါတ်ဆီ gasoline
dut hsee kon ဓါတ်ဆီကုန် ran out of gas
dut pone ဓါတ်ပုံ photograph (n)
dut pone yite ဓါတ်ပုံရိုက် to take photos

E

et khayah အက္ခရာ alphabet

G

Gabah ကမ္ဘာ Earth (planet)
gabah hlaet khayee thae ကမ္ဘာလှည့်ခရီးသည် globetrotter, world traveler

gabite hnite ခါးပိုက်နှိုက် pickpocket

gadi ကတိ promise (n)

gadi pay ကတိပေး to make promises

gado ga ကူးတို့ခ ferry fee

gah wune ဂါဝန် skirt

gate hsone ဂိတ်ဆုံး last stop, end of the line

gaung mah ခေါင်းမာ stubborn

gaung shaw yay ခေါင်းလျှော်ရည် shampoo

gaung zin ခေါင်းစဉ် title, headline

gaut ဂေါက် golf (n)

gaut thee ဂေါက်သီး golf ball

gaut yaik ဂေါက်ရိုက် to play golf

gazar ကစား to play

gazar gwin ကစားကွင်း playground

gitah ဂီတာ guitar

gitah tee ဂီတာတီး to play guitar

H

haw tae ဟော်တယ် hotel

haw tae lait sah ဟော်တယ်လိပ်စာ hotel address

hin in ဟင့်အင်း no [informal]

hla လှ pretty

hlae လှည်း cart (drawn by animal)

hlae လှဲ to lie, recline horizontally

hlu လှူ to donate

hlute လွတ် to free (someone or something)

hlute taw လွှတ်တော် parliament

hman မှန် mirror

hman မှန် to be correct, to be right

hman baloo မှန်ဘီလူး magnifier, magnifying glass

hmar မှား to be wrong

hmah မှာ to order

hmah jin dae မှာချင်တယ် I'd like to place an order.

hmat မှတ် to memorize

hmat mi မှတ်မိ to remember

hmaung မှောင် dark

hmoh မှို mushroom

hmut mi dae မှတ်မိတယ် I remember

hmut taing မှတ်တိုင် bus stop, train stop

hmway မွှေး fragrant, aromatic

hmya ta မျှတ just, fair

hmyaw မျှော် to wait for someone or something, to hope for, to anticipate

hnay နေး slow

hngar ငှား to rent

hnin နှင်း snow

hnin htote နှင်ထုတ် to ban, to banish someone

hnin ze နှင်းဆီ rose

hnit နှစ် year

ho hah ဟိုဟာ that object, that thing

ho hmah ဟိုမှာ there

hsar ဆား salt

hsan ဆန် rice (uncooked)

hsae ဆဲ curse, cuss

hsah ဆာ hungry

hsaing ဆိုင် store, shop

hsaing pait chaing ဆိုင်ပိတ်ချိန် business closing hour

hsaing phwint jain ဆိုင်ဖွင့်ချိန် business opening hour

hsaint ဆိမ့် flavorful, rich in taste

hsait ဆိတ် goat

hsait thar ဆိတ်သား goat meat

hsaung bar ဆောင်းပါး article (news, magazine)

hsaung yah thi ဆောင်းရာသီ Ccold season

hsaut ဆောက် to build, to construct

hsay ဆေး medicine

hsay ဆေး to wash

hsay zaing ဆေးဆိုင် pharmacy

hsay bawt lait ဆေးပေါ့လိပ် cheroot

hsay byin lait ဆေးပြင်းလိပ် cigar

hsay dan ဆေးတံ smoking pipe

hsay hmin jaung ဆေးမင်ကြောင် tattoo (n)

hsay hsayah ဆေးဆရာ medicine man, healer

hsay lait ဆေးလိပ် cigarette

hsay lone ဆေးလုံး pill

hsay thauk ဆေးသောက် to take medicine

hsay yon ဆေးရုံ hospital

hsayah ဆရာ boss, teacher, master, mentor

hsayah daw ဆရာတော် abbot

hsayah ji ဆရာကြီး head nun of a nunnery

hsayah lay ဆရာလေး nun

hsayah wun ဆရာဝန် doctor

hsi ဆီ oil

hsin jay ဆင်ခြေ excuse

hsin jay pay ဆင်ခြေပေး to give an excuse

hsin yae ဆင်းရဲ poor

hson ဆုံ to meet

hsone ma ဆုံးမ to admonish, to teach (matters of morality)

hsu dae ဆူတယ် It's noisy.

hsu taung pyaet ဆုတောင်းပြည့် wish comes true

hsut pyah ဆပ်ပြာ soap

hsut pyah hmont ဆပ်ပြာမှုန့် laundry detergent

hsut pyah yay ဆပ်ပြာရည် liquid soap

hsu ဆူး thorn

htaing ထိုင် to sit

htaing jin dae ထိုင်ချင်တယ် I want to sit.

htamain hsaing ထဘီဆိုင် woman's sarong shop

htamin jet ထမင်းချက် cook (n)

htamin sar gun ထမင်းစားခန်း dining room

htar ထား to put (something) in a place

htaung ထောင် prison

htaung ထောင် to raise, to erect

htaung jaut ထောင်ချောက် trap

htaung or **daung** ထောင် thousand

htaut pant ထောက်ပံ့ to support

htay ထေး rich

htee ထီး umbrella

htee hsaung ထီးဆောင်း to carry an umbrella

hti ထိ to touch

htin yuu or **htin shoo** ထင်းရှူး pine

htoo jar ထူးခြား distinct

htoo zan ထူးဆန်း strange

htote ထုပ် to bundle up, to pack

htote ထုတ် to take out, to bring out

htuh ထူ thick (as in books)

htut ထပ် again, more

htwar ထွား stocky

htway ထွေး to spit out

htwet ထွက် to leave, to depart

htwet ngway ထွက်ငွေ expense (lit., money spent)

I

inga nayt အင်္ဂါနေ့ Tuesday

Ingalake sah အင်္ဂလိပ်စာ English language

Ingalake zagar အင်္ဂလိပ်စကား English language (spoken)

Isalam အစ္စလမ် Islam

J

jaboe ကြမ်းပိုး flea

jah nae ဂျာနယ် journal

Japan asar asah ဂျပန်အစားအစာ Japanese cuisine

Japan zagar ဂျပန်စကား Japanese language (spoken only)

Japan zah ဂျပန်စာ Japanese language

Jarmun sah ဂျာမန်စာ German language

Jarmun zagar ဂျာမန်စကား German language (spoken)

jin ဂျင်း jeans

jone ဂျုံ flour

K

ka က to dance

kan jay ကမ်းခြေ shore, beach

kan nar ကမ်းနား beach

Kachin ကချင် Kachin (ethnic nationality)

kah ကာ to cover

kaing ကိုင် to handle, to hold

kait ကိုက် to bite

kala htaing ကုလားထိုင် chair

Kalar asar asah ကုလားအစားအစာ Indian cuisine

kalaung ကလောင် pen, scribe

kalaung nam mae ကလောင်နာမည် pen name

kan ကန် to kick

kar bain ကားဘီး car tire

kar chaung ကားချောင် bus isn't crowded

kar ga ကားခ bus fare, passenger fare

kar gate ကားဂိတ် bus terminal

kar hmut taing ကားမှတ်တိုင် bus stop

kar hsayah ကားဆရာ driver

kar kyut ကားကြပ် bus crowded

kar let hmut ကားလက်မှတ် bus ticket

kar maung ကားမောင်း to drive car

kar nauk kya dae ကားနောက်ကျတယ်
the car/bus was late

kar pyet ကားပျက် the car broke down

kar see ကားစီး to ride a car

kari yah ကြိယာ verb

kauk ကောက် crooked

kaung ကောင်း fine, good, well

kaung bi ကောင်းပြီ all right, OK

kaung kin ကောင်းကင် sky

kaut kyit ကောက်ကျစ် dishonest

kaw ကော် glue (n)

kaw naet kaat ကော်နဲ့ကပ် to glue

kaw phe ကော်ဖီ coffee

kawlah hala ကောလာဟလ rumor

Kayar ကယား Kayah (ethnic nationality)

Kayin ကရင် Karen (ethnic nationality)

kha lay ကလေး child

kha yee ခရီး trip, journey

kha yee htwet ခရီးထွက် to go on a trip

kha yee pan ခရီးပန်း to suffer from jet lag
(lit., travel fatigue)

kha yee thae ခရီးသည် traveler

kha yee thwar ခရီးသွား to travel

kha yee thwar loke ngan
ခရီးသွားလုပ်ငန်း travel agency

khan ma ခန်းမ hall

khae dan ခဲတံ pencil

khalay daine ကလေးထိန်း nanny, babysitter

khalay hsan ကလေးဆန် immature, childlike

khamyar ခင်ဗျား you [formal, used by
male speaker]

khan nar ခမ်းနား ceremonious, festive

khant ခန့် handsome

khar ခါး bitter

khauk htee ခေါက်ထီး umbrella
(collapsible type, to fit handbags, etc.)

khaw ခေါ် call

khayar ကရား kettle

khayay ခရေ star flower

khayee thae ခရီးသည် passenger

khayee way ခရီးဝေး long-distance travel

khayee phyaungt bah zay ခရီးဖြောင့်ပါစေ
May your journey be safe! (blessing)

khayin ခက်ရင်း fork

khet khae ခက်ခဲ difficult

khin boon ခင်ပွန်း husband [formal]

khin min ခင်မင် friendly

khoe ခိုး to steal

khone ခုံ desk

khone ခုန် to jump, to leap

khote ခုတ် to chop

khwae ခွေး dog

khwae ခွဲ to split apart, to separate

khwae khwah ခွဲခွာ to part ways

khwet ခွက် cup

kimar palata ကီးမားပလာတာ keema
paratha (Indian food)

kin ကင် grill

ko ကို prefix for adult male

ko baing ကိုယ်ပိုင် private, self-owned

ko baing kar ကိုယ်ပိုင်ကား private car

Ko ree yan sah ကိုရီးယန်းစာ Korean
language

Ko ree yan zagar ကိုရီးယန်းစကား Korean
language (spoken)

ko yay ko dah ကိုယ်ရေးကိုယ်တာ personal
affairs

kon kya zayait ကုန်ကျစားရိတ် cost,
expense

kon pyu tah ကွန်ပျူတာ computer

kon thae ကုန်သည် merchant

kone lan ကုန်းလမ်း land travel, land route

kone tin kar ကုန်တင်ကား truck

kone zone zaing ကုန်စုံဆိုင် grocery store,
general goods store

kor phe zaing ကော်ဖီဆိုင် coffee shop

kote ကုတ် to scratch

dote kha ဒုက္ခ misery, trouble

koyin ကိုရင် novice

ku ကု to heal, to cure

ku ကူ to help

ku thoh ကုသိုလ် merit

kune yah ကွမ်းယာ betel quid

kuu ကူး to cross

kwae kwah ကွဲကွာ to be apart, to be
separated

kwae lun ကွယ်လွန် to pass away [die]

kwune thee ကွမ်းသီး areca nut

kyanawt atwet ကျွန်တော့အတွက် for me
(male speaker)

kyae ကျယ် loud
kyae ကျယ် broad, wide
kyae ကြယ် star
kyae ကြ to scatter, sprinkle
kyah be ကြာပြီ it's been a while; it's been too long
kyah thah baday nayt ကြာသပတေးနေ့ Thursday
kyait ကြိုက် to like
kyama ကျွန်မ my [formal, used by female speaker]
kyama ကျွန်မ I (formal, female speaker]
kyan ကြမ်း rough
kyan mar bah zay ကျန်းမာပါစေ May you be healthy! (blessing)
kyanaw ကျွန်တော် I [formal, male speaker]
kyanawt ကျွန်တော့ my [formal, used by male speaker]
kyar ကျား tiger
kyauk ကြောက် to be afraid
kyauk ကျောက် rock
kyauk hsu ကျောက်ဆူး anchor (for ship)
kyauk sayah kaung ကြောက်စရာကောင်း scary
kyaung ကျောင်း school, monastery
kyaung ကြောင် cat
kyaung hsaut ကျောင်းဆောက် to build a school
kyaung hsayah ကျောင်းဆရာ school teacher
kyaung nay bet tha nge jin ကျောင်းနေဘက်သူငယ်ချင်း schoolmate, classmate
kyaung oak ကျောင်းအုပ် headmaster, principal
kyaung oak hsayah ma ကျောင်းအုပ်ဆရာမ headmistress, female principal
kyaung thar ကျောင်းသား student
kyaung thu ကျောင်းသူ student (female)
kyaut saine ကျောက်စိမ်း jade
kyaw ကြော် to fry
kyee ကြီး big
kyet ကြက် chicken
kyet oo byote ကြက်ဥပြုတ် boiled (chicken) egg

kyet oo jaw ကြက်ဥကြော် fried egg
kyet thar ကြက်သား poultry, chicken meat
kyet thon kyaw ကြက်သွန်ကြော် onion fritter
kyi ကြည့် to look, to watch
kyin ကျဉ်း narrow, cramped
kyin nah ကြင်နာ to have sympathy for (someone)
kyit ကျစ် dense
kyut ကျပ် kyat (Burmese currency denomination)
kyut ကျပ် tight
kyute ကြွပ် crunchy
kywae ကျွေး to feed
kywet ကြွက် rat
kywon kyin ကျွမ်းကျင် fluent, skillful

L

la လ month
la kyut လကြတ် lunar eclipse
la pyayt nayt လပြည့်နေ့ full moon day
la pyayt nya လပြည့်ည full moon night
la yaung လရောင် moonlight
lan လမ်း road, street
lan ma jee လမ်းမကြီး main road
lan shauk လမ်းလျှောက် to take a stroll
lan zone လမ်းဆုံး end of the line
lae လယ် farm (n)
lae bin လည်ပင် neck
lae htune လယ်ထွန် to farm
lae thamar လယ်သမား farmer
lah လာ to come
lah chin dae လာချင်တယ် want to come
lain လိမ် to lie, to deceive
lain လိင် sex
lain mah လိမ္မာ well-behaved
lait sah လိပ်စာ address
lan bya လမ်းပြ travel guide, tour guide
lan zan လန်းဆန်း fresh, vitalized
lan jar လမ်းကြား alley
laphet thoke လက်ဖက်သုပ် tea leaf salad
laphet yae လက်ဖက်ရည် Burmese tea
laphet yay zaing လက်ဖက်ရည်ဆိုင် tea shop
law လော to hurry, to be in a hurry

lay လေ air
lay လေး richly flavored
lay လေး heavy
lay aye set လေအေးစက် air conditioner
lay htee လေထီး parachute
lay yin byan လေယာဉ်ပျံ airplane
lay yin hmoo လေယာဉ်မှူး pilot
lay yin let hmut လေယာဉ်လက်မှတ် plane ticket
lay yin mae လေယာဉ်မယ် flight attendant, female
lay yin maung လေယာဉ်မောင် flight attendant, male
lay yin nauk kya dae လေယာဉ်နောက်ကျတယ် the plane was late
lay zait လေဆိပ် airport
lay zar လေးစား to respect
let လက် arm, hand
let ait လက်အိတ် glove
let hmu loke ngan လက်မှုလုပ်ငန်း craft-making business, selling homemade goods
let hmu pyin nyah လက်မှုပညာ handicraft making skills
let hmut လက်မှတ် ticket
let hnate dut mee လက်နှိပ်ဓါတ်မီး flashlight
let hsaung pyitsee လက်ဆောင်ပစ္စည်း gift items
let hsay လက်ဆေး to wash one's hands
let kaing pawah လက်ကိုင်ပဝါ handkerchief
let kaing phone လက်ကိုင်ဖုန်း mobile phone
let khan လက်ခံ to accept
let khote tee လက်ခုပ်တီး to applaud
let ma လက်မ thumb
let ma လက်မ inch
let net လက်နက် arm, weapon
let pat nah yi လက်ပတ်နာရီ wristwatch
let phet yay လက်ဖက်ရည် sweet tea
let sar chay လက်စားချေ to avenge
let shawt လက်လျှော့ to give up
let soot လက်စွပ် ring
let thee လက်သီး fist
let thote pawah လက်သုတ်ပဝါ hand towel

let war လက်ဝါး palm
let yway zin လက်ရွေးစင် top choice, top selection
like kah လိုက်ကာ curtain, partition
lin လင် husband
lin လင်း bright
lin ban လင်ပန်း tray
lin mayar လင်မယား married couple, husband and wife
lite လိုက် to follow, to chase
lo aut လိုအပ် need, necessary
lo jin dae လိုချင်တယ် I'd like, I want
loke ar pay လုပ်အားပေး volunteer (v)
loke ar bay လုပ်အားပေး volunteer (n)
loke ngan လုပ်ငန်း business
loke phor kaing bet လုပ်ဖော်ကိုင်ဘက် coworker
lone wa လုံးဝ not at all
lu လူ person
lu လု to rob
lu byoh လူပျို single man, bachelor
lu hmu yay လူမှုရေး social
lu jee hsan လူကြီးဆန် mature, adult-like
lu ji လူကြီး adult
lu myar dae လူများတယ် to be crowded
lu myoe လူမျိုး race, ethnicity, nationality
lu myoe khwae jar yay လူမျိုးခွဲခြားရေး racism
lu nay hmu ahsint atan လူနေမှုအဆင့်အတန်း living standard
lu ngae လူငယ် youth
lu ngae လူငယ် young people
lu thar လူသား human
lu zain or **thazain** လူစိမ်း or သူစိမ်း stranger
lute လွတ် to escape
lwan လွမ်း miss (someone)

M

ma မ prefix for young woman
ma ar boo မအားဘူး I'm not free, I'm busy
ma hmut mi boo မမှတ်မိဘူး I don't remember
ma hote မဟုတ် not true
ma kait phoo မကိုက်ဘူး no deal ([slang], literally, "It doesn't add up")

ma kaung boo မကောင်းဘူး

ma lo boo မလိုဘူး not necessary

ma nit မိနစ် minute

ma pyaw dat phoo မပြောတတ်ဘူး
I cannot speak [this language]

ma thay jah boo မသေချာဘူး I'm not sure
of it

ma thwar dat phoo မသွားတတ်ဘူး I don't
know how to get there

ma twaet jin boo မတွေ့ချင်ဘူး I don't
want to meet [with …]

ma wa thay boo မဝသေးဘူး I'm not full yet

mah မာ hard

main ma မိန်းမ woman, female

maint gon မိန့်ခွန်း speech

maint gun pyaw မိန့်ခွန်းပြော to give a speech

mait hset မိတ်ဆက် to introduce

mait sway မိတ်ဆွေ friend [formal word]

makhant lay zar lote မခန့်လေးစားလုပ်
to mock, to show disdain

manar loh မနာလို envious

manet မနက် morning

manet sah မနက်စာ breakfast

mashi maphyit မရှိမဖြစ် essential

mataw lo မတော်လို့ I didn't mean to; it
was an accident

maung မောင် younger brother (if you're a
woman)

maung မောင်း gong (musical instrument)

maung မောင်း to drive (a vehicle)

maung မောင် prefix for young male

may မေး to ask

may gun မေးခွန်း question

may zi မေးစေ့ chin (anatomy)

mayar မယား wife

mayt မေ့ forget

mee မီး fire, light

mee ban မီးပန်း fireworks

mee bo jaung မီးဖိုချောင် kitchen

mee boh မီးဖို oven

mee bone မီးပုံး lamp

mee bone pyan မီးပုံးပျံ hot air balloon

mee gan thit tah မီးခံသေတ္တာ safebox

mee htun bwae မီးထွန်းပွဲ Light Festival

mee jit မီးခြစ် lighter

mee nay thae မီးနေသည် pregnant woman

mee pait မီးပိတ် to turn off the light

mee phwint မီးဖွင့် to turn on the light

mee pyet မီးပျက် have a power outage

mee thut thamar မီးသတ်သမား firefighter

mee thway မီးသွေး coal

mi ba maet မိဘမဲ့ orphan

mi point မီးပွိုင့် traffic light

mi yoe phalah မိရိုးဖလာ traditional,
hereditary

min မင်း you [familiar, intimate]

min galah hsaung မင်္ဂလာဆောင် wedding

min galah hsaung မင်္ဂလာဆောင် to get
married, to marry someone

minthamee မင်းသမီး princess, actress

minthar မင်းသား prince, actor

mite tae မိုက်တယ် It's cool! [slang]

mi thar zu မိသားစု family

moe မိုး rain

moe gah ain ji မိုးကာအင်္ကျီ raincoat

moe gote set wain မိုးကုပ်စက်ဝိုင်း horizon

moe joe မိုးကြိုး thunder

moe joe pyit မိုးကြိုးပစ် thunder strikes

moe oak မိုးအုံ့ overcast

moe phwa bwae kya မိုးဖွဲ့ဖွဲ့ကျ to drizzle (rain)

moe thae မိုးသည်း to rain heavily

moe yah thi မိုးရာသီ rainy season

moke မုခ် gate (of a religious place)

moke hingha မုန့်ဟင်းခါး catfish chowder
with noodles

mon lwae မွန်းလွဲ late afternoon

mone မုန်း to hate

mont မုန့် snack

mont zaing မုန့်ဆိုင် snack shop

moo dae မူးတယ်။ to be dizzy, drunk

mote hsait yait dar မုတ်ဆိတ်ရိတ်ခါး
razor blade

mote hsoe မုဆိုး hunter

mote thone yah thi မုတ်သုန်ရာသီ
monsoon season

mway မွေး to breed, give birth to

mway zar မွေးစား to adopt

myu မြူ fog, mist

myan မြန် fast

myan myan မြန်မြန် quickly

myan myan shauk မြန်မြန်လျှောက် walk fast

Myanmah asar asah မြန်မာအစားအစာ Burmese cuisine

Myanmah zar မြန်မာစာ Burmese language

myar များ many, much, a lot

myaut phet မြောက်ဘက် north, northern

myay jee မြေကြီး earth (the ground)

myet hlaet မျက်လှည့် magic

myet hlaet hsayah မျက်လှည့်ဆရာ magician

myet hman မျက်မှန် reading glasses

myet hna thote pawah မျက်နှာသုတ်ပဝါ face towel

myet hnah မျက်နှာ face

myet hnah thit မျက်နှာသစ် to wash one's face

myet lone မျက်လုံး eye

myin မြင်း horse

myin hlae မြင်းလှည်း horse-drawn cart

myint မြင့် tall, high

myo မြို့ city

myo daw မြို့တော် capital

myo daw khan ma မြို့တော်ခန်းမ city hall

myoe yoe မျိုးရိုး ancestry, heritage

myoe zet မျိုးဆက် generation

N

nae nae နည်းနည်း a little

nae nae chin dae နည်းနည်းချဉ်တယ် a little bit sour

nae nae cho dae နည်းနည်းချိုတယ် a little bit sweet

nae nae khar dae နည်းနည်းခါးတယ် a little bitter

nae nae kyae dae နည်းနည်းကျဲတယ် a little thin (as in liquid)

nae nae kyi dah နည်းနည်းကြီးတာ something a bit bigger

nae nae mar dae နည်းနည်းမာတယ် a little hard

nae nae pyawt dae နည်းနည်းပျော့တယ် a little soft

nae nae pyit tae နည်းနည်းပျစ်တယ် a little bit thick (as in liquid)

nae nae shay dah နည်းနည်းရှည်တာ something a bit longer

nae nae sut tae နည်းနည်းစပ်တယ် a little bit spicy

nae nae thay dah နည်းနည်းသေးတာ something a bit smaller

nae nae to dah နည်းနည်းတိုတာ something a bit shorter

nah နာ to feel hurt

naing နိုင် to win, to defeat

naing ngan နိုင်ငံ nation

naing ngan jar thar နိုင်ငံခြားသား foreigner

naing ngan yay နိုင်ငံရေး politics

naint နိမ့် low

nan byah နံပြား naan bread

nan daw နန်းတော် palace

nan yan နံရံ wall

nar နား to rest

nar aye dae နားအေးတယ် It's quiet

nar jin dae နားချင်တယ် Want to rest

nar lae dae နားလည်တယ် I understand

nar lae hmu နားလည်မှု understanding

nar ma lae boo နားမလည်ဘူး I don't understand

nah yi နာရီ hour

nat gadaw နတ်ကတော် spirit medium

nauk နောက် to tease

nauk hsone နောက်ဆုံး the last, the final (in a series)

nauk hsone zay နောက်ဆုံးဈေး last offer, final price

nauk kya နောက်ကျ to be late

naung da နောင်တ remorse, regret

naut နောက် next, later, after that, then

naut hlae နောက်လှည့် turn around, turn back

nay နေ to live

nay gah myet hman နေကာမျက်မှန် sunglasses

nay hlone နေလှုံ to sunbathe

nay htwet chaing နေထွက်ချိန် sunrise

nay jar ban နေကြာပန်း sunflower

nay kaung dae နေကောင်းတယ် I'm fine; I'm well

nay kyut နေကြတ် solar eclipse

nay laung နေလောင် sunburn

nay win jain နေဝင်ချိန် sunset

nay yaung နေရောင် sunlight

nayt lae နေ့လည် midday, noon

nayt lae zah နေ့လည်စာ lunch

nee နီး close, near

nee pyin nyah နည်းပညာ technology

nee pyin nyah loke ngan နည်းပညာလုပ်ငန်း technology business

nga ငါ့ my [familiar, intimate]

nga yoke thee ငရုတ်သီး chili

ngae ငယ် young

ngae tha ngae jin ငယ်သူငယ်ချင်း childhood friend

ngalyin လျှင် earthquake

ngalyin hlote လျှင်လှုပ် to quake

ngan ငံ salty

ngapyaw thee ငှက်ပျောသီး banana

ngar ငါး fish

ngay ငေး to gaze at

ngway ငွေ silver

ngway ငွေ money [formal]

ngway chay ငွေချေ to settle the bill

ngway chay jin dae ငွေချေချင်တယ် I'd like to settle the bill

ngway htote ငွေထုတ် to withdraw money

ngway sayin or ban sayin ငွေစာရင်း or ဘက်စာရင်း bank account

ngway thwin ငွေသွင်း to deposit money

no နို့ milk (n)

noe lah နိုးလာ to wake up

nu နု tender, youthful

nun နာမ် noun

nun နံ stinky

nut နတ် spirits, angels

nwar နွား cow

nwar hlae နွားလှည်း ox-drawn cart

nwar no နွားနို့ milk (from cow)

nway yah thi နွေရာသီ hot season

nya ည night

nya nay ညနေ evening

nya nay zah ညနေစာ dinner

nya zay dan ညဈေးတန်း night market

nyain jan yay ငြိမ်းချမ်းရေး peace

nyant ည့ံ to be bad at (something)

nyar choe ညာချိုး turn right

nyi ညီ younger brother (if you're a man)

nyi lay ညီလေး little brother

nyi ma ညီမ sister

nyi ma lay ညီမလေး little sister

nyin ငြင်း to argue

nyit pat ညစ်ပတ် dirty

O

oak choke အုပ်ချုပ် govern, administrate

oak kah gae ဥက္ကာခဲ meteor

oak ka hta ဥက္ကဋ္ဌ chairman, chief

oh အို old

oh အိုး jar

ohn no khauk swe အုန်းနို့ခေါက်ဆွဲ coconut noodle soup

one no အုန်းနို့ coconut milk

one thee အုန်းသီး coconut

one yay အုန်းရည် coconut juice

oo lay ဦးလေး uncle

P

pa hsain ပုဆိန် ax

paat tee ပတ်တီး bandage

pae byote ပဲပြုတ် boiled beans

pah ပါ to include

pah dae ပါတယ် it's included; it's in there

pat hsan or pite hsan ပိုက်ဆံ money

pat hsan phyone or pite hsan phyone ပိုက်ဆံဖြုန်း to waste money

pa hta ma zone ပထမဆုံး the first, the foremost (in a series)

pain ပိန် thin

paing shin ပိုင်ရှင် owner

pait ပိတ် to close, to turn off

pakhone ပုခုံး shoulder

palae ပုလဲ pearl

palat satit ait ပလတ်စတစ်အိတ် plastic bag

palata ပလာတာ paratha

palet kala htaing ပက်လက်ကုလားထိုင် reclining chair

pan jan ပန်းခြံ garden, park

pan thee ပန်းသီး apple

par ပါး thin, flimsy

par ပါး cheek

para hita ပရဟိတ nonprofit

pasoe hsaing ပုဆိုးဆိုင် man's sarong shop

pat, bat ပတ် week

pauk zay ပေါက်ဈေး current price, market price

paung ပေါင်း to add

paung ပေါင်း to steam (cook)

paung mont ပေါင်မုန့် bread

paung mote htaw but thoke ပေါင်မုန့်ထောပတ်သုပ် buttered bread

paw ပေါ inexpensive, cheap, abundant

pawah ပဝါ towel

pawt ပေါ့ lightly flavored, underseasoned

pay ပေး to give

pe dawt ပြီးတော့ after that, then

pe yin ပြီးရင် ffter that, then

phan ဖမ်း to arrest

phae ဖဲ playing card

phait ဖိတ် to invite

phalar ဖလား bowl, goblet

phanut ဖိနပ် footwear

phanut chute ဖိနပ်ချွတ် to remove one's footwear

phat ဖတ် to read

phauk thae ဖောက်သည် patron, regular customer

phayae the ဖရဲသီး watermelon

phayar ဘုရား pagoda

phayar ဘုရား God

phayar boo ဘုရားဖူး pilgrimage, visiting shrines and temples

phayar jaung ဘုရားကျောင်း church, temple, place of worship

phayar zin ဘုရားစင် altar, shrine

phayaung daing ဖယောင်းတိုင် candle

phet ဖက် to hug, to embrace

phi ar ဖိအား pressure

phi ar pay ဖိအားပေး to put pressure on

phon htu ဖုံထူ dusty

phone hset ဖုန်းဆက် to make a phone call

phone ji kyaung ဘုန်းကြီးကျောင်း monastery

phone khor ဖုန်းခေါ် to make a phone call

Phone Phone ဘုန်းဘုန်း Monk [less formal address]

phwet ဖွက် to hide (something)

phwint ဖွင့် to open, to turn on

phyae phyae ဖြေးဖြေး slowly

phyae phyae shauk ဖြေးဖြေးလျှောက် walk slowly

phyaet ဖြည့် to fill

phyah ဖျာ mat

phyar ဖျား to be sick

phyar nay dae ဖျားနေတယ် I'm sick

phyay ဖြေ to answer

phyet ဖျက် to destroy

phyit ဖြစ် to happen, to be, to occur

phyone ဖြုန်း to squander, to waste

pin ban ပင်ပန်း to be tired, to be weary

pin lae ပင်လယ် ocean

po ပို့ to send

po ga ပို့ခ delivery fee

poe ပိုး insect

poh ပို to exceed

pon byin ပုံပြင် fable

pone ပုန်း to hide (from people)

pone hnate set ပုံနှိပ်စက် printer, press

pout si ပေါက်စီ meat bun

pu ပု short (in height)

pu pu lay ပုပုလေး Really short! (in height)

put wun kyin ပတ်ဝန်းကျင် surroundings, environment

pwae zar ပွဲစား broker (for business negotiation), go-between

pya ပြ to show

pya dike ပြတိုက် museum

pya zut ပြဇာတ် play (n) (theatrical)

pyaet ပြည့် to be full

pyah ပြာ ash

pyah gwet ပြာခွက် ashtray

pyan ပြန် to go back (to one's home or point of origin)

pyan ပျံ fly

pyan nyah yay ပညာရေး education

pyar yay ပျားရည် honey

pyauk ပျောက် to lose something

pyaung ပြောင်း change

pyaw ပြော to speak

pyaw ပျော် happy

pyaw dat ပြောတတ် can speak (a certain language)

pyaw za yar ji ပျော်စရာကြီး So much fun!

pyawt ပျော့ soft

pyay ပြေး to run

pyet ပျက် to be destroyed, to be ruined, to fall apart

pyet gadain ပြက္ခဒိန် calendar

pyet thanah ပြဿနာ problem

pyin ပြင် repair, to fix

pyin ပျဉ် lumber

pyin pay bah ပြင်ပေးပါ please fix it for me

pyin dae ပျင်းတယ်။ bored

Pyinthit sah ပြင်သစ်စာ French language

Pyinthit zagar ပြင်သစ်စကား French language (spoken)

pyit sote pan ပစ္စုပ္ပန် the present

pyoe htaung ပျိုးထောင် to nurture

pyone ပြုံး to smile

pyote ပြုတ် boil (cooking)

pyu zu ပြုစု to nurse, take care of

R

ray diyoh ရေဒီယို radio

S

sah စာ mail, letter

sah jote စာချုပ် contract, treaty

sah kyi taik စာကြည့်တိုက် library

sah lone baung စာလုံးပေါင်း spelling

sah oak hsaing စာအုပ်ဆိုင် bookshop

sah po စာပို့ to send a letter

sah po thamar စာပို့သမား postman

sait စိတ် mind

sait badee စိပ်ပုတီး prayer bead string

sait dut kya dae စိတ်ဓါတ်ကျတယ် I feel disappointed, let down

sait hlote shar စိတ်လှုပ်ရှား to be excited

sait kan ဆိပ်ကမ်း beach

sait kauk စိတ်ကောက် To pout, to brood

sait koo စိတ်ကူး imagination

sait ma hman စိတ်မမှန် to be crazy [polite]

sait mapah boo စိတ်မပါဘူး not interested, half-hearted

sait mashi bah naet စိတ်မရှိပါနဲ့ Please excuse me! Please don't mind me

sait nyit စိတ်ညစ် to be depressed

sait pain dae စိတ်ပိန်တယ် I feel deflated [slang]

sait pote စိတ်ပုပ် ill-tempered, malicious

sait pu စိတ်ပူ to worry

sait shay စိတ်ရှည် to be patient

sait to စိတ်တို short-tempered, angry

sakhan စခန်း camp

sakhan cha စခန်းချ to set up camp

sanay nayt စနေနေ့ Saturday

saphoh hmuu စားဖိုမှူး chef

sar စား to eat

sar jin dae စားချင်တယ် I want to eat

sar jin za yar ji စားချင်စရာကြီး Looks so delicious! (for food)

sar thauk hsaing စားသောက်ဆိုင် restaurant

sar thone thu စားသုံးသူ diner, restaurant customer

sar zayah စားစရာ food, eatables

saung စောင် blanket

saung စောင်း barp

saungt စောင့် to wait

saungt shaut စောင့်ရှောက် to guard, to take care of

saunt စောင့် to wait

saw စော to be early

say danah စေတနာ charitable spirit, goodwill

sayt zut စေ့စပ် to engage, to be engaged to

see စီး to ride (a vehicle)

see စေး sticky

see bwar yay စီးပွားရေး economy

see kan စည်းကမ်း rules

set bain စက်ဘီး bicycle

set bain pyet စက်ဘီးပျက် the bicycle broke down

set bain see စက်ဘီးစီး to ride a bicycle

set hmu loke ngan စက်မှုလုပ်ငန်း manufacturing business

set ku စက္ကူ paper (writing material)

set ku ait စက္ကူအိတ် paper bag

set yone စက်ရုံ plant, factory

shaet tae tae ရှေ့တည့်တည့် straight ahead

shah လျှာ tongue

shah ရှာ to find, to look for

shah shay လျှာရှည် long-winded
Shan ရှမ်း Shan (ethnic nationality)
Shan khauk swe ရှမ်းခေါက်ဆွဲ Shan noodle
salad
shauk လျှောက် to walk
shawt zay လျှော့စျေး discounted price
shay ရှည် long
shay haung pyitsee ရှေးဟောင်းပစ္စည်း
antique
shayt hmah ရှေ့မှာ in front of
shayt nay ရှေ့နေ lawyer
shi ရှိ to have, to exist
shin ရှင် you [formal, used by female
speaker]
shin ရှင်း to explain
shin ရှင်း to clean up, to tidy up
shin bayin ရှင်ဘုရင် king
shin lin ရှင်းလင်း to clarify
shin pya ရှင်းပြ to explain
shin pyu ရှင်ပြု novitiation, ordination to
become a monk
shote ရှုပ် messy, confusing
shuu phanut ရှူးဖိနပ် shoe
shway ရွှေ gold
shwayt pyaung ရွှေ့ပြောင်း to move
si htamin ဆီထမင်း Burmese style sticky
rice
si zin စီစဉ် to arrange, to plan
sike kar ဆိုက်ကား sidecar (trishaw)
simun gain စီမံကိန်း project
sit စစ် war
sit thar စစ်သား soldier
site စိုက် to plant
soh စို wet
sone zan စုံစမ်း investigate
su စု to collect
sut စပ် spicy

T

tae တည်း to stay, to lodge somewhere
tae kho gan တည်းခိုခန်း guesthouse, inn,
motel
tah won တာဝန် duty, obligation
taik khaik တိုက်ခိုက် to attack
taing pyi တိုင်းပြည် country

tait sait တိတ်ဆိတ် quiet
tait tait sait sait တိတ်တိတ်ဆိတ်ဆိတ်
quietly
takhah talay တစ်ခါတစ်လေ sometimes
tan ta တမ်းတ to long for
tanin ga nway nayt တနင်္ဂနွေနေ့ Sunday
tanin lah nayt တနင်္လာနေ့ Monday
tar တား to prevent
tar myit တားမြစ် to forbid
tarait hsan တိရစ္ဆာန် animal
tarait hsan yone တိရစ္ဆာန်ရုံ zoo
taung တောင်း to ask for, to request,
to demand
taung တောင် mountain
taung တောင်း basket
taung ban or taung man တောင်းပန်
to apologize
taung ban bah dae or taung man bah dae
တောင်းပန်ပါတယ်။ I apologize
taung bet တောင်ဘက် south, southern
taw တော် to be good at
taw တော wood (forest)
tayar htaing တရားထိုင် meditate
tayar swae တရားစွဲ to sue
tayar thu jee တရားသူကြီး judge
tayar yone တရားရုံး court (judiciary)
Tayoke sar တရုတ်စာ Chinese language
Tayote asar asah တရုတ်အစားအစာ
Chinese cuisine
tet တက် to come up
tha baw tu သဘောတူ to agree
tha na khar သနပ်ခါး thanakha (aromatic
wood paste used as a cosmetic)
tha ngae jin သူငယ်ချင်း friend [informal
word]
tha htay သူဌေး rich person
thabaw kaung သဘောကောင်း good-
natured
thaboot tan သွားပွတ်တံ toothbrush
thachin သီချင်း song
thachin hsoe သီချင်းဆို to sing songs
thachin hsoh bwae သီချင်းဆိုပွဲ concert
thadi htar သတိထား be careful
thadi ya သတိရ remember
thadin သတင်း news

thadin dauk သတင်းထောက် reporter

thadin zah သတင်းစာ newspaper

thae သယ် to carry

thay thay lay သေးသေးလေး Really small!

thae chay သည်းခြေ liver

thae yu po hsaung yay သယ်ယူပို့ဆောင်ရေး transportation

thagaung or than
gaung သန်းခေါင် midnight

thaghar atu သကြားအတု artificial sweetener

thaik သိပ် very

thaik chin dae သိပ်ချင်တယ် very sour, too sour

thaik cho dae သိပ်ချိုတယ် very sweet, too sweet

thaik hla dae သိပ်လှတယ် very beautiful

thaik khar dae သိပ်ခါးတယ် very bitter, too bitter

thaik kyae dae သိပ်ကျဲတယ် very thin, too thin (as in liquid)

thaik mar dae သိပ်မာတယ် very hard, too hard

thaik pyawt dae သိပ်ပျော့တယ် very soft, too soft

thaik pyit tae သိပ်ပျစ်တယ် very thick, too thick (as in liquid)

thaik sut tae နည်းနည်းစပ်တယ် very spicy, too spicy

thain သိမ်း to keep, to confiscate

thajar သကြား sugar

thajar lone သကြားလုံး candy

thakhoe သူခိုး thief

thama kyan သမ္မာကျမ်း Bible

thamaing သမိုင်း history

thamar daw သမားတော် specialist (medical)

than gaung သန်ကောင် parasite

than ma yah သံပရာ lemon, lime

than yone သံရုံး embassy

thanar သနား to have sympathy for, to feel sorry for

thanar dut သနားတတ် kindhearted, sympathetic

thanar zayah lay သနားစရာလေး Poor thing!

thant shin yay သန့်ရှင်းရေး clearing, clear-up

thant shinn သန့်ရှင်း clean

thar thamee သားသမီး offspring, children

thatti သတ္တိ courage

thauk သောက် to drink

thauk chin dae သောက်ချင်တယ် I want to drink

thauk chin za yar ji သောက်ချင်စရာကြီး Looks so delicious! (for drinks)

thauk kya nayt သောကြာနေ့ Friday

thauk sayah သောက်စရာ drinks, refreshment

thawt သော့ key

thawun to သဝန်တို jealous

thay သေး small

thay သေ to die (blunt, not polite)

thay jah သေချာ to be sure, certain

thay jah dae သေချာတယ် I'm sure of it

thay pauk သေးပေါက် to urinate

thayaw သရော် to mock, to satirize

thayay gwin သားရေကွင်း rubber band

thayet thee သရက်သီး mango

thee khan သည်းခံ to tolerate

thee thant သီးသန့် exclusive

thet thut lwut သက်သတ်လွတ် vegetarian

thi la shin kyaung သီလရှင်ကျောင်း nunnery

thin သင် to teach

thin gan သက်န်း a monk's robe

thin maw သင်္ဘော boat, ship

thin maw thar သင်္ဘောသား sailor, seaman

thinbaw zait or thin maw zait သင်္ဘောဆိပ် harbor, pier

thinn jaing သချိုင်း cemetery

thit pin သစ်ပင် tree

thit thar သစ်သား wood

thoe thar သိုးသား lamb (meat)

thone သုံး to use

thu nah byu သူနာပြု nurse (n)

thut သတ် kill

thut yut သပ်ရပ် neat, tidy

thwaa jaa htoo dan သွားကြားထိုးတံ toothpick

thwae သွယ် slim, willowy

thwar သွား to go

thwar သွား teeth

thwar dat dae သွားတတ်တယ် I how how to get there

thwar dite hsay သွားတိုက်ဆေး toothpaste

thwar jin dae သွားချင်တယ် I want to go

thwar lae သွားလည် to visit

thwar tike သွားတိုက် to brush one's teeth

thwar zo သွားစို့ let's go

thway သွေး blood

thway doe သွေးတိုး high blood pressure

thway doe shi သွေးတိုးရှိ to have high blood pressure

thwin kon htote kon သွင်းကုန်ထုတ်ကုန် import-export

ti htaung တည်ထောင် to establish

tin bah တင်ပါ yes (only used in conversations with monks and nuns)

tin tain တင်းတိမ် to be content

tinbar တင်ပါး buttock

to တို short (in length)

to hoo or to foo တိုဟူး tofu

to to lay တိုတိုလေး Really short! (in length)

toat တုတ် chubby

toe တိုး increase

toe တိုး to push into a crowd

toe tet တိုးတက် to improve

tu တူ chopsticks

TV တီဗွီ TV

TV kyi တီဗွီကြည့် to watch TV

twaet တွေ့ to meet

twayt တွေ့ to meet

twayt jin dae တွေ့ချင်တယ် I want to meet [with …]

U

u ဥ egg (can be used for any type of egg, e.g., snake egg, duck egg, quail egg, turtle egg)

u ဦး prefix for mature man

u baday ဥပဒေ law

U zin ဦးဇင်း Monk [formal way to address a monk]

Urawpa ဥရောပ Europe

ut အပ် needle

W

wa ဝ fat

wa bi ဝပြီ I'm full (can't eat anymore)

wae ဝယ် to buy

wah thanah ဝါသနာ hobby

wah thanah pah ဝါသနာပါ to be interested in something

war ဝါး to chew

war ဝါး bamboo

waw hah ra ဝေါဟာရ vocabulary

way ဝေး far

way li way lin ဝေလီဝေလင်း predawn, early morning, wee hours

wayan byay ဝရမ်းပြေး outlaw, fugitive

wet ဝက် pig

wet thar ဝက်သား pork

win baut ဝင်ပေါက် entrance

win jay ဝင်ကြေး admission fee

win ngway ဝင်ငွေ income

wun dan ဝန်ထမ်း staff, clerk

wun nae ဝမ်းနည်း to be sad

wun thah dae ဝမ်းသာတယ် I'm happy

wut kya ဝါကျ sentence

wute ဝတ် to wear (clothing, jewelry)

Y

ya dae ရတယ် acceptable

ya htar ရထား train

ya htar nauk kya dae ရထားနောက်ကျတယ် The train was late.

ya htar pyet ရထားပျက် The train broke down

ya ma lar ရမလား Can I get it? Is it doable? (Slang)

yadanah ရတနာ treasure, jewel

yadanah zaing ရတနာဆိုင် jewelry shop

yah thi ရာသီ season

yah ye lait sah ယာယီလိပ်စာ temporary address

yah zawin ရာဇဝင် history (formal word)

ya htar let hmut ရထားလက်မှတ် train ticket

yaing ရိုင်း rude

yait ရိုက် to strike, to hit

yar ယား to itch

yauk ရောက် to arrive

yauk kyar   ယောက်ျား   man, male
yauk pe   ရောက်ပြီ   Here we are! We've arrived!
yaung   ရောင်း   to sell
yaw gah   ရောဂါ   disease
yay   ရေး   to write
yay bawae   ရေဘဝဲ   octopus
yay choe   ရေချိုး   to take a bath, to shower
yay choe gan   ရေချိုးခန်း   shower room
yay dagon   ရေတံခွန်   waterfall
yay gae jaung   ရေခဲချောင်း   popsicle
yay hmway   ရေမွှေး   perfume
yay kan   ရေကန်   lake
yay khae   ရေခဲ   ice
yay khae mont   ရေခဲမုန့်   ice cream
yay khae yay   ရေခဲရေ   ice water
yay koo   ရေကူး   swim
yay koo kan   ရေကူးကန်   swimming pool
yay lan   ရေလမ်း   sea travel, sea route
yay ngat tae   ရေငတ်တယ်။   I'm thirsty
yay nway jan   ရေနွေးကြမ်း   plain tea
yay thu ma   ရေသူမ   mermaid
yaygae thit tah   ရေခဲသေတ္တာ   refrigerator
yet   ရက်   day
yin khone dae   ရင်ခုန်တယ်   I'm excited (lit.
  my heart is jumping)
yin khone thaan   ရင်ခုန်သံ   heartbeat
yin kyay   ယဉ်ကျေး   polite
yin kyay hmu   ယဉ်ကျေးမှု   culture
yint   ရင့်   ripe
yoe thar   ရိုးသား   honest
yoe yah   ရိုးရာ   traditional
yoke shin yite   ရုပ်ရှင်ရိုက်   to shoot a movie
yoke thay   ရုပ်သေး   marionette, puppet
yone   ရုံး   office
yone   ယုံ   to believe
yoe   ရိုး   simple
yoo   ရူး   to be crazy, insane
yote hsoe   ရုပ်ဆိုး   ugly
yote shin   ရုပ်ရှင်   cinema, movie
yu   ယူ   to take

yu mae   ယူမယ်   I'll take it
yut   ရပ်   to stand
yut   ရပ်   to stop
yut kwet   ရပ်ကွက်   neighborhood
ywah   ရွာ   village

Z

zabae   စပယ်   fasmine
zabar   စပါး   paddy (rice grain with husk)
zabin   ဆံပင်   hair
zabin hnyut hsaing   ဆံပင်ညှပ်ဆိုင်
  hairdresser's shop
zabin phee   ဆံပင်ဖီး   to fix or comb one's hair
zabwae   စားပွဲ   table
zabwae doe   စားပွဲထိုး   waiter, waitress
zagabone   စကားပုံ   proverb
zagabyan   စကားပြန်   translator
zagar   စကား   spoken word, language
zagar kywae   စကားကြွယ်   eloquent
zagar myar   စကားများ   to quarrel
zagar myar   စကားများ   talkative
zagar nae   စကားနည်း   (a person) of few
  words
zah pana   စျာပန   funeral (formal)
zanee   ဇနီး   wife (formal)
zaung dan   စောင်းတန်း   corridor, walkway
  (of a religious site)
zawgyi   ဇော်ဂျီ   wizard
zay   စျေး   market
zay hsaing   စျေးဆိုင်   shop
zay kyi   စျေးကြီး   expensive
zay oo bauk   စျေးဦးပေါက်   first sale for the
  day
zay thae   စျေးသည်   vendors, merchants
zay wae   စျေးဝယ်   to shop
zedi   စေတီ   shrine, pagoda
zin gyan   စကြံ   corridor
zit myit   ဇစ်မြစ်   root, origin
zune   ဇွန်း   spoon
zut lan   ဇာတ်လမ်း   story, plot

Published by Tuttle Publishing, an imprint of Periplus Editions (HK) Ltd.

www.tuttlepublishing.com

Copyright © 2019 Periplus Editions (HK) Ltd.

Library of Congress Control Number: 2019931655

ISBN: 978-0-8048-4961-6

Distributed by

North America, Latin America & Europe
Tuttle Publishing
364 Innovation Drive,
North Clarendon,
VT 05759-9436, USA
Tel: 1 (802) 773 8930;
Fax: 1 (802) 773 6993
info@tuttlepublishing.com
www.tuttlepublishing.com

Asia Pacific
Berkeley Books Pte Ltd
3 Kallang Sector #04-01
Singapore 349278
Tel: (65) 6741 2178;
Fax: (65) 6741 2179
inquiries@periplus.com.sg
www.periplus.com

First edition
22 21 20 19   6 5 4 3 2 1   1904RR

Printed in China